TABLE OF CONTENTS

DEDICATION

To my husband, Dimitri, and my family, for their never-ending confidence and support.

To my friends and colleagues, for their wisdom and encouragement.

To Abby, Adam, Adrian, AJ, Allen, Alex, Alyx, Allison, Amanda, Andrew, Anthony, Austin, Ben, Bobby, Brad, Brenden, Brent, Brian, Bryan, Catherine, Chris, Christina, Charlie, Colin, Connor, Corbin, Craig, Daniel, David, Drew, Dylan, Eric, Evan, Ewan, Franklin, Glen, Gordon, Daniel, David, Gretchen, Henry, Isabel, Jacob, Jacqueline, Jared, Jason, Jay, Jeff, Jeffrey, Jeremy, John, Joe, Jonathan, Joseph, Joshua, JT, Justin, Karly, Katie, Kelsey, Ken, Kenneth, Kip, Kyle, Lance, Lee, Luke, Mark, Matt, Matthew, Michael, Mickey, Mikey, Mitchell, Natalie, Nathaniel, Nicholas, Philip, Rob, Sam, Sara, Scott, Shauna, Stephen, Steven, Steve, Thomas, Tom, Tony, and Zachary, who gave me the opportunity to learn, whose enthusiasm and energy confirm what I am doing, and without whom this book would not be possible.

Thank you.

PREFACE

have had the privilege of working with children and teens with autism spectrum disorders (ASD) and their families for over 20 years. In this book ASD refers to children with autistic disorder, Asperger Syndrome and pervasive developmental disorder-not otherwise specified (PDD-NOS). My experiences have been challenging at times, but always stimulating and enlightening.

The Super Skills program was created out of my attempts to help children with ASD develop social competency. In the mid-1980s, when I started group training sessions, specific educational programs for children with ASD were not available. My early attempts to teach this group were guided by Goldstein et al. (1980), McGinnis and Goldstein (1984), and Jackson, Jackson, and Monroe (1983). Although not specifically designed for children with ASD, these programs offered a course of action.

Nevertheless, the children with ASD struggled with components of the lessons. Contributing to discussions, role-playing and completing group activities were often difficult, and there was little generalization to "real" settings outside of the group. The youngsters did not consistently make friends or fit in with their peers at school and in their neighborhoods, despite my best efforts and the efforts of others around them.

In retrospect, traditional social skill training programs are too sophisticated for children with basic and severe social deficits. Such programs typically assume a beginning level of social competence and skill unknown to the child with ASD, who usually does not understand and cannot navigate the simplest social interaction.

The challenges that these children experience in the group setting are directly related to the complexities of the disorder. How can one expect a child to contribute to a discussion of a specific social skill when she does not understand the rules of reciprocal conversation? How can she role-play when she does not know how to pretend? How can she participate in a group setting when she does not acknowledge another's body language, feelings or point of view? It gradually became clear to me that an alternative program with distinct and special objectives was needed to effectively address these unique and complex problems.

In spite of my early disappointment, I continued to believe that a peer group was essential to successful learning. Social skills, by their very nature, could not be taught in isolation. Contrary to popular opinion, which was to include children with ASD with more typically developing children, I believed that children with ASD could learn with each other. Based on my experiences, children needed the support of evenly matched peer partners facing similar challenges to feel secure enough to practice new behavior. They needed to develop competence in social relationships. When placed with more socially competent peers, the children with ASD were "out of their league." Despite the efforts of leaders and others to support mutual satisfaction in the relationship, children with ASD were never "equal partners," and thus never experienced the satisfaction of sustaining a relationship on their own. And worst of all, if a child could not sustain a relationship in a controlled group setting, how could he ever sustain a friendship in the real world?

I knew from personal experience that peers with ASD had the potential to be compassionate and caring. I believed that with strategic guidance they could encourage and motivate new skills in each other, whereas peers without ASD could only surmise their personal and unique understanding of the issues.

UNIQUE FEATURES OF SUPER SKILLS

Shaped over many years of clinical experience, and influenced by the major works of McGinnis and Goldstein and Jackson, Jackson, and Monroe, Super Skills targets the fundamentals of social behavior for each child in a group, considering the child's unique profile of social interaction.

Super Skills:

- ◆ builds upon strengths while teaching prosocial exchanges with evenly matched peer partners
- ◆ unscrambles each social skill into separate and tangible actions that have meaning for every student
- ◆ orchestrates the right mix of role-plays and practice activities
- ◆ creates a nonthreatening environment
- ◆ encourages new social behavior and mutually satisfying relationships

As a result of Super Skills, children with ASD have developed new social competencies and begun to make use of them in their homes, schools and communities. As they become more comfortable with their newly acquired skills, they are able to cautiously apply them in additional settings. Progress takes many hours of dedicated, coordinated, repetitive practice.

Super Skills developed from a desire to make a difference in the lives of children with ASD and their families. It has not undergone the rigid tests of empirical research but continues to develop. This book is my effort to share what I have learned from many years of practice. The book is written with the novice practitioner in mind, one who has little understanding of how to begin to develop a social skills training program. It is meant to be practical and straightforward. Readers with more experience will find new ideas to try in your practice settings.

– Judith Coucouvanis

FOREWORD

uring the past few years, many social skills curricula have been published for children and adolescents with autism spectrum disorders (ASD). However, few of them address thoroughly the multifaceted needs of children with high-functioning autism, Asperger Syndrome, and pervasive developmental disorders-not otherwise specified. Although it is easy to be critical of many of these recent curricula, it should be recognized that developing a comprehensive social skills program is a Herculean task that is not within the purview of many practitioners and researchers who work with individuals with ASD.

Judith Coucouvanis is one of those rare people whose understanding of the characteristics of individuals with ASD and their needs is evident in her social skills curricula, *Super Skills: A Social Skills Group Program for Children with Asperger Syndrome, High-Functioning Autism and Related Challenges.* This program is phenomenal on many levels.

First, Super Skills goes beyond teaching basic, mechanical social skills. In 30 lessons, Coucouvanis introduces four types of skills necessary for social success: (a) fundamental skills, (b) social initiation skills, (c) getting along with others, and (d) social response skills. Fundamental skills consist of several skills, such as eye contact, facial expressions, voice volume and tone. Social initiation skills address several areas, including greeting and starting a conversation. The program area of getting along with others focuses on skills often not addressed, such as recognizing teasing, negotiating, reciprocity, irony, and adjusting one's mood to that of others. Finally, social response skills include acknowledging others, following directions, offering encouragement, and reading others' body language.

The author's knowledge of ASD is also evident in the instruments she provides to easily assess students' social skills levels. One such instrument, Creating Success: Know the Student Checklist, is alone worth the purchase of this book! This profile identifies the student's current interests, stress responses, language abilities, academic skills, sensory issues, health issues, and overall social profile. Coucouvanis emphasizes the importance of knowing the child before he or she starts participating in a social skills group. Other assessments include the Profile of Social Difficulty, Super Skills Grouping Profile, and the Target Behavior Practice Checklist.

Several introductory chapters precede the cornerstone of this impressive resource: the 30 lessons mentioned above. One of these chapters is devoted to behavioral issues often experienced by individuals with ASD. I believe that the author's view of behavioral challenges is one that should be embraced by all. According to Coucouvanis, "When such disruption occurs regularly, it is usually a signal that the leader needs to intervene and change some aspect of the group structure. It does *not* mean that a child is intentionally misbehaving, willful or manipulative" (p. 39). No emphasis is placed on blaming or punishing. Rather, the social skills instructor is directed to modify the environment to ensure student success and minimize behavioral challenges. Coucouvanis has also included a form to identify the reason why a given behavior occurs, along with a strong reinforcement system. These are key to teaching individuals with ASD in a social skills group, in a classroom or at home.

Each of the 30 social skills lessons is presented in an identical format, making it easy to follow and implement the ideas. As is evidenced in the Steps to Success, Thoughts Before Starting, and Introducing the Skill portions of the lessons, Coucouvanis ensures that the social skills leader is prepared to lead the group. Other lesson plan components include (a) Read and Review Steps to Success, (b) Warm-Up Activity, (c) Role-Play (with home, community, and school options), (d) Practice Activities, (e) Supplies, (f) Supporting Skills to Prompt and Reinforce, and (g) Extending Skill Development.

Super Skills is a strong and comprehensive curriculum that I strongly support. It has been integrated into the graduate program in autism spectrum disorders at the University of Kansas – a program I proudly co-direct. Although not yet empirically validated, Super Skills' foundation is sound and its activities meet the complex needs of children and youth with ASD.

– *Brenda Smith Myles, Ph.D., associate professor at the University of Kansas*
Author and co-author of numerous publications, Myles' recent books include *The Hidden Curriculum: Practical Solutions for Understanding Unstated Rules in Social Situations, Asperger Syndrome and Adolescence: Practical Solutions for School Success, Asperger Syndrome and Sensory Issues: Practical Solutions for Making Sense of the World* and *Asperger Syndrome* and *Difficult Moments: Practical Solutions for Tantrums, Rage, and Meltdowns – New Revised and Expanded Edition.*

INTRODUCTION

astering social skills is a formidable challenge for persons with autism spectrum disorders (ASD), who do not have an innate ability to make and keep friends, to "fit in" or to work effectively with others. To them, social rules of behavior and interaction are often confusing and frequently overwhelming. Generally, they lack knowledge about appropriate social behavior and have little understanding of the unwritten rules of social conduct. This difficulty in understanding social norms affects all situations and is interwoven in all aspects of human relationships (Moore, 2002; Myles & Southwick, 2005; Quill, 1995; Stewart, 2002). Moreover, it often results in social isolation, ostracism, failure to maintain successful employment, misunderstanding, depression and anxiety (Ghaziuddin, 2002; Meyer & Minshew, 2002; Myles & Simpson, 2002).

WHAT IS SUPER SKILLS?

Super Skills is a group approach to teaching social competence to children with ASD. It is a social skills curriculum for elementary-aged children who have functional language. For lack of better terminology, it targets youngsters with "higher-functioning" ASD. This typically includes diagnoses of autistic disorder, Asperger Syndrome (AS) and pervasive developmental disorder-not otherwise specified (PDD-NOS).

The premise behind Super Skills is that children who have severe social deficits must be taught specific, desirable actions for social inclusion in a setting where they cannot fail. It teaches these actions with equal peer partners who share similar deficits. Everyone is set up to succeed, one step at a time. In the supportive and nonthreatening environment provided by Super Skills, peers share the experience of mutual learning. Discovering that others share problems similar to their own is a tremendous relief to most children. Secure in the knowledge that they will be supported, they are urged to try out new ways of interacting. With repetition and persistence, most experience success and eventually feel pride and joy in their progress.

The Super Skills approach targets specific social deficits unique to each child and teaches appropriate prosocial behavior in a straightforward, optimistic and positive way. Each social skill is subdivided into separate actions or characteristics that are easy for a child to methodically practice. With time, children recognize that some actions are

present in most social interactions (e.g., "Use a friendly voice" or "look at the person"). Thus, although skills are taught one at a time, it quickly becomes apparent that they are interrelated. Many overlap when used in similar situations. Starting and Entering a Conversation, for example, have corresponding and unifying conditions of use – they are used to initiate social interaction. An associated skill is Showing Interest in Others. It suggests how and why to converse, while Reading Body Language offers a method to help regulate the conversation.

Unlike typically developing children, who spend thousands of hours experimenting and practicing with relationships, children with ASD miss out. Recent literature suggests that a primary problem is a lack of experience sharing (Gutstein & Whitney, 2002). As a result, while typically developing children are experiencing social inclusion, youngsters with ASD are experiencing social isolation.

Super Skills is orchestrated to give everyone an opportunity to practice new social behavior through modeling, rehearsal and practice activities. Guided by the group leader and supported by their peers, children feel secure enough to practice new behaviors that help develop competence in social relationships. Specifically, the program targets deficits in reciprocity, communication and understanding. Children are taught the skills needed to develop relationships while emphasizing the experience of being part of a common unit, and the value of each person's contributions.

As children with ASD learn with each other, their unique perspective on the challenges they face is invaluable. They gradually begin to encourage each other to try new behavior without fear of ridicule or embarrassment. They learn the value of trust and slowly recognize what it means to be an equal partner in a relationship and to sustain that relationship over time. Frequently these friendships survive outside of the group setting. Thus, Super Skills ultimately builds competency in a multitude of social situations.

WHAT MAKES SUPER SKILLS UNIQUE?

1. **Super Skills is structured.** Super Skills uses many of the teaching strategies found in traditional social skills training groups, such as modeling, role-play, reinforcement and rehearsal. Some of the major works that influence the Super Skills program are listed in the reference list. Unlike more traditional groups, however, Super Skills is very structured. Each skill is subdivided into a list of concrete and tangible steps, called Steps to Success. Especially for young children, these steps must be simple to visualize and understand. Sometimes pictures illustrating the words accompany the steps (see examples, pages 335-342). Children are taught what the skill looks like and sounds like. While some traditional group programs also define the components of a skill, the steps are usually too abstract for children with ASD.

2. **Super Skills follows a specific lesson format.** Although the core curriculum is fluid, the diversity of what is taught is based upon the needs of the students. Through careful collaboration between parents, teachers, leaders and the child, specific priorities or "target behaviors" are identified for each child. Together, this collection of target behaviors determines what social skills will be the essential curriculum. One primary skill is chosen as the central focus for each session.

3. **No two Super Skills groups are alike.** As students make progress, new target behaviors receive concentrated attention. Consequently, the focus of each group is regularly changing. By comparison, more typical skills training groups have a specific curriculum to follow and each group repeats the complete curriculum.

4. **Super Skills is designed to make learning fun and successful.** The specialized practice activities create enthusiasm and excitement, provide structured opportunities for intense interaction and help children to thrive. They are a vital part of Super Skills. Most children with ASD have problems using and understanding language, so relying solely upon language-based teaching methods will likely be ineffective. In addition, young children lose attention easily and usually do not understand the issues well enough to contribute to a discussion. Thus, activities help to "show" how a specific skill is performed. Super Skills provides abundant opportunities to rehearse real-life social situations. In brief, Super Skills is not talking, but doing.

CHAPTER 1

SETTING UP

n the following chapter we will take a brief look at some of the basics of Super Skills, including the characteristics of ideal session leaders and potential student participants. Important for smooth-running and successful sessions are also group composition, physical space as well as session length and frequency.

WHO CAN LEAD SUPER SKILLS SESSIONS?

Effective group leaders have come from a wide range of preparation and backgrounds, including social workers, psychologists, nurses, speech and language therapists, counselors, teachers, occupational therapists and consultants. Thus, no single professional group qualifies as the most effective group leader for Super Skills. Nonprofessional leaders have included parents, teaching assistants and university students.

It is possible to lead Super Skills with one leader; however, a co-leader, assistant or helper is desirable, particularly if the leader is a novice. The assistant can offer positive feedback to students, set up activities, lead small groups and help manage rewards. With some guidance and direction, parents, teaching assistants or older students can be effective helpers. The well-prepared leader can direct a small group of 4-8 participants alone. However, here too, a helper is a welcome support. Because many leaders will not have the luxury of a helper, this curriculum is written specifically for the single leader.

Regardless of who leads the Super Skills sessions, some essential leader qualities are necessary for the Super Skills curriculum to be effective. These are:

◆ **Understanding of and experience with children with ASD.** Understanding of the disorder and how social deficits are expressed is essential to correctly interpret a child's behavior. When beginners lead a group, they must be careful not to interpret behavior as manipulative, willful or calculating – a common mistake. The more experience the leader has in interacting with children with ASD, the greater the likelihood he or she will understand what is happening in any situation that arises. Experienced leaders will likely recognize that not all children with ASD are alike and react accordingly.

◆ **Flexibility.** The leader must learn to "read" the group and know when to change the pace or move on to an alternative or different activity. Recognizing when to participate and when to merely observe, letting the children take the lead, is a skill that comes with practice. Inherent in this is also the knowledge that the group must remain actively engaged. Super Skills is generally fast-paced to maintain instructional control. Once this control is lost, the leader loses many valuable minutes dealing with behavior problems and trying to regain control. Do not be afraid to deal positively with the diverse problems that arise (discussed in Chapter 4).

◆ **Positive energy, enthusiasm.** Giving frequent praise and encouragement is essential to the program. Therefore, the leader must be enthusiastic and believe in and respect the children. When the leader is encouraging, children are more willing to try. Reinforcing attempts and rewarding successes is crucial to the children's progress. Finally, children with ASD frequently mirror the mood of those around them. When the mood is positive, they are more likely to reflect that positive attitude in their personal behavior.

◆ **Sense of humor.** Invariably problems will occur, and a session may not go as planned. A sense of humor helps to manage these challenges. In addition, by modeling an appropriate use of humor, the leader helps students learn about humor.

WHAT CHILDREN ARE CANDIDATES?

Potential Super Skills participants can be identified in several ways. In the school setting the resource teacher, counselor, social worker, psychologist or other support person will likely be aware of children with social impairments and might approach teachers and parents to discuss the children's participation in a Super Skills program. Alternatively, the Super Skills leader who recognizes a need for the program might ask teachers and other personnel to select specific children they believe might benefit. A classroom teacher might identify one child or a small group of children, or elect to use the Super Skills curriculum to teach appropriate social behavior to the entire classroom. Although designed for children with ASD and other social impairments, Super Skills has been used to help typically developing children improve their social skills as well.

When the leader is in a private setting, such as a clinic or private office, colleagues might refer children. Notices that advertise the beginning of the program might be posted in local newspapers, on web sites, and in Internet chat rooms. Referrals can be screened by the therapist.

The Super Skills curriculum is primarily designed for elementary students with ASD. These include children with HFA, AS and PDD-NOS. Children who do not have these formal diagnoses, but have severe social deficits, also benefit from the program. Within

this context the following variables are considered relevant:

◆ **Language:** Although functional language use is variable in children with ASD, the ideal participant in this curriculum demonstrates milder language impairments only. Specifically, the child must demonstrate the language necessary to answer direct questions, participate in a discussion to some degree and offer ideas and opinions.

◆ **Reading and Writing:** Reading and writing skills, although helpful, are not essential. Activities can be easily modified with the use of pictures for children who do not read. Others can share reading responsibilities. And children who do not write can dictate their answers to a scribe or forego certain activities altogether.

◆ **Age:** The targeted age group for this curriculum is 7-11 years, or generally students in second to fourth or fifth grade.

◆ **Behavior Challenges:** Some behavior challenges are usually inherent in a diagnosis of ASD. These are not reasons for exclusion from Super Skills. In fact, specific lessons are included that teach how to manage anger, deal with mistakes and be more flexible – behaviors that are often the origins of behavior difficulty. Chapter 4 describes how to set up the group sessions to minimize behavior difficulties and deal with problems when they arise. Individual lessons also suggest how to manage specific problems. The leader will likely find it helpful to initially limit the number of children with severe behavior challenges in a group to one or two. When the leader is more knowledgeable about children with ASD and comfortable with the curriculum and its behavior support strategies, the number of students with behavior challenges may be increased.

SETTING

There is no ideal setting for Super Skills. Groups have been taught in homes, clinics, conference rooms, church schoolrooms, classrooms and outdoors at recess. The curriculum is designed for a group of 4-8 participants, led by 1-2 staff members. The small-group format allows for more individual attention, guidance and practice. It also encourages supportive relationships between the children, thus more easily creating opportunities for them to work as partners and teams. When more leaders are available, the group size can be increased and the curriculum adapted by expanding activities or separating the larger group into smaller subsets.

For example, one elementary school requested a Super Skills program for a group of 18 children who had social difficulties at recess. Some had ASD and did not have the skills necessary to play in a group whereas others had problems with impulse control and aggression. One leader (the author) and four assistants (autism consultant, speech therapist, two paraeducators) successfully led six sessions. While the group met outside

during recess, it was common for other nonidentified children to ask to join in. They were easily included.

SESSION FREQUENCY AND LENGTH

Completing the role-plays and activities in Super Skills takes a group of six children up to 90 minutes if the entire lesson is taught in one session as presented. Of course, this depends to some degree on how much time is spent at each activity. Also, the amount of teaching time will vary with the setting. The curriculum is designed to allow for such flexibility.

If only one activity is included, the group may conclude in 45 minutes or less, or a minimum of 20 minutes may be used if several sessions are planned to teach one skill each week. For example, the skill could be introduced in the first session, role-plays in the second, with the activities carried out in the remaining sessions. This approach works well in a school setting. When longer sessions are planned, such as in a clinic or private practice, the pace must be quick-moving to sustain the children's attention and interest. When I am leading a clinic group, I plan for 90 minutes. I teach for 75-80 minutes and meet with parents for the last 10 minutes while the students finish up their last activity (see discussion of parent meeting in Chapter 5).

PROGRAM DURATION

Some Super Skills programs targeting very specific skill deficits are brief, lasting 4-6 weeks for 30 minutes a session. Some are longer, lasting 90 minutes per week during an entire school year. Others are open groups and continue for years. That is, new participants join after others leave or graduate to middle school, thereby creating openings. The participants who elect to remain in Super Skills for years generally realize the most progress. These students often repeat lessons on the same target behaviors while continuing to develop new skills.

SEATING

The ideal physical space includes a round table and chairs. With this arrangement, a single leader can more effectively observe what is happening in the group, give immediate reinforcement and notice matters that require urgent attention. This arrangement also fosters eye contact between members and encourages a sense of "we," making it more difficult for one member to isolate him- or herself. A separate table should be nearby for divided group activities. This can be a small card table or another round

table. Some empty space is necessary for activities that require moving around.

Generally, let members sit where they choose; however, sit particularly distractible children next to the leader so that he or she can easily use physical and visual prompts. If observers are present, sit them away from the group unless they will be participating. Direct them to be silent until asked to participate; otherwise their presence may be distracting.

HOW TO PREPARE THE ROOM

Minimize distractions in the room to focus children's attention on the leader and each other. Close windows and doors if possible. Cover windows or open shelving, if children are particularly distractible. Place supplies in containers near the leader on the floor or behind the leader on a chair within easy reach. Be proactive when possible. One spring a few ladybugs found their way into my room through cracks in the windows and doors. The bugs became quite a distraction to one group member whose special interest was insects. For several weeks, I completed a ladybug check and removed the bugs prior to the start of each group to eliminate this unexpected distraction.

SUPPLIES

The necessary supplies are listed, in alphabetical order, separately for each session of the curriculum. Many of the sessions use games. These can be purchased from toy or department stores, or may be found at garage sales or loaned from families. (A list of games and their manufacturers is included in the Appendix, page 299.)

Be sure to prepare the games and supplies in advance. I carry supplies in plastic tubs and cloth bags. An easel may be necessary if a flipchart is used rather than a black or whiteboard. Always plan for more activities than might be used to allow the most flexibility. I have found it helpful to provide a pocket folder for each group member, where children carry homework, schedules, notes, etc. They receive extra points for remembering to bring their folder to Super Skills.

CHAPTER 2

GETTING STARTED

electing where to begin teaching social interaction skills to a child with ASD or related challenges can appear overwhelming. There is a seemingly limitless number of skills and associated rules to be mastered. Given the myriad social deficits and the variety of ways they are manifested, there are numerous possibilities for one child, let alone a group of children.

The issue with these children is not whether or not social deficits are present, but to what degree. The Profile of Social Difficulty (POSD) (see Table 2.1 and blank forms in the Appendix, pages 342-348), coupled with other measures such as observation and parent, teacher and child interviews, guides the selection of priority skills for each member of the group and the group as a whole. These priority skills are also called target behaviors.

WHAT IS THE PROFILE OF SOCIAL DIFFICULTY (POSD)?

The POSD is a list of skills necessary for effective social interaction that are typically difficult for children with ASD. The list reflects my clinical experience and the work of others in social skills, including McGinnis and Goldstein (1984, 1990, 1997), Jackson, Jackson and Monroe (1983) and Gajewski, Hirn and Mayo (1993, 1994, 1996). The POSD is not an inclusive list of all possible behaviors but a tool to help determine a child's current social skill profile. Once completed for a given student, the POSD indicates the challenges a child faces in social situations and identifies gaps in skill development. It also reflects social behaviors that are relatively easy for the child to perform.

Not every child will have difficulty using all of the skills, and a few will have social problems in areas that are not listed. Each child will need more help with some skills than with others. A few children will experience difficulty in a number of circumstances but not every circumstance. For example, a child may be able to join a conversation at home, but unable to do so at school. The individualized profile that results from com-

pleting the POSD identifies the ease and difficulty of four pro-social behavior components: Fundamental Skills, Social Initiation Skills, Social Response Skills and Getting Along with Others. These four areas form the foundation of the Super Skills program. For most, but not all, of the skills, corresponding teaching lessons are found in the second half of this book.

The following is a brief overview of the four major areas of the POSD, which in turn serve as the foundation for the skills taught in the Super Skills lessons.

◆ **POSD: Fundamental Skills.** Fundamental Skills are required for effective communication. Eye contact, suitable volume and tone, as well as appropriate facial expression are key to positive social relations. These behaviors do not come naturally or easily for many children with ASD. Limited use of these skills as well as misunderstanding their importance leads to misperception and misinformation. Without these basic skills individuals can miss important cues. Communication breakdown is the ultimate outcome.

> John, an 8-year-old child with AS, greets his classmate Alex on the playground. Alex is carrying a soccer ball towards a group of children who are waiting for him. John begins urgently describing his favorite book about the Titanic. He doesn't look at Alex and doesn't notice that Alex is rolling his eyes and pursing his lips. He also doesn't realize that Alex is heading towards a group of peers to play soccer. When Alex runs off and leaves him standing alone, John does not understand why.

◆ **POSD: Social Initiation Skills.** Social Initiation Skills involve approaching another person to start a communication or social interaction. They are difficult for children with autism, who tend to be shy and fail to recognize when these skills are useful. For children with AS, the skills are difficult because these children tend to be domineering.

Typical social initiation skills include greeting, starting a conversation, entering a conversation, giving a compliment, inviting someone to play or asking for help. In the previous example, John wants to join his classmate at recess; however, he does not realize that he might be more successful if he asks to join in the soccer game rather than talking about his special interest.

Social initiation is extremely important in school settings where peers are the focus of relationships. Often children with ASD want to make friends but are unsuccessful in their attempts without knowing why. Children with ASD are often socially intrusive or awkward.

> Miguel, a 6-year-old child with PDD-NOS, raises his hands in the air and waves them over his head during a group discussion. He yells "guys, guys,

my turn." He wants to tell his classmates about the television show *Blues Clues* that he had watched that morning, but his comment is not related to the current topic of conversation and his method of getting the group's attention is too forceful and invasive. As a result, he is unsuccessful.

Some children with AS or PDD-NOS engage in disrespectful behavior, clueless of its offensive nature. For example, they might make offensive personal comments, rudely remarking on another's shortcomings or physical imperfections. Many appear uncaring and aloof. Others intrude into personal space. By the elementary years some children have learned to initiate interactions by using inappropriate behavior. These behaviors might include touching or hitting others, making lewd comments or using inappropriate gestures.

Keisha, a 12-year-old child with AS, consistently enters the room with arms crossed and a frown, clueless that her actions distance her from her peers and make her appear unfriendly.

Engaging in one-sided conversations about narrow or unusual interests is another manifestation of problems with social initiation. Special interests may include a specific sports team, historical event or time period, video game, violent act, gun collection, means of transportation, animal species or electrical appliance, among many others. Commonly the child acquires vast amounts of knowledge about this single topic, and, like John, uses this knowledge to attempt to interact with others. He typically recites a specific script and does not ask his partner for an opinion or wait for a comment or question. Children must be taught to ask questions to show interest in others and their activities.

Finally, some children remain passive and shy. Typically these are children with high-functioning autism. They usually make no effort to initiate interaction and have no clue about how to do so, preferring to remain isolated in their own world.

Thomas, a 9-year-old child with HFA, does not join in small-group conversations with peers. He sits alone, stares off into space and plays with his fingers. When someone asks him a question, his response clearly shows that he has not been following the discussion.

◆ **POSD: Social Response Skills.** As the term implies, Social Response Skills are used in response to a verbal or nonverbal communication or interaction initiated by someone else, or in response to an event in the environment. For example, when a peer approaches and greets with "Hey, John," a suitable reply might be "Hey, Mark," to give a "high five," or smile and wave hello.

Social Response Skills usually include acknowledging others, following directions, staying on task, waiting or offering help or encouragement. The child must be able

to "read" the person's body language and correctly interpret what is said to be able to respond appropriately. Some children with ASD do not recognize that a response is necessary, while others do not know how to respond. As a result, they are frequently viewed as rude or unfriendly.

> Sasha, an 8-year-old child with HFA, gets on the bus. Her neighbor greets her and asks Sasha to sit next to her. Sasha proceeds to sit next to her neighbor but without acknowledging her friend or her invitation.

> Ismahl, a 10-year-old with HFA, responds to peers who come near him by saying, "Go away."

> Sarah, an 11-year-old child with AS, is quite knowledgeable and loves to read, especially about history. When her teacher quotes a fact of Greek civilization, Sarah stands up and corrects her.

◆ **POSD: Getting Along with Others.** Getting Along with Others includes the skills necessary to foster positive relationships. They require a certain amount of reciprocity, or being able to adjust personal behavior to relate to what another person is saying or doing. Children with ASD do not understand the social rules of reciprocity. For example, students with AS may try to dominate and monopolize an interaction. Dictating a play activity, setting the rules for games and controlling the outcome are common methods of monopolizing. They may also choose to play alone rather than join in a group where they must give up control of the activity, or they may argue and refuse to see their part in a problem, frequently blaming others and refusing to take responsibility for their own behavior.

> Anthony, age 11, misses the school bus. He blames his mother because she took too long fixing breakfast.

> Steven, age 10, gets in a fight at school. He blames his friends because they are "stupid."

Temper tantrums and outbursts are not uncommon in young children if they cannot be first at something, or when they do not win.

> Darrel, a 7-year-old child with AS, insists he should win the game of *Chutes and Ladders*. When he realizes he might lose, he tips the game board over and runs out of the room.

Children with HFA tend to passively ignore others. They might fail to comment when a peer completes an especially difficult task, encourage another who is feeling discouraged, comfort someone who is sad, show interest in a friend's activities or give someone else a chance to talk.

Frequently unable to take another's perspective, to "walk in someone else's shoes," youngsters with ASD often react inappropriately. For example, if a classmate trips and falls, they may not realize the classmate is hurt. Instead they might laugh because they think the fall was funny. Also, children with ASD do not recognize and understand how others might perceive them. Thus, if a child starts a conversation about a favorite interest in electricity and the peer looks bored, he generally does not acknowledge this response. The lack of reciprocity as well as the lack of ability to take another's perspective often leads to isolation, rejection, and at times, ostracism.

Included in Getting Along with Others is the ability to handle teasing and to understand jokes, metaphors and irony. Individuals with ASD tend to interpret words and phrases literally, so the meaning of humor is often lost to them. They may become the victims of cruel jokes and tricks and are easily taken advantage of because they do not perceive that others sometimes lie or trick them. If others in the environment do not understand what is happening, they may perceive the child or adult with ASD as particularly disturbed. For example, at the urging of his male peers, one young child was encouraged to touch the chests of girls in his class, while another was encouraged to urinate on the playground, and a third to tie up a classmate with a jump rope.

The myriad unique and diverse ways that social skill impairments can manifest are at times difficult to capture. Moreover, no two children are alike. The boundaries created by the four behavior components, Fundamental Skills, Social Initiation, Social Response and Getting Along with Others are somewhat artificial, as they all interrelate. However, these categories help when conceptualizing problems and planning the final curriculum. The POSD is not perfect, but it offers a way to begin understanding the deficits so that effective intervention can begin.

◆ **Who Completes the POSD?** Individuals who know the child well and are familiar with his or her social interaction skills complete the POSD. This usually includes parents, teacher(s) and occasionally siblings. Each view represents a personal perception of the child's strength and weaknesses in circumstances that are familiar to the recorder. Each individual will have a different perspective, and these furnish valuable information when determining target behaviors and designing the Super Skills curriculum. Therefore, getting POSDs from a variety of sources is helpful. When possible, parents should complete the POSD independently so that each parent's perspective is known. Siblings offer a wealth of information and can contribute distinctive opinions that may differ from those of their parents. Teachers and others can provide valuable information regarding a child's social behavior at school. Finally, when possible, a child's self-report is desirable (see the Appendix, page 348). Many children have very accurate perceptions of what is difficult and

easy for them. Occasionally, children have specific requests, such as "I want to get Matt to quit teasing me" or "I want Sarah to be nice to me." These are important considerations when determining target behaviors.

Table 2.1 shows the completed POSD for Ben, a 10-year-old child with AS. The POSD was completed by his fifth-grade teacher. As indicated, it reveals many strengths in Social Initiation Skills and challenges with Social Response Skills. Ben has particular difficulties dealing with teasing and anger (also marked on both parents' POSDs). For these reasons, his teacher and parents requested that these be his target behaviors. Ben agreed.

The POSD should not be the only tool or measure used to guide the selection of skills to be taught in Super Skills groups, as it does not always capture the restrictions of the setting or biases of the rater. Because rules of social interaction vary by setting, it is difficult to capture on paper those differences. Consequently, it is best to work in cooperation with a child's teachers and parents to determine readiness for learning a skill as well as specific preferences for priorities. Directly observing the child is valuable when there is a question about whether or not a child might benefit from Super Skills or to help determine target behaviors.

The POSD is a useful observation tool and allows the observer to record observations directly onto it. For example, a recorder observing Pavel's conversation skills at school notes that Pavel does not initiate conversation with peers but does so easily with adults. The observer writes *adults* in the "very easy" column and *classmates* in the "difficult" column under the heading "Starting a Conversation." However, if Pavel is never observed starting a conversation, even though he has opportunities to do so, the observer might simply check "very difficult."

WHY SELECT TARGET BEHAVIORS?

Identifying target behaviors is an essential component of Super Skills. Target behaviors help keep everyone focused on the priority social skills for a specific child. They are also the focus of reinforcement programs and intensive teaching when the class is not in session. When there are no priorities, teaching becomes haphazard, the focus for each child is lost and deficits seem insurmountable and hopelessly futile to address. Using Super Skills, mastery of target behaviors temporarily takes precedence over other social deficits, which in turn become of secondary importance. Once target behaviors are achieved, or sufficient progress has been made so that everyone agrees they are no longer a priority, new target behaviors are selected. The Target Behavior Practice Chart in Table 2.2 (see blank form in the Appendix, page 350) is used to encourage children to practice target behaviors between sessions. Its use is further described in Chapter 5.

Table 2.1: SUPER SKILLS PROFILE OF SOCIAL DIFFICULTY FOR BEN

Child's Name: __Ben__   Age: __10__

Recorder: __Mrs. Tate__   Relationship to child: __teacher__   Date: __9/6/04__

Here are some social skills that people sometimes have difficulty with. Please mark the column you think applies to this child at present.

	Very Difficult	Difficult	Somewhat Difficult	Neither Difficult nor Easy	Somewhat Easy	Easy	Very Easy
Fundamental Skills	0	1	2	3	4	5	6
Eye Contact							x
Correct Facial Expression					x		
Correct Voice Volume			x				
Correct Voice Tone			x				
Correct Timing					x		
Social Initiation Skills	0	1	2	3	4	5	6
Using Person's Name							x
Using Farewells						x	
Greeting					x		
Introducing Self						x	
Asking for Help				x			
Giving a Compliment					x		
Starting a Conversation					x		
Joining a Conversation			x				
Ending a Conversation			x				
Exchanging Conversation				x			
Inviting Someone to Play							
Introducing Others				x			
Joining In		x					
Talking About Self							
Making a Complaint					x		
Asking Appropriate Questions				x			
Offering an Opinion					x		
Expressing Basic Feelings					x		
Expressing Complex Feelings			x				
Social Response Skills	0	1	2	3	4	5	6
Responding to Greeting					x		

Table 2.1: SUPER SKILLS PROFILE OF SOCIAL DIFFICULTY FOR BEN (cont.)

	Very Difficult	Difficult	Somewhat Difficult	Neither Difficult nor Easy	Somewhat Easy	Easy	Very Easy
Social Response Skills	0	1	2	3	4	5	6
Responding to Compliments				x			
Listening					x		
Following Directions				x			
Making Short Comments		x					
Staying on the Topic		x					
Waiting		x					
Staying on Task			x				
Offering Help					x		
Giving Encouragement				x			
Reading Body Language		x					
Reading Feelings of Others		x					
Dealing with Mistakes				x			
Dealing with Anger			x				
Refusing When Appropriate				x			
Getting Along with Others	0	1	2	3	4	5	6
Taking Turns			x				
Sharing					x		
Playing by the Rules							
Apologizing					x		
Being Fair					x		
Being a Good Sport					x		
Using Kind Talk					x		
Being Flexible				x			
Asking Permission					x		
Cooperating				x			
Dealing with "No"			x				
Compromising			x				
Dealing with a Problem			x				
Receiving a Suggestion			x				
Giving a Suggestion			x				
Letting Others Talk							
Showing Interest in Others		x					
Using Humor							
Disagreeing Politely			x				
Dealing with Teasing		x					

◆ **How Many Target Behaviors?** As mentioned, target behaviors should reflect the input of parents, teachers and the child. Generally, two to three target behaviors per group member are optimum. However, if the group meets for fewer than six sessions, only one or two target behaviors are needed. Target behaviors must be a mixture of easy and complex skills. Do not choose skills that are "very difficult" when a child is just beginning Super Skills. The child should achieve some success relatively quickly so that the prospect of learning social skills appears fun and easy. Selecting only "very difficult" skills will likely lead to discouragement.

> Costas is an 8-year-old child with Asperger Syndrome. His POSDs reveal that it is difficult for him to deal with mistakes. His teacher reports this is creating problems in the classroom, and his mother reports trouble with music lessons and chores. Costas admits that he cannot deal with mistakes and would like to be able to do so. Therefore, dealing with mistakes becomes one of his target behaviors.

> The Super Skills leader recognizes that this will be a challenging skill for Costas to master so she considers another target behavior that will likely be easier for him. She recognizes that helping Costas achieve success relatively quickly at one skill will encourage him to try harder to master the more difficult ones. Costas is greeting occasionally at home. Greetings are a relatively straightforward skill, so greetings are selected as his second target behavior.

> Finally, Costas is good at starting conversations because he has many special interests, but he cannot join conversations on the topic. So this is chosen as his third target behavior. It will be challenging, but with some guidance and direction he will likely show progress.

◆ **Defining Target Behaviors** Target behaviors are defined by their behavioral components. These are the Steps to Success found in each lesson plan. Essentially, these steps explain what the skill consists of when it is used appropriately. The Steps to Success can be altered to fit the circumstances of an individual group member.

For example, Step 5 of Entering a Conversation (see page 115) might have to be modified for a child who monopolizes conversation and does not pause long enough for others to join in. "Speak for a short time on the topic" might be changed to:

- Speak for 10-20 seconds on the topic.

- Speak for 10-20 seconds on the topic and pause.

- Speak for 10-20 seconds on the topic. Pause for 5 seconds.

There are a number of ways to make steps more specific when needed, such as

Table 2.2: Super Skills Target Behavior Practice Chart

Name: **Kimberly**

Each time you practice one of your target behaviors, you receive credit towards a bonus prize. Write in the target behavior that you practiced below. Tell me where you practiced it and how well you think you did. Have your parent, teacher or friends initial it. Return the completed chart to me for credit. The more you practice, the more you earn!!

Date	Target behavior	Situation	How did I do?	Initials
10/13	Join In	Asked Marie to play with her on the computer	good	BL
10/14	Start a conversation	Told dad about school field trip	Well	CL
10/14	Join a conversation	Grandma's birthday party, joined conversation about vacation	OK	MB
10/18	Start a conversation	Hiking in park, told mom about gym class	Good	BL
10/19	Join In	My house; joined cousins playing tag outside	Great	MB
10/21	Join a conversation	School lunch: joined kids talking about Halloween plans	Good	DR
10/22	Join In	Tried to join kids playing basketball at park	Not so good	BL

Awesome!! You did it!!

specifying a time limit, changing or deleting a step, offering additional information or a definition.

> Dimitri, age 10, is learning to deal with teasing. Because of poor impulse control, he is unable to ignore and walk away when teasing occurs. Therefore, Step 4, Choice D (accept it gracefully), is targeted as the priority strategy to teach. To help Dimitri understand more clearly what this means, the choice is further defined as "Pretend the person said something nice." In this way he learns to respond calmly without overreacting. Eventually he learns to make a joke of the teasing (Choice E).

◆ **Changing Target Behaviors** Should target behaviors stay the same? Succeeding in social skill development may appear to be a formidable task; however, it is not impossible. Some students make relatively quick progress whereas others require years of diligent practice. Becoming a socially competent individual may be a life-long struggle.

The Profile of Social Difficulty offers information that can be compared over time to help monitor a child's progress. However, deciding when a target behavior is "mastered" is relatively subjective. A skill may become easier in some circumstances, but remain difficult in others.

> Iris has been working on the skill of exchanging conversation for several months. She has mastered the steps of waiting for a pause before speaking and saying something on the topic. She can converse for several "turns" when calm and when the topic is of low interest to her. However, when the topic is her special interest in Japanese films, it is difficult for her to remember to give others a chance to comment or ask questions.

Changing target behaviors should be a cooperative decision that involves parents, teachers and the child. It is not uncommon to choose a new target behavior even though a previous one has not been completely mastered. This happens, for example, when the child knows how to perform a skill but needs more practice in real-life settings. Parents, teachers and others continue to work with the child to develop his expertise in the skill area while he focuses on a new skill in Super Skills. Sometimes parents elect to continue reinforcement programs for both skills so the child remains motivated to keep using the former target behavior.

> Being a Good Sport is one of Rolo's target behaviors. He bowls every Saturday but has major meltdowns when his total score is lower than his partner's. Through Super Skills and regular practice, Rolo has eventually

learned to deal with the disappointment of a lower score by congratulating his partner and saying "good game." However, he continues to have meltdowns at home when he loses at board games. As a result, Being a Good Sport remains a target behavior, but a new target behavior is added.

On occasion, for new students especially, expectations are set too high and a selected skill is too complex. As a result, it may have to be replaced with a simpler, more basic target behavior.

Angela is a 9-year-old child with autism. Her parents and teachers want her to work in a group as she usually sits passively by herself. So Cooperating is selected as one of her target behaviors. However, after working with Angela in the group, the leader quickly realizes that she does not understand the more basic skill of Joining in a Conversation. After this discovery is discussed with teachers and parents, Entering a Conversation becomes Angela's new target behavior, even though she has not yet mastered the skill of cooperating.

POSD AND SUPER SKILLS LESSONS

You may wonder why there is not a corresponding lesson for each skill on the POSD. Some skills, like Fundamental Skills, are essential to every skill and, therefore, can be practiced in each session if necessary. They are included in the POSD so that any problems in these core areas are easily recognized. Most of the Social Initiation, Social Response and Getting Along with Others skills have corresponding teaching lessons, but some do not. Some of the Social Response skills, such as Responding to Greetings and Compliments, can be taught in conjunction with initiating them. Further, some of the POSD skills are more suitable for a preschool/kindergarten curriculum and are not included here. These include sharing, taking turns, using farewells, playing by the rules, apologizing, and so on. Nevertheless, they are included in the POSD because problems in these areas must be acknowledged and rectified. On the other hand, some skills are included because they typically cause problems for children with ASD, such as Staying on the Topic, Giving Short Comments, or Asking Appropriate Questions. These skills can be addressed through lessons of how to join and exchange conversation.

Although this book presents teaching strategies for a selected group of skills, the reader may utilize the strategies to develop additional programs, as needed for individual students. Any of the "extra" skills that do not have corresponding teaching lessons may be designated as target behaviors.

SELECTING LESSONS

Once target behaviors have been determined, how are lessons selected for the overall curriculum? Among the 30 lessons in this book, do not begin with Lesson 1 and proceed to the end. Teach skills the children need, rather than teaching a curriculum to the children. Thus, the individually selected target behaviors determine which lessons to select. This is essential to the program's success.

Nevertheless, some subjectivity goes into determining the final schedule of lessons to include. In general, the more sessions that are planned, the greater flexibility the leader has. Invariably, I want to include more skill lessons than there is time. The following strategy offers a place to start and ensures that everyone's priority skills are included.

1. Use the Super Skills Grouping POSD (see the Appendix, page 342) and summarize the POSD scores for each child (see Table 2.3). Do this by averaging individual scores for each social skill when you have multiple POSDs for one child (see the example in Table 2.4) or record each POSD score with different-colored ink. For example, record the teacher's scores in red, mother's scores in blue, father's scores in black, child's scores in green and other scores in orange. Be consistent across group members.

2. Indicate each child's potential target behaviors with a special mark, such as a star or the letter T.

3. Look for the greatest degree of agreement between preferred target behaviors and similar deficits.

4. Based upon the number of sessions planned, work from the most agreement to the least agreement.

5. Assign a skill for each session, in general starting with simpler moving towards more difficult skills. The schedule in Table 2.5 was developed from the POSD Grouping Profile in Table 2.3. The eight sessions listed include target behaviors as well as related skills. Notice that Manuel's target behavior of "correct voice tone" is not on the schedule. This is because using a friendly voice is a component of every Super Skills lesson.

Table 2.3 SUPER SKILLS GROUPING PROFILE OF SOCIAL DIFFICULTY

*=target behavior; empty cells indicate no data were available.

To identify shared social skill difficulty among a group of children, summarize their POSD scores below. Assign a numerical value to each level of difficulty on the POSD, starting with 0 for very difficult and ending with 6 for very easy. The higher the total score the easier it is for a child to perform.

Children's Names	Ben	Richard	Alex	Marcos	Manuel			
Fundamental Skills								
Eye Contact	4	2	2	2	3			
Correct Facial Expression	3	3		3	4			
Correct Voice Volume	2	3	2	2	2			
Correct Voice Tone	2	3	3	2	1*			
Correct Timing	3	2	2	3	3			
Social Initiation Skills								
Using Person's Name	5	4	5	1	4			
Using Farewells	4	4	5	1	5			
Greeting	3	3	4	1	4			
Introducing Self	3	2	4	1	3			
Asking for Help	2	2	5	0*	3			
Giving a Compliment	3	4	5	2	3			
Starting a Conversation	3	4	1	2	3			
Joining a Conversation	2	2	1	2	2			
Ending a Conversation	2	1	1	1	2			
Exchanging Conversation	2	1	2*	2	2			
Inviting Someone to Play	2	2	3	3	1			
Introducing Others	3	4	4	2	1			
Joining In	3	4	4	2	1			
Talking About Self	5	4	4	3	2			
Making a Complaint	4	6	5	2	5			
Asking Appropriate Questions	4	2	2	1	3			
Offering an Opinion	4	5	3	1*	2			
Expressing Basic Feelings	3	2	3	2	3			
Expressing Complex Feelings	1	1	2	1	2			
Social Response Skills								
Responding to Compliments	3	2	4	3	3			
Listening	2	2	4	3	3			
Following Directions	3	1	2	2	3			

Table 2.3 SUPER SKILLS GROUPING PROFILE OF SOCIAL DIFFICULTY (cont.)

Children's Names	Ben	Richard	Alex	Marcos	Manuel
Social Response Skills					
Making Short Comments	1	4	3	3	3
Staying on the Topic	1		3	3	3
Waiting	1	2	3	4	3
Staying on Task	2	1	3	3	2
Offering Help	4		2	2	3
Giving Encouragement	3	1	4	3	3
Reading Body Language	1	2	3	3	2
Reading Feelings of Others	1	2	3	2	2
Dealing with Mistakes	3	2	2	1	1
Dealing with Anger	1*	2	2	1	2
Refusing When Appropriate	3	4	2	2	2
Getting Along with Others					
Taking Turns	3	2	3	4	4
Sharing	4	2	4	4	4
Playing by the Rules	3	2	4	4	2
Apologizing	3	2	4	4	5
Being Fair	4	2	5	4	3
Being a Good Sport	3	2	4	4	1*
Using Kind Talk	3	2	5	3	4
Being Flexible	2	1*	2*	3	1
Asking Permission	4	4	4	4	4
Cooperating	3	1	5	4	3
Dealing with "No"	2	1	2	4	3
Compromising	2	1	3	4	2
Dealing with a Problem	2	2	2	3	2
Receiving a Suggestion	2	2	3	3	2
Giving a Suggestion	4	5	3	3	3
Letting Others Talk	2	2	4	3	3
Showing Interest in Others	2	2	1	1*	3
Using Humor	4	3	3	5	5
Disagreeing Politely	3	2	2	3	2
Dealing with Teasing	1*	0*	2	3	1

Table 2.4: Averaging POSD Scores											
	Ben				Alex			Marcos			
	M	F	T	Ave	M	F	Ave.	M	T	T	Ave
Greeting	2	2	4	3	4	4	4	2	0	2	1
Introducing Self	4	1	5	3	4	4	4	2	0		1
Using Farewells	4	4	5	4	5	4	5	2	0	2	1

M= mother, F= Father, T= Teacher.

Note. Alex does not have a POSD from his teacher. Marcos does not have a POSD from his father but has POSDs from two different teachers. In cases like this, simply average the available POSD scores.

Table 2.5: Curriculum Schedule

1. Showing Interest in Others
2. Exchanging Conversation
3. Asking for Help
4. Dealing with Teasing

5. Being Flexible
6. Dealing with Anger
7. Dealing with a Problem
8. Being a Good Sport

GROUPING

In general, group children together who share similar skill deficits, including language, academics (reading and writing) and behavior. Another important variable is the skill of the leader. If the leader is a novice, I do not recommend working with a group of children all of whom have skill deficits in Getting Along with Others. In such instances, the leader may end up managing challenging behaviors rather than teaching social skills. Instead, it would be far better to mix the children into less homogenous groups.

PLANNING FOR DIFFERENT TARGET BEHAVIORS AMONG MEMBERS IN THE GROUP

Although target behaviors are the primary focus of a child's involvement in Super Skills, they are not always the sole focus. As we have seen, not everyone in the group shares the same target behaviors. While Joining in a Group might be a target behavior for some, others might focus on Cooperating or Reading Body Language. This is the flexibility of the Super Skills program. Teaching one main skill for each session, or sessions, provides ample opportunity to practice components of target behaviors, even when they are not the main point of the session. Generally, children with ASD gain from repetition in many different circumstances and from different points of view.

Occasionally, a child has mastered a skill and does not need more practice. Or perhaps a skill is not a deficit for a given child. In such cases, the child has an opportunity to excel, to help the leader model the skill and demonstrate this strength to his peers. This builds up self-confidence and helps the student to feel good about her progress. With some advance planning, there are almost always ways to build meaningful practice opportunities into the session.

> Asking for Help and Giving a Suggestion are target behaviors for Tasha, age 8, who has autism. She is not bothered when she loses at a game. So, when the main lesson is Being a Good Sport, which is a target behavior for others in the group, the focus for Tasha is to ask for help during the game and give a suggestion to a peer during the game.

CHAPTER 3

CREATING SUCCESS

or most children with ASD, learning new material is difficult. These children see themselves faced with confusing demands, obscure expectations and misunderstandings, leading to the same dismal conclusion – failure (Stewart, 2002). Although the child would like to succeed, he often finds it safer to relax into a familiar routine. This routine might be to wait so long that others end up doing the task for the child, to watch others do the task repeatedly and then sit down and do it perfectly or to use well-established behaviors that succeed in ultimately evading frustration and failure.

These behaviors might include escaping to the bathroom or hall, yelling out, crying, becoming silly, attempting to change the task expectations, blurting out, fidgeting, becoming restless, staring off, replaying internal dialogues, shutting down, refusing, damaging or destroying property or hurting others. The child is managing her distress the best way she knows how – by using a tactic that successfully reduces fear and anxiety. When a child engages in such a familiar routine, she expects the same ultimate conclusion: reducing her stress. Thus, contrary to all appearances, she is not being manipulative or noncompliant.

In the same way that any new task or learning experience can be fear-provoking, new social experiences are frightening to children with ASD. Learning Super Skills is no exception. The fear of failure is strong. Asking a child to "try" a role-play or to "try" an unfamiliar activity where there is a chance of error frequently induces or increases stress. Other common causes of increased tension in Super Skills include being asked a question, losing at a game, not being called upon after volunteering, being corrected by a peer, not being first, being asked to do a difficult task (write, read, draw), loud voices, transitions between activities or being in close physical proximity to others.

There is no cookie-cutter child with ASD. Every single one is different. Therefore, the causes of stress are varied, and how one student copes with frustration and anxiety may be very different from the way another child does. Unless a child has experienced

the fun of succeeding that motivates more typical children to learn, he will at least hesitate, and at most, oppose participating in Super Skills. In other words, just because we are ready to teach the child to play with others, or to join a conversation, doesn't mean that he will be ready to learn.

We want to replace failure and frustration with success and satisfaction. It is our job as leaders and teachers to set kids up to succeed one step at a time. We must make it impossible for them to fail.

KNOW THE STUDENTS

The more information leaders know and understand about students in a group, the more effective they will be. This does not mean that a comprehensive life history of the child is needed. However, some basic information is essential. This includes the following.

◆ **Current interests:** Knowing current interests helps to individualize role-plays, design activities and arrange partners for a session. When two students enjoy drawing, pairing them for a cooperative drawing activity increases their interest and participation. It will be easier for them to converse because they are mutually interested in the drawing and it captures their attention. Knowing hobbies and favorite activities also helps when choosing tangible reinforcers. For example, a child who collects foreign coins or stamps might be highly motivated to participate successfully when he realizes he can earn one of his favorite items.

◆ **Stress response:** It is important to know the general situations each student perceives as anxiety-provoking and how she manages stress, regardless of whether her particular methods are effective or not. Such knowledge helps determine strategies to minimize stress and frustration when necessary but also, and more important, to purposefully and carefully design activities that cause some degree of anxiety so a student can gradually learn to cope. Often children indicate stress by excessive fidgeting, distractibility or restlessness. Watching for these cues and responding with stress-relief measures helps to create a successful session.

◆ **Language abilities:** Communication problems are inherent characteristics of children with ASD. Having knowledge about strength and weakness areas in language helps to understand how children may contribute to discussions as well as interact with peers. Supports, such as visual schedules or picture cues that help to understand language, can be prepared in advance, given this information. Knowledge of language abilities is necessary to prepare individualized scripts for role-plays. Finally, the child with limited abilities can be taught the exact language to use in given situations if his or her language abilities are known ahead of time.

◆ **Academic skills:** A child's ability to read and write impacts whether or not the leader calls upon the child for such tasks. Some children know how to read but are uncomfortable reading aloud. In this instance, it is good practice to offer the child a choice of reading or not. If writing is not one of a child's strengths, or he simply cannot do it, divide the group into pairs with one person acting as the scribe, or direct the child to dictate his answers to another.

◆ **Sensory issues:** Understanding sensory issues goes a long way in preventing problems with children with ASD. For example, recognizing that a loud group session might negatively impact someone who is sensitive to sound, that an activity that requires touching might be stressful to somebody who is sensitive to touch, or that a bright room might bother a child who is sensitive to light, is essential to a successful session. Some signals of sensory dysfunction include the following:

- Overreaction to touch

- Over/underreaction to pain

- Unusual reaction to noise

- Too heavy or too light pressure when using writing implements

- Sitting on knees

- Hiding

- Acting tired

- Disorganization, inattentiveness, fidgeting

◆ **Health concerns:** Knowing relevant medical issues is important to planning activities and reinforcers. For example, if a child has food allergies or diet restrictions, alternative snacks may be required. If a child stares off or is unresponsive, she may be having a seizure. If she is exceptionally tired or irritable, it may be because she is taking medication that causes such reactions.

◆ **Social profile:** Finally, knowing each child's social profile is essential. This was discussed in detail in Chapter 2.

This basic knowledge about the students is vital for creating a successful Super Skills program by helping to decipher how children with ASD react to the world. An effective leader uses this information to begin to look at the world from the student's point of view and plan accordingly. Use Table 3.1: Creating Success: Know the Student Checklist to begin gathering basic information about each student in Super Skills (a blank copy is found in the Appendix, page 294).

Table 3.1: Creating Success: Know the Student Checklist

Child's Name: Miguel   **Date:** 1/3

Current Interests: What are the child's current interests and favorite activities? Check all that apply and list or highlight as needed.

☑ Art: clay, crafts, drawing, <u>painting</u>, sand, wood Other:	☑ Sports activities: Baseball, basketball, bike riding, hockey, horseback riding, outdoor play, skating, soccer, swimming, tennis, <u>gymnastics</u>
☑ Pet(s): Dog: Clue	☐ Movies: (list) Spy Kids
☑ Collections: beads, books, dolls, cards, coins, comics, insects, rocks, stamps, t shirts, Other: crystals	☑ Television show(s): (list) memorizes commercials
☑ Play activities/games: (list) running, tag	☐ Music: (list)
☐ Computer activities: (list)	☐ Transportation: airplanes, boats, cars, trains, trucks, ships
☐ Special topics: animals, dinosaurs, event(s), famous person(s), geography, historical era, insects, plants, solar system Other:	☐ Other comments:
☑ Electronic games: (list) Play station 2: racing games, would play games all day if allowed	

Stress Response: How does the child usually indicate he/she is becoming anxious or stressed? Check all that apply and add details as needed.

☐ Asks inappropriate questions/makes inappropriate comments	☐ Distractibility increases
☐ Leaves seat/room	☐ Shuts down
☐ Becomes off task	☐ Facial expression/posture changes
☐ Has meltdown	☐ Stares off
☐ Becomes silly	☐ Fidgeting/restlessness increases
☐ Noises/humming increases	☑ Voice tone/volume changes
☑ Blurts out, calls names: stupid, liar	☑ Hurts self/others: kicks, shoves
☐ Reduces eye contact	☑ Yells out
☐ Cries/tearful	☑ Other comments: unpredictable events are usual triggers
☐ Refuses requests	
☐ Damages property	
☐ Repeats self	

Academic Skills: Indicate the child's broad reading and writing skills. Check those that apply and add details as needed.

☑ Reads at age/grade level	☑ Writes below age/grade level
☐ Reads below age/grade level	☐ Writing skills minimal
☐ Reading skills minimal	☐ Does not like to write
☐ Does not like to read aloud	☐ Likes to write
☐ Likes to read aloud	☑ Other comments: math above grade. Slow to complete school work
☐ Writes at age/grade level	

Language Ability: In general, how do the child's language expression and comprehension abilities relate to typical peers? Are there specific problems with language use? Check all that apply and add details as needed.

☐ Language expression at age/grade level	☐ Monopolizes conversation
☐ Language expression slightly below age/grade level	☐ Repeats self (perseverates)
	☐ Slow to respond (needs more time)
☐ Language expression below age/grade level	☐ Script required for discussion/role-plays
☐ Comprehension of spoken language at age/grade level	☐ Difficult to understand when speaks
	☐ Voice volume: soft, loud
☑ Comprehension of spoken language slightly below age/grade level	☑ Visual supports helpful but not required
☐ Comprehension of spoken language below age/grade level	☐ Visual supports required: pictures/ written words
☑ Argues when doesn't want to do the same thing that others do	☑ Other comments: more trouble responding to open-ended questions. Trouble understanding intentions of others
☐ Blurts out	

Sensory Issues: Does the child have any significant sensory issues? Check those that apply and add details as needed.

☐ Sensitive to bright lights	☑ Sensitive to smells/tastes
☐ Sensitive to touch	☑ Other comments: wears long-sleeved shirts and pants
☐ Sensitive to loud sounds/voices	
☐ Sensitive to infringement into personal space	
☐ Sensitive to textures	

Health Concerns:

☐ Activity restrictions:	☑ Diet restrictions: dairy products
☐ Medications:	☐ Sleep problems:
☐ Allergies:	☑ Other comments: healthy
☐ Seizures:	

Social Profile: Complete the POSD (Appendix, page 346)

Misc: Prefers to be alone, has good days and bad days; bad days are multiple episodes of screaming and name calling. Responds well to rehearsal in advance of new situations and is beginning to ask for help in both familiar and unfamiliar situations when the unusual happens.

PLAN AND PREPARE

Advance planning is key to smooth management of a group session. Although the sessions are detailed in the second half of this book, leaders have to make certain decisions beforehand. These include:

- Which discussion questions?

- Which role-plays?

- Which activities?

- What supplies?

- What supports?

- What homework, if any?

In Super Skills, there is no such thing as too much preparation. The structure provided by the lessons helps to maximize instructional control and minimize behavior challenges. However, advance planning is critical to success. Arrange the details for each session in advance and be prepared for any eventuality. Know available options. The ability to be flexible within Super Skills comes from planning ahead. Making spontaneous decisions that keep the group progressing becomes easier the more familiar you become with the students, their responses and the Super Skills format.

Structure

The Super Skills format provides the consistency and routine children with ASD need to feel secure and comfortable. Once established, this structure should not be varied. Children come to predict the sequence of the group activities and rely on the routine, even though they do not know the exact nature of all of the activities, how long they will last or how many there will be. Surprises and significant changes in the routine can lead to anxiety and disrupt the group goals. If changes are necessary, be sure to discuss them before the group starts.

Part of this structure includes the use of visual supports. Effective for many, but not all children with ASD, visual supports help to ensure that everyone has identical information. This includes knowledge of rules, Steps to Success and reinforcement activities. They are a continual reminder of what to do. According to Show and Beisler (1997), visual supports work because they:

- are stationary, not transient

- maintain concise and systematic presentation

- are easily understood by most people

- improve our organization

- highlight key concepts

- decrease verbal directives and repetition

- change our expectations for child success

In Super Skills, picture supports are added for children who cannot read to offer support to the Steps to Success (see samples in the Appendix, pages 335-342). Picture stories may also be used to further individualize a skill for students.

Finally, visual supports may be used to help regulate behavior. This is further discussed in Chapter 4, Dealing with Disruptive Behavior.

CREATE A POSITIVE ENVIRONMENT

A positive learning environment is essential for children to thrive and increase their social interactions skills. To create such an environment the leader must be able to:

- Be a participant leader

- Make learning fun

- Keep up the pace

- Emphasize the positive

- Give clear, concrete directions

Such abilities will influence whether Super Skills develops positively or deteriorates into a negative and potentially alienating experience.

◆ **Be a participant leader.** Central and pivotal to an affirmative learning environment is the relationship between the leader and the students. This relationship must be supportive and exceptionally positive (see Table 3.2: Leader Do's and Don'ts). The students rely on the leader to organize the session, provide consistency, keep them from failing and be the chief problem solver. To fulfill all these roles, a leader cannot simply observe and wait for opportunities to teach, but must be an active participant in the group. This includes orchestrating well-structured situations for social interaction, anticipating problems and being prepared to actively model, prompt, facilitate, coach and encourage successful student-to-student interactions.

Table 3.2: Leader Do's and Don'ts	
Do's	**Don'ts**
• Stay calm and neutral	• Raise voice
• Show, model	• Lecture
• Use positive reinforcement	• Bribe, punish
• Offer choices	• Command, demand
• Refer to rules, Steps to Success	• Nag, preach
• Ask questions when problems arise, find out what happened	• Make assumptions
• Respect refusal	• Force compliance
• Agree to disagree	• Argue
• Understand ASD	• Blame the child

◆ **Make learning fun.** Some of the practice activities in the lessons may feel threatening, especially at first. Therefore, children must feel supported in their efforts and know that you as leader recognize their struggles. When the activities are pleasant, the environment is conducive to learning. Make the group so much fun that children are disappointed when they miss a session because of illness or conflicting plans.

It is not uncommon for older children new to the program to resist attending or to initially refuse certain tasks. In my experience, however, even those who are initially resistive begin to realize that they too can participate successfully when the learning is enjoyable.

◆ **Keep up the pace.** Super Skills is meant to be quick and fast-paced. Don't give children a chance to get bored or lose attention. Vary the learning tasks so interest is maintained and a child is not continuously frustrated. Sometimes discussions get bogged down with details, or one child monopolizes the discussion. In such situations, be ready to cut the discussion short. Although important, discussion is not the main teaching strategy. *Super Skills is learning by doing.* Don't wait for behavior to degenerate so that you spend your time reacting to misbehavior. Be alert, look around and maintain instructional control. If an activity is not working the way you want, swiftly wrap it up and move on.

◆ **Emphasize the positive.** A dangerous mistake when working with kids with ASD is to be overly critical and focus on shortcomings. While it is true that a child may have to be reminded of his errors, do not dwell on mistakes. When correction is needed, it is more effective to tell the youngster what to do. For example, if the child is practicing how to join a conversation and forgets to wait for a pause, instead of correcting her by saying: "You forgot to wait for a pause," say, "Yes! You joined in on the topic. Now let's try again, and this time I'd like you to wait for a pause before joining in." In this way, the child is encouraged to try once more. Similarly, if a child is having trouble sitting still, ignore his fidgeting and focus on listening, following directions, effort or volunteering. If the fidgeting is too distracting, silently hand him a rubber ball to squeeze.

Use praise continuously when students are attempting new behavior. When the leader is upbeat and encouraging, students are more willing to try. In addition, they imitate the language and soon encourage each other. Respond with some form of encouragement to every child: "I like the way you looked at me." "Your voice was very friendly," and so on. Table 3.3 gives examples of praise.

Table 3.3: Praise			
Good try!	Good answer!	Yes!	Give me 5!
You did it!	You can do it!	Great!	Good choice!
Good job!	Super job!	Terrific!	I like that.
Fantastic!	That's wonderful	Excellent!	First rate!
A-One!	I like how you . . .	Superb!	Outstanding!

◆ **Give clear, concrete directions.** Be clear in your own mind about what you want the children to do and why. Then speak clearly and simply using a neutral tone of voice. "John said 'hi.' What do you say to John?" Be concrete and explicit and tell what to do, rather than what not to do, whenever practical. Examples are included in Table 3.4. Frequently praising compliance helps children to understand exactly what they are doing right and encourages them to continue.

Avoid questions with a choice unless the child really has a choice and you are ready to accept "no" as an answer. Examples to avoid include "Can you put your coat in your locker?" "Are you ready for Super Skills?" "It's time to put your toys away, O.K.?" Instead, say: "Please put your coat in your locker." "It's time for Super Skills," and "Please put your toys under your chair."

Table 3.4: Giving Directions	
Say ...	*Instead of ...*
Ask Jimmy if you can use a marker.	Don't grab the marker from Jimmy.
Put your hands on the table.	Stop fidgeting.
Please read Step 1.	Pay attention.
Watch Mary role-play.	Stop talking.

When possible, use group directions instead of singling out one child. If one child is playing with a pencil, direct everyone to put their pencils on the table, then collect them and put them away.

Constant repetitions of directions teach children eventually not to listen to words. Instead, point to a rule on the rules chart when a child needs a specific reminder about a rule, rather than constantly reminding the child. If this is unsuccessful, try a personalized visual prompt. Alan, age 9, had difficulty remembering to use a quieter voice. When a visual prompt was placed in front of him, he soon got the message and was better able to comply with the directions. This was also much less distracting to the rest of the group. See Figure 3.1.

Figure 3.1: Personalized Visual Prompt

Shhhhh too LOUD

Hurts ears

The Picture Communication Symbols ©1981-2005 by Mayer-Johnson LLC. All rights reserved worldwide. Used with permission.

USE POSITIVE REINFORCEMENT

When using Super Skills, positive reinforcement, a powerful method of behavior change, is vitally important to shape behavior. Reprimands and punishment are not recommended. Since learning new behavior is seldom stress-free for children with ASD, incentives are needed to promote new behavior and to encourage them to practice new skills.

Positive reinforcement occurs when a reward is provided following a behavior contingent on the occurrence of the behavior (Fouse & Wheeler, 1997). Simply stated, behavior that is followed by a reward is more likely to occur again. This includes prosocial behavior, positive and negative behavior. For example, reinforcing a child who willingly participates in a role-play with praise, a sticker, high five, or extra points increases the likelihood the child will continue to participate in role-play scenarios.

Maxine, age 7, was new to Super Skills and had never role-played before. After watching several students role-play the steps used to introduce oneself to another, she volunteered to go next. She was praised with "nice volunteering, Maxine!" and given an extra sticker for her reinforcement chart.

Unfortunately, many children have learned about negative reinforcement. Negative reinforcement occurs when an event is withdrawn following a behavior (Fouse & Wheeler, 1997). For example, a child has a temper outburst because he is asked to participate in a role-play, and the teacher excuses him from the role-play (event removed). In this case, the temper outburst was negatively reinforced and the likelihood of the child using a temper outburst in the future to escape role-plays is increased. Attention, escape, tangibles and sensory input will reward (maintain) inappropriate or disruptive behavior.

Rewards are used to shape behavior alternatives in addition to praise, discussed earlier. Although most adults have some understanding of how to use rewards, many have told me privately that they believe that children should be able to act appropriately without a reward. Others perceive rewards as bribes and use them inappropriately. Bribes are given "after the fact" and used to stop a negative behavior already in progress. "If you stop screaming, I will take you outside."

A sound reinforcement program, planned in advance, keeps the adult in control and teaches acceptable behavior. Anthony, a child with autism, touches others, especially when he is excited. The Super Skills leader makes an agreement with Anthony. "If you keep your hands in your pockets during your role-play, I will give you a bonus sticker for your chart." A common mistake is to reward a child when he is not performing the desired behavior, such as Anthony does not put his hands in his pockets and the leader gives him a bonus sticker anyway. Another mistake is to reward a child when he is doing something other than the defined, desired behavior; for example, Anthony takes his hands out his pockets and waves them in his partner's face. The leader gives him a bonus sticker telling herself, "Well, he didn't touch his partner." The correct response in this scenario is to reward Anthony with a bonus sticker only if he tries to keep his hands in his pockets, perhaps he takes them out and then quickly puts them back again, or if he successfully keeps his hands in his pockets for the entire role-play.

What to reward:
◆ Child does nothing: No
  Anthony does not put his hands in his pockets.
◆ Child is doing something other than the assigned task: No
  Anthony waves his hands in the air.
◆ Child tries a skill: Yes
  Anthony puts his hands in his pockets and remembers to put them back if he forgets and takes them out.
◆ Child is successful: Yes
  Anthony keeps his hands in his pockets during his entire role-play.

USING SYSTEMATIC REWARDS

There are countless approaches to using systematic rewards. Many include the use of tokens such as stickers, initials, points, chips or tickets. The system used in Super Skills meets three basic criteria. It:

1. *Is easy to administer*

   The straightforward system is easily mastered by the youngsters who quickly grasp the meaning of the rules, the purpose of the timer and the use of tokens.

2. *Is simple to monitor*

   The leader quickly and easily monitors each child's performance. New expectations may be added to each reinforcement chart when necessary.

3. *Uses time efficiently*

   Minimal time is needed to identify expected behaviors, dispense rewards and oversee the program. Therefore, the majority of group time can be spent in teaching.

PREFERRED SUPER SKILLS REINFORCEMENT SYSTEM

After experimenting with numerous reinforcement methods and a variety of approaches, the following simple earn-and-exchange token system is recommended for use with elementary-age students.

1. Give each child a 5x7 reinforcement card (see Figure 3.2). Modeled after the Picture Exchange Communication System (PECS) program (Frost & Bondy, 1994), each card states "I am working for" followed by a place for the child to write in the reward of her choice and her name. Typical choices include candy, toy, coin or pencil. Suggested rewards are listed in Table 3.5.

2. Review the rules with the children at the beginning of every Super Skills session. Using written rules, such as a poster, makes it easy to refer to rules when needed later in the group session. For example, the Rules for Good Listening poster (Carson-Dellosa Publishing, www.carsondellosa.com) is simple and to the point. It states: Eyes Are Watching, Ears Are Listening, Lips Are Closed, Hands Are Still, Feet Are Quiet. Ask the children to quickly demonstrate each rule as it is read and praise appropriate responses. This prompts the group to show learning readiness at the beginning of each session.

3. Divide the total length of the Super Skills session into equal time segments, anywhere from 5 minutes to 15-20 minutes each. For example, a session of one hour

might be divided into three 20-minute intervals or four 15-minute intervals. For younger students, more frequent reward intervals may be necessary, whereas older children should be able to sustain longer intervals. Set a timer at the beginning of each time interval. When the timer rings, briefly stop the session and praise the children who have been following the rules and participating. Then place a sticker or initial in the designated place on each child's reinforcement card.

4. At the end of the group session, distribute the reward of choice to the students who have received all stickers or initials. It is rare for a child not to receive a reward because you are setting children up to succeed. However, there are occasions when a child does not receive all of the stickers, but has made an effort to follow the rules. Give this child a small reward, such as a piece of candy or a sticker, for effort and instruct him to try again next time.

5. Children may be assigned "bonus" behaviors, or goals to reach during a session. These are added at the leader's discretion and written directly on each child's card at the beginning of the lesson. A child who frequently interrupts others might have a goal of "I waited for a pause before speaking" or "I waited until I was called upon to speak." For another child who demonstrates an explosive temper, the goal might be to "Use only nice talk" or "Use a quiet voice." A third child might not volunteer, instead spending too much time "in his own world." This child might receive a bonus for "Volunteering three times" or "Speaking out."

   In this way each session can be individualized to target specific social skills for each student. Never single out one student for this approach but assign all students something extra to work at. Place a bonus sticker at the end of the session on the card and give the child an extra reward of his or her choice.

6. The final component of the reinforcement system involves applying stickers spontaneously for exceptional actions. Give such bonus stickers to students who spontaneously demonstrate uncommon but positive social behavior. This might include those who give a peer a sincere compliment, make a gesture of friendship such as offering to partner with a student who everyone knows has trouble reading or volunteer to help clean up. Praise the specific behavior and give an extra sticker.

   Michael, age 10, never greeted the leader and peers without prompts, despite many reminders to do so. One day he entered the group with a spontaneous greeting. He was lavishly praised and given a bonus sticker before the group had even started.

Table 3.5: Typical Rewards				
Comic books	Action figures	Foreign coins	Stamps	Art supplies
Markers/pens	Small cars	Marbles	Legos	Small models
Jewelry	Maze books	Stickers	Candy/treats	Silly putty
Seasonal items	Bead kits	Stationery	School supplies	Posters

Figure 3.2: Reinforcement Chart

Name: John

I am working for: coin

In the above example, John has chosen to earn a coin as his preferred reward. So far he has earned two of the four tokens needed to earn this reward. There are two time intervals remaining in the group session.

CHAPTER 4

DEALING WITH DISRUPTIVE BEHAVIOR

Behavior problems inevitably occur during Super Skills sessions, no matter how well planned and organized. When considering the myriad challenges facing children with ASD and similar challenges, this is not surprising. Usually the problems that come up in Super Skills sessions replicate the problems the children experience in more typical daily environments.

Experiencing these challenges first-hand gives leaders a snapshot view of the communication breakdowns and stress reactions that occur at home and at school. This information is invaluable when trying to help children with ASD develop new coping skills and succeed in their efforts to use them.

WHAT IS DISRUPTIVE BEHAVIOR?

In general, disruptive behaviors in Super Skills are those that interfere with the progress of the group. They interrupt the normal movement and growth of the group to the point that it becomes challenging to continue with planned activities. When such disruption occurs regularly, it is usually a signal that the leader needs to intervene and change some aspect of the group structure. It does not mean that a child is intentionally misbehaving, willful or manipulative.

Sometimes children can explain the rules or list appropriate behavior but are unable to apply them when the situation arises. The presence of disruptive behavior indicates the need to teach the child when and how to use alternative, more appropriate means of interaction. Typical disruptive behaviors include temper outbursts or rage attacks, destructiveness, refusal, hitting and other types of aggression, self-injurious behavior, excessive fidgeting or restlessness, and arguing or monopolizing.

COMMON FUNCTIONS OF DISRUPTIVE BEHAVIOR

Disruptive behavior usually occurs for a reason; that is, it fulfills a need. Common functions of disruptive behavior include the following: to request attention; to escape, avoid, refuse or protest; to access something; to engage in sensory feedback/rituals; to express an emotional state; to gain power and control; to intimidate; to express perceived loss; to reflect obsessional thoughts (Myles & Southwick, 2005).

◆ **Request attention.** Children who have restricted language use may resort to outbursts, hitting or other types of aggression to receive attention. Others may request attention by talking about their special interests. These examples of social initiation indicate that the child must be given opportunities to receive attention through other means. Give the child opportunities to "shine," to show off knowledge about a subject, to be the model or the leader. Single the child out for a special task. Typical alternative skills to teach include using proper names, asking someone to play, asking for help and exchanging conversation.

◆ **Escape, avoid, refuse, protest.** Learning new skills is rarely easy, so disruptive routines that allow a child to escape, avoid or refuse are common, particularly for children with AS, who often have a strong need to control circumstances that directly affect them. It is frequently difficult for a child with AS to accept direction from others. To eliminate or reduce such disruptive behaviors, setting achievable expectations, allowing the child some control and using positive reinforcement are all critical in these situations. The child who uses disruptive behavior to protest must be taught alternative means of coping, such as dealing with anger, being flexible, dealing with mistakes or being a good sport.

◆ **Access something, such as food, an activity or an object.** When children use disruptive behavior to gain access to something, it usually means that this has been a successful strategy for them in the past. That is, the child has learned to use an outburst to force a parent to purchase a desired item in a store, to argue with others to control an activity or outcome or to be aggressive to get a toy. The skill alternatives depend upon the circumstances of the disruptive behavior.

Jeremy, a child with AS, collects sets of building blocks. Every time his parents shop at a local variety store, he lies on the floor and screams if they do not purchase one of these sets. Jeremy must be taught to deal with anger, follow directions, ask permission and deal with "no."

◆ **Engage in sensory feedback/rituals.** Rituals are behaviors that are performed in the same sequence and in the same way across time. Rituals are determined by the child and are usually perceived as unusual by others in the environment. One ritual might be to close all cupboard doors in a specific order, color all pictures in a coloring book a predetermined color sequence, such as red, yellow, green, or systematically line up favorite toys. These behaviors are usually mildly disruptive and can be dealt with ahead of time or ignored.

◆ **Express emotional state: Stress, confusion, boredom, frustration, fear, anger.** This common function of disruptive behavior is demonstrated in many ways. Behaviors may be aggressive, destructive, loud and impulsive. Some children shut down and retreat within themselves. Others fidget and become restless. Children with sustained problems in emotional expression are often referred to Super Skills groups in order to learn self-control and alternative coping strategies. Most frequently, these children have a diagnosis of AS. Fear of failure or of making a mistake is especially strong. Those with chronic anger and frustration management problems are frequently prone to rage attacks. Intensive work is required, and the assistance and support from everyone working with the child is essential if progress is to be made.

Note: The novice leader should not include more than one student with chronic rage attacks in a group. Their presence can be very disruptive unless extra support is present.

◆ **Gain power and control; intimidate.** Sometimes disruptive behavior is an attempt to retain control of a situation – to intimidate others or show power. An example is the child who routinely uses foul language, upends the game or destroys a group project that is not going the way he wants it to. Sometimes this behavior can be dealt with by using the prevention strategies described below. In other cases, a more individualized approach is required, using strategies to reduce chronic disruptive behavior discussed later in this chapter. Typical skills to learn include being a good sport, dealing with anger, cooperating, playing by the rules, disagreeing politely, using kind talk, giving and receiving a suggestion, apologizing and being flexible.

◆ **Express perceived loss.** In other children, loss of face or perceived position as the smartest, best game player, best artist, and so on, precipitates disruptive behavior. Thus, the child's self-esteem is compromised, and her reaction is an expression of discomfort.

◆ **Reflect obsessional thoughts.** The need to protect an irrational thought, often viewed as rules dictating behavior by individuals with AS, can also be the function of a disruptive behavior. Examples of such rules might be:

- I always choose a blue playing piece.
- I always role-play first.
- Only Sam can be my partner.
- I cannot have a pink folder.

Thoughts like these indicate the need to learn skills such as being flexible, taking turns and cooperating.

STRATEGIES TO REDUCE MILD DISRUPTIVE BEHAVIOR

There are no "typical" behavior challenges of children with ASD. Each child perceives the world in his own special way and reacts accordingly. However, several strategies may be used to help a child manage short-term stress and frustration that often lead to disruptive behavior. First suggested by Redl and Wineman (1957), re-reported by McGinnis and Goldstein (1997), and re-re-reported by Myles and Southwick (2005), these techniques are generally effective in reducing mild problems. Below we will briefly look at planned ignoring, proximity control, signal interference, interest boosting, use of humor, restructuring the program, removing seductive objects, antiseptic bouncing and reality appraisal.

◆ **Planned ignoring.** When a Super Skills group first begins, it is important to ignore many mildly disruptive behaviors. Most children demonstrate such a multitude of deficits that the group will quickly spiral into a negative experience for everyone if every problem is attended to. It is much better to focus on positive behaviors and thereby increase the frequency of positive responses.

Clarify ahead of time, by reviewing group members' POSDs, which disruptive behaviors you will likely encounter and determine those you plan to ignore. Typical situations to ignore in the early stages of a group include blurting out answers, negative or loud tone of voice, monopolizing, minor teasing, rituals, hoarding supplies and leaving the group to use the bathroom. While mildly disruptive, such behaviors can be shaped once more serious challenges have been resolved. Making a conscious effort to initially ignore mildly disruptive behavior while reinforcing appropriate behavior as described in Chapter 3 can go a long way towards establishing a positive group experience for everyone.

◆ **Proximity control.** Proximity control, moving near the student, is an essential preventive strategy but is also indispensable when a child has become stressed or upset.

Placing yourself in close proximity so they are acutely aware of your presence helps many children calm when they start becoming agitated. For the most beneficial support, intentionally sit next to children who have behavior control issues. Move closer to anyone who is becoming agitated if the child is not already near you. It is not uncommon for children who recognize that they might become anxious to sit next to the leader when the group first begins. For some children, placing a firm hand on a shoulder is reassuring, while others react negatively to touch. In some cases, it is a good idea to ask a parent to sit next to or in close proximity to the child. Sitting the parent in a corner of the room, within eyesight of the child, and gradually fading his or her presence is often helpful for new students in the group.

◆ **Signal interference.** These nonverbal signals, gestures or warning signs cue children to change behavior. They are used without accompanying language when children engage in mildly disruptive behavior, or when the leader wants to signal a child that the leader is aware the child is troubled or distressed. A signal can be a secret between the leader and a specific student, but it is often difficult to keep it a secret from other students. I prefer to teach a signal to the entire group and then use it universally with any student who needs it. Teaching can occur briefly at the beginning of a session where behavior and a signal are "practiced" by the entire group. When a private signal is needed, teach it in private. Examples of signals include the following:

- *Fidgeting, touching others, distracting:* Look at the child, slowly shake your head "no" and silently fold your hands in front of you. Give a silent O.K. sign (index finger pressed to thumb) when the child complies.
- *Talking too loudly:* Place one hand in front of you, palm down. Slowly lower your palm to signal a child to speak softer.
- *Talking too quietly:* Turn your palm upward and raise it to signal a child to speak louder.
- *Being impatient, blurting out, interrupting:* Hold an index finger in the air to signal a child to wait.

◆ **Interest boosting.** It is common for children with ASD to have problems attending, especially when they are not interested in the subject matter. Some of the strategies used in situations like that were discussed earlier in this book, but they are worth mentioning again. Strategies to enhance attention include:

- Use special and unique interests in discussion, role-plays, and activities.
- Ask direct questions. Don't let one person monopolize.
- Keep everyone involved. Assign everyone a task.
- Keep up the pace. Don't allow idle time.
- End undesirable activities.

◆ **Humor.** A sense of humor can go a long way in reducing problems. However, children with ASD often do not understand humor. Super Skills group is a safe place to learn more about how to use and understand humor. Some children laugh too loudly, others inappropriately, and some are clueless about the nature of humor in a given situation. Laugh when something is funny. Explain humorous events when they occur to those who do not understand what is happening.

◆ **Restructuring the program.** Generally, stick to the structure and routine you have established. However, at times a chosen activity does not turn out the way you had expected. It may be too complicated or too boring. As a result, the children become edgy and their attention wanes. When this occurs, end the activity quickly and move on to something else. Do not continue with an unproductive activity. For this reason, it is important to be well prepared with alternatives.

Sometimes a student enters the group with a pressing personal problem or experience, perhaps the death of a grandparent or the pending separation of her parents. This creates a spontaneous opportunity to practice how to respond to such events. Use some of the discussion time and prompt and guide other group members in what to say, taking advantage of the opportunity to practice Reading the Feelings of Others.

◆ **Removing seductive objects.** Toys and other objects brought by students to Super Skills group may be distracting. In general, direct children to give such items to a parent for safe keeping, or put them under a chair or in some other designated spot for the duration of the session. If children have brought objects at your request for a specific purpose, such as a family photo for a general discussion of brothers and sisters, collect them and place them within easy reach to be brought out when appropriate.

Sometimes a youngster needs a fidget object to calm down and be able to concentrate better. This is perfectly acceptable. Provide a special soft ball or squishy toy for such occasions.

◆ **Antiseptic bouncing.** This strategy is practical before a student loses control (Myles & Southwick, 2005). When a change in behavior indicates an impending crisis, such as flexing and tensing muscles, facial grimacing, change in voice tone, excessive tapping or fidgeting, direct the student to run an errand, get supplies you "forgot," take a note to someone, find out a piece of information or get a drink. In my experience, most children recognize when they need a break and usually ask to use the bathroom. They successfully rejoin the activity when they return.

◆ **Reality appraisal.** The intent of reality appraisal is to explain to the group why a behavior is inappropriate or unacceptable. It involves explaining consequences. "If" you do this, "then" this will happen.

1. If you do not follow the rules, you will not earn a sticker. In Super Skills, everyone earns a prize when they earn all of their stickers.

2. If you talk all the time, no one else will have a chance. In Super Skills, we take turns talking.

3. If you do not participate in a role-play, you will not earn a sticker. In Super Skills, everyone participates in role-plays.

STRATEGIES TO REDUCE CHRONIC DISRUPTIVE BEHAVIOR

Max, age 10, is a new student in Super Skills and not well known to the leader. He is adamant that he will not read aloud the Steps to Success and participates only minimally in discussions. His affect is usually angry. He regularly shouts "shut up" to the group leader and peers when he is upset. Nevertheless, he enjoys most activities as long as they are going his way.

After a few weeks in Super Skills, Max becomes more cooperative. He is not pressed to read aloud and eventually begins volunteering to read. He starts to offer ideas in discussions and partners well with a quieter group member. He is praised regularly for his contributions and allowed to be the last main actor to role-play. He likes earning foreign coins. But despite significant improvement, Max's behavior continues to disrupt the group. He impulsively shouts "shut up" when he is upset – now two or three times each lesson. This behavior is ultimately targeted for individual intervention.

The leader decides to add an individualized behavior goal to each group member's reinforcement chart. "No saying 'shut up,' say 'be quiet'" is added to Max's reinforcement chart while other individualized goals are written on the other students' cards. Each child is able to earn a bonus sticker and prize if they accomplish their targeted behavior goal.

At the first session this strategy is implemented, Max tries hard to curb his behavior, but he is unsuccessful and does not earn an extra foreign coin. Most of his peers earn their bonus prizes. At subsequent sessions Max earns the bonus coin, and his disruptive behavior is successfully altered.

Chronic disruptive behavior is often prevented or minimized by using the strategies mentioned in Chapter 3 as well as the strategies to reduce mild disruptive behavior mentioned above. It is recommended that the Super Skills leader familiarizes him- or herself with these approaches and uses them naturally, rather than resorting to more punitive approaches such as time-out, isolation or physical restraint, which do not focus on the

intent of the behavior. Max says "shut up" primarily to express anger and frustration. Sending him to time-out after the fact is not a good strategy because Max needs to practice self-control. Being angry is O.K.; how he expresses his anger is the problem. The better strategy is to begin teaching him what to say and to focus on dealing with anger.

When disruptive behavior is occurring regularly in a group, the leader should consider modifying or changing several aspects of the group structure. The best approach seldom uses a single intervention to address a single disruptive behavior. In most cases effective intervention involves the simultaneous manipulation of many variables.

Teaching Strategies

When a student demonstrates chronic disruptive behavior, reevaluate your expectations and teaching plan. You may need to present information differently, considering these potentially useful strategies:

- Increase visual supports. Try pictures, lists, personal cue cards or gestures.
- Reduce the number of reading or writing activities.
- Use stories. They are often helpful for younger students.
- Shorten or eliminate discussions altogether.
- Shorten role-plays.
- Change partners.
- Make sure the child understands what you are asking him to do.
- Simplify verbal directions. Get to the point in as few words as possible.
- Evaluate the reward intervals. In some cases intervals have to be shortened, so that students perhaps earn reward stickers after 5 minutes rather than 10 or 15 minutes. This may be true for a particularly young group where students are highly distractible.

It is best to operate on the assumption that a student who is chronically disruptive must be taught alternatives. Do not take disruptive behavior personally. This is not about punishment or control. The child will likely not perform disruptive behaviors if she has a more socially acceptable way to get what she needs – not simply because she wants to avoid being punished.

Hypothesize the Function of the Disruptive Behavior: Functional Analysis

Developing a hypothesis about the function, or purpose, of a behavior is sometimes referred to as a functional analysis (Fouse & Wheeler, 1997; Myles & Southwick, 2005). In the case of disruptive behavior there may be multiple functions. Determining what these functions are is central to teaching alternative actions that address the reason for the behavior in the first place. Clues to the function of a behavior are obtained from evaluating the events that immediately precede the behavior. These are called the antecedents. They may be an action, event, person's tone of voice, or another aspect of the environment.

Sometimes an intervention addresses one aspect of a disruptive behavior, but not all. A child may have a temper outburst after losing a game (antecedent). The leader develops a teaching plan to Be a Good Sport, and the outburst is successfully eliminated. However, this same child might have a temper outburst when the group becomes too noisy (antecedent). Just because the child has learned to remain calm when losing does not mean she will realize the need to remain calm in other situations. She will have to be taught directly what to say and do when the group is noisy; for example, calmly tell the group "It's too loud in here" or "I need a break, it's getting too loud." Addressing the function of the behavior is key to successfully altering it.

Table 4.1 is an example of a functional analysis. (See also blank form in the Appendix, page 296.)

> Jared, a 9 year-old child with AS, has temper outbursts quite regularly during the first few Super Skills sessions. The leader decides to record the circumstances in order to determine potential reasons for them. The functional analysis for the session indicates that a primary antecedent to a temper outburst is an unanticipated or unexpected event.
>
> This indicates to the leader that Jared needs to learn alternative strategies to express frustration and to deal with problems. In addition, Jared may be bothered by sensory stimuli, such as touch and loud noises. In this case, the leader might decide to collect data for another session to see if her hypotheses are on target.

Determine the Alternative Behavior or Skill

Defining the desired behavior that is to replace the disruptive behavior is crucial when dealing with chronic disruptive behavior. Simply determining that you want the child to stop a behavior such as screaming, fidgeting or arguing is not defining the alternative or replacement behavior. Decide exactly what you want the child to do instead. For example, to say "be quiet," walk away, fidget with a sponge ball, use a friendly voice, and so on. There may be several alternatives to choose from.

Find Out if the Replacement Behavior Is in the Child's Repertoire

Can the child do what you are asking? Make sure the child understands the desired behavior and that he can carry it out. Be explicit in your expectations and explanations. Children with ASD do not understand abstract concepts. Those with AS are

Table 4.1: Functional Analysis

Name: _Jared_

Challenging/Disruptive Behavior: _Screaming/Temper Outburst_

Date	Place/Circumstances (Describe what the child is doing)	Time Began	Time Ended	Antecedent: What happened immediately prior to the behavior?	Intensity (0-5) low-high	Consequence: What happened immediately after the behavior? (adult action)
10/6	Discussion	9:05	9:06	Several group members talking at once, room is loud	2	Ignored
10/6	Role-plays	9:15	9:16	Was not chosen to go first	3	Ignored
10/6	Activity: Art project	9:30	9:32	Did not get marker of first choice	4	Taken through steps of problem solving
10/6	Activity: Art project	9:40	9:41	Was bumped on the arm by another student	2	Ignored
10/6	Activity: Prize distribution	10:00	10:03	Preferred treat was all gone	4	Taken through steps of problem solving

prone to argue and often do not take responsibility for their behavior, preferring to blame and find excuses. Visuals often help the child to process and remember information as well as concretely display, in black and white, the expectation (Hodgdon, 1999). Max was capable of saying, "Be quiet," but needed to practice self-control to apply it. Adding the desired behavior to his reinforcement chart cued this explicit expectation and left little room for discussion or arguing.

When the child does not have the replacement behavior in her repertoire, break the expectation into components that are manageable for the child and gradually introduce the components one at a time. Set up multiple opportunities to teach.

> Felice, age 8, has a 5-minute temper outburst every time she loses a game. Being a Good Sport is targeted as the replacement skill she needs to master. The leader decides to increase the opportunities for Felice to practice this skill and adds a short game to every Super Skills session for a few weeks. At the beginning of the game, the group leader places a visual support in front of Felice (see Figure 4.1).

Figure 4.1: Being a Good Sport		
game	I win!	happy
I like to play games.	Sometimes I win.	I might feel happy.
I lose	sad	good sport
Sometimes I lose.	I might feel sad.	I am a good sport.
calm	sad	"Good game."
I am calm.	I think: "It's O.K. Everybody cannot win."	I say: "Good game."

Felice quickly reviews the support with the leader. "Stay calm when losing" is added to her reinforcement chart. During the game the leader praises Felice for staying calm, and gives her a bonus sticker at the end of the game for remaining calm. After several sessions, when this step is mastered, the next step, "Say good game," is added to her chart, and over time, expectations to deal with anger appropriately are increased.

◆ Reinforce the Desired Behavior

Adding the replacement behavior to a child's reinforcement chart is a simple and effective way to remind the child of the new expectation as well as to reinforce success. If a disruptive behavior is frequent, bonus stickers may be applied at each timed reinforcement interval (e.g., every 10 minutes). Gradually increase the intervals as the frequency of the desired behavior increases and the disruptive behavior decreases.

COMMON QUESTIONS ABOUT DISRUPTIVE BEHAVIORS

"How Should I Deal with Refusal?"

Refusal is often the result of fear of failing or of "being wrong." For a new student, the best approach is to allow the student to watch others before proceeding with her turn. Then, matter-of-factly ask the student if she is "ready" for her turn. When the child says no, say something like, "O.K., I'll ask you again in a bit" or "O.K., maybe next time." Pick battles wisely. Participating in a role-play is the only "mandatory" Super Skills activity and the first hurdle for many students to cross. Therefore, do not insist children greet, read, answer questions, or participate in a warm-up activity during their first or second session. Let them sit and watch these activities if needed. They are learning and should earn a sticker as long as they are listening. Most children will eventually volunteer.

Occasionally, a child waits until all others have finished and then refuses to role-play, her "last chance," so to speak. In such instances, try the following:

1. Explain, "In Super Skills, everyone participates in a role-play. You have to do this before the group ends. Let me know when you are ready."

2. When the timer signals the end of the time segment that includes role-play, remind the child that she has to complete a role-play before earning a sticker on her reinforcement chart. Leave this space in her chart blank.

3. Set up the practice activity and offer the student the choice of participating or not participating. When the next timed reinforcement interval is completed, praise her and apply a sticker if she participated.

4. When the group ends, praise the children for participating, following the rules and earning their rewards. Pass out rewards to those who have earned them.

5. Give the child who did not role-play one more chance to complete a role-play. Usually she will do it at this point. Quickly set up a brief role-play, act it out and reward the child.

6. Tell the child who does not role-play, "I'm sorry you were unable to earn your prize today. I'm sure you will next time."

7. At the beginning of the next session, state the universal rule: "Remember, in Super Skills everyone participates in role-plays." Proceed normally through the group format.

8. The child will likely volunteer to answer a question, read and role-play. Enthusiastically praise her efforts.

In some instances, refusal is an expression of a child's need for greater control. In these circumstances, try asking for volunteers and call on the child when he volunteers. "Who wants to read step number one? Who wants to be first? Who . . . ?"

When refusal indicates a protest, such as when the child did not get the game piece he wanted and, therefore, does not want to play, matter-of-factly begin the activity without him. Usually the child will join in after a few minutes. Next time, use the opportunity to decide as a group how to choose game pieces, decide who will go first, and so on.

"How Should I Deal with Temper Outbursts?"

Temper outbursts or rage reactions usually occur in response to stress and frustration. Because of their rigidity, children with ASD often have difficulty coping when situations do not go according to their expectations, such as losing at a game, not being first, or not being able to control an activity.

If the child is new to Super Skills, it is best to wait out short outbursts if possible and conduct an informal functional analysis noting the antecedents, frequency and duration. Using the functional analysis form (see the Appendix, page 296), record the circumstances of the outbursts. *Antecedents* are events that occur immediately prior to the outburst and give clues to the reason for the outburst. *Frequency* is how often the outbursts occur, whereas *duration* is the length of the outburst. This information is useful when determining alternative skills to teach and when measuring a child's progress at learning those new skills. The frequency of Max's outbursts of "shut up," three to five times per session, often disrupted the group. The alternative behavior was "please, be quiet." Once the frequency of "shut up" had reduced to 0 while the frequency of "please, be quiet" increased, it was determined that Max had successfully mastered the new skill.

Before an outburst occurs, planned ignoring, proximity control, reality appraisal, signal interference or antiseptic bouncing (described on pages 42-45) are practical and convenient. They are also valuable when introducing a child to replacement behaviors and alternative skills when dealing with frustration and anger. Being a Good Sport, Dealing with Anger, Being Flexible or Dealing with Mistakes are frequently the alternative skills that must be taught. Once the alternative skill has been identified, gradually begin to teach the skill steps, starting with one, as described for Felice previously.

An increase in tantrums or disruptive behavior usually indicates an increase in stress. Many times the stress can only be alleviated if the child is allowed to remove himself from the group and then return later. Set up a safe place for a student to go to. Do not call it "time-out." Simply ask the student who is angry, "Do you need a break?" and let him go. Welcome his return and ask him if he is ready to be included. Let him take the initiative.

"Should I Use Time-Out?"

Although there are times when time-out seems to be an appropriate intervention strategy, it is rarely used in Super Skills. In general, time-out is a teacher-directed punishment strategy and means time-out from reinforcement (Patterson, 1975). When used wisely, it can be effective as a behavior management tool in some environments, such as when a child hits, kicks or pushes another student, throws an object at another person, bites or scratches. However, if such aggressive acts are a regular occurrence in the group, it is a signal to the leader to conduct a functional analysis, evaluate his teaching strategies and carry out crucial prevention techniques discussed in Chapter 3 and earlier in this chapter.

Since the focus of Super Skills is on teaching alternative skills, the assumption is that children have to be present in the environment in order to learn those skills. In many cases, time-out encourages escape rather than learning. When children need a break, it is best for them to learn their personal signals and initiate the break on their own. For example, they can be cued with, "Do you need a break?" This implies need for rest rather than need for punishment.

The decision to implement a time-out program must be made very carefully. Time-out is labor-intensive and is difficult for the novice leader to use successfully while keeping a group going. Time-out can quickly escalate into a power struggle, particularly with older students, thus subtracting from valuable group instruction time. Time-out is most effective for one or two target behaviors, not as a general behavior management strategy. Its use is reserved for behavior that usually cannot be ignored, such as hitting or property destruction. The length of time-out is typically 1 minute for each year of the child's age, and a timer is desirable to keep track of time. The time-out place must be safe and free of distractions. Sometimes a chair in the corner of the room can be used, but most often a separate place is necessary. Once time-out is implemented, it is required every time the targeted, disruptive behavior occurs in order to be effective. Time-out must never be used in isolation, but always coupled with a reinforcement program.

"How Do I Deal with Monopolizing?"

Review the skill of Exchanging Conversation (page 124) with the child, emphasizing that a conversation means that everyone takes turns talking and listening. Typically the child who monopolizes does not really listen to what others say. He needs to be taught to notice their words, to comment and to ask questions on the topic. Gradually limit the amount of time per group the child can talk by limiting the number of times he can volunteer and the number of minutes he can talk. Use a timer if necessary. Don't be afraid to cut the child off, but be sure to set up a bonus reinforcement program that rewards him for asking questions about others and using appropriately brief comments.

FINAL THOUGHTS

When disruptive behavior is present in Super Skills sessions, it is likely that the same behavior is present in other environments as well. Keep regular contact with parents and others involved in the child's team. Keep everyone up-to-date on the child's progress and notify them immediately if there is a concern. Work together to establish specific goals and objectives that include using replacement behaviors in all affected environments. This ensures that everyone is teaching replacement behaviors intensively when Super Skills is not in session.

> While Felice used her visual chart in Super Skills, her parents and teacher had duplicate charts to use at home and school. The objective to "stay calm when losing" was included in her individualized educational program and during daily play with friends or siblings at home. Felice was required to "practice" her new skill at least once a day. Her successes were rewarded with tokens that she exchanged for a sleep-over with a friend, a favorite activity.

CHAPTER 5

HOW TO USE THE LESSON PLANS

n this chapter we will discuss how to use the Super Skills lesson plans presented in Chapters 6-8 using the format of each lesson plan: Steps to Success, Thoughts Before Starting, Introducing the Skill, Read and Review Steps to Success, Warm-Up Activity, Role-Plays, Practice Activities, Supportive Skills to Prompt and Reinforce, Supplies and Extending Skill Development.

STEPS TO SUCCESS

To use the lesson plans effectively, you:

1. **Read these instructions.**
2. **Read Chapters 1-4.**
3. **Stay positive.**

THOUGHTS BEFORE STARTING

Each Super Skills lesson is divided into the following parts: Thoughts Before Starting, Introducing the Skill, Read and Review Steps to Success, Warm-Up Activity, Role-Plays, Practice Activities, Supportive Skills, Supplies and Extending Skill Development.

Thoughts Before Starting explains the skill deficit and gives information useful to the leader when preparing each lesson. For example, it discusses special issues to consider when teaching a given skill as well as recurrent themes that help understand the unique challenges of the skill for the child with ASD.

The following icons are used:

☑ **To do, include in teaching the lesson**

☐ **Make a selection and mark it**

✖ **Potential problem**

Some of the lesson plans include potential problems, but not all. These are typical problems that might occur while teaching. How to deal with the problem when it occurs is addressed in the lesson by the following icons:

☹ **Poor solution to the problem, do not use**

😐 **O.K. solution to the problem, use if necessary**

☺ **Best solution to the problem, use when possible**

Expressions in italics. Suggested leader text appears in places. The words are suggestions only. The group leader may prefer a different choice of language. Use what feels natural to you so long as you keep within the parameters of the lessons and the principles of Super Skills.

Beginning Each Session

Begin each session in the same manner according to the following format.

◆ Greet children as they arrive and wait for, or prompt, reciprocal greetings.

◆ Insist that all members greet each other, using the correct names. If someone forgets a name, coach the child in how to find out (Ask). Nametags are helpful to leaders and children who can read. Picture nametags may also be used.

◆ Collect folders and briefly review homework and target behavior practice charts. Award points and bonus prizes, as appropriate.

◆ Collect or put away toys that children may have brought.

◆ Prepare reinforcement charts, review rules and set the timer.

INTRODUCING THE SKILL

Introducing the Skill presents suggestions for how to begin teaching the lesson. Sometimes a brief activity is used to introduce a skill, at other times a short discussion is preferred. Each session includes several discussion questions. In most circumstances, choose only a few questions for each session. The words in italics provide the leader with an optional script to use to lead the discussion.

Usually children with ASD are not skilled in contributing to a discussion, and therefore benefit from the opportunity to develop these skills. Briefly exchange conversation on a few well-chosen topic questions. Discussion can be painstakingly slow and laborious and can quickly set a negative tone for the group. Therefore, it is important to keep the discussion brief and to the point.

Strategies to facilitate discussion include the following:

1. Speak clearly and simply.

2. Keep up the pace. Don't wait long for replies.

3. Keep the discussion brief.

4. Use visuals such as pictures, posters, charts and lists to help keep the discussion focused.

5. Call on different members to contribute. Don't let one person monopolize. Accept all contributions.

6. Frequently praise volunteering, answering questions and listening.

7. To encourage more participation, say something like, "That's possible," "What else?" "What is a different answer?" or "Who can think of another way?"

8. Take an active part in the discussion. Offer ideas, opinions and cues to move the discussion along. Do not lecture!

9. If the discussion is not going well, end it. Move on to Read and Review Steps to Success.

READ AND REVIEW STEPS TO SUCCESS

Copy the Steps to Success onto a flipchart, whiteboard, posterboard or blackboard and place them so they are in full view of the children for the entire session. They serve as a quick visual reminder of the components of the skill. Use them to prompt and cue children throughout the session. Also, provide two copies of the Steps to Success to children at the close of the session (see the Appendix, pages 303-334). One copy is for parents, the other for the child's teacher. When needed, a copy of the picture steps may be substituted (see sample in the Appendix, pages 335-342).

In this part of the lesson, students read the Steps to Success aloud, clarifying the intent and meaning of each step. This happens relatively swiftly and promptly. The typical format is:

1. Introduce the Steps to Success. Point to Step 1.

2. Ask for a volunteer to read Step 1.

3. Ask the group for a demonstration of the step, such as "show me your friendly face," "show me looking." Or ask for an explanation, such as "what is a pause?"

4. Proceed clockwise around the group or continue asking for volunteers, reading one step at a time and reviewing its meaning.

5. Frequently praise participation, volunteering and cooperation.

If a step is unfamiliar or requires information that is unknown to the group, provide the explanation. For example, when reviewing Steps 3 and 4 of Ending a Conversation (Skill 6-10), show the students the list of explanations and farewells from the end of the lesson to help describe explanations and farewells.

Some children may be poor readers or unable to read at all. They may participate in the following manner.

1. Read the easiest step, such as "look."

2. Read with the leader or a peer.

3. Practice reading the step ahead of time to memorize the words.

Problem

✖ A child refuses to read when it his turn.

Solutions

☺ Don't insist the child read. Matter-of-factly ask the child if he is passing his turn to the next person and, if so, move on to the next reader. Do not force participation. Continue to offer the opportunity to read in each session. My experience has been that eventually everyone will participate.

☹ Removing points, punishing in any way, coercing, chastising.

WARM-UP ACTIVITY

The **Warm-Up Activity** is a brief activity used to reinforce the Steps to Success. It is a straightforward activity that can be introduced prior to discussion to actively engage the group.

ROLE-PLAYS

The purpose of the **Role-Plays** is to rehearse the Steps to Success. School, home and community scenarios are included with each lesson, and are indicated as follows.

 Alternative School Scenarios

 Alternative Home Scenarios

 Alternative Community Scenarios

You do not need to use the role-plays suggested here. In fact, it is preferable to use role-plays that are realistic to the personal experiences of group members. To establish more personal and realistic role-plays, ask students to think of a situation where they might use the skill and to describe the circumstances to the group. This strategy works well in long-standing groups whose members are very familiar with the Super Skills format. In newer groups, an alternative strategy is to ask parents or teachers to write out a role-play situation in advance for the child.

Everyone is expected to participate in a role-play as both a main and a supporting actor. Some members may be reluctant to participate, preferring to observe before taking a turn, whereas others want to go first. Always ask for volunteers. Giving the students some control over when they role-play helps to reduce anxiety and foster cooperation.

Role-Play Format

1. Ask for a volunteer to go first.

2. Describe the role-play scenario.

3. Ask for volunteer supporting actors and assign roles.

4. Assign all remaining students a specific Step to Success to watch for. These students are called the observers.

5. Perform the role-play.

6. If necessary, coach actors to keep the role-play going.

7. Provide immediate praise, such as "Nice job," "Good role-play," "Excellent," and so on.

8. Ask observers to comment on whether the steps they were asked to observe for were followed.

9. Provide specific feedback. Point out what was done correctly, enthusiastically emphasizing the positive.

10. If a step is missed or completed incorrectly, ask the students to repeat the role-play and tell them exactly what to do instead.

    ☺ I'd like you to do the role-play once more. This time I want you to wait for a pause before joining in.

    ☺ Nice job. I'd like you to try the role-play again, and this time I'd like to see a big smile.

    ☺ Try the role-play once more and move closer.

    ☹ You didn't do it right. Do it over.

    ☹ You forgot to wait for a pause. Do it again.

    ☹ You were wrong. Try again.

PRACTICE ACTIVITIES

The ***Practice Activities*** provide an alternative atmosphere where students can perform the current skill as well as previously taught skills. The activities should be fun!! They are designed to create spontaneous interaction that in turn provides teaching opportunities.

They are informal, yet remain structured. Examples include pre-arranged games, art projects and similar activities that are well-thought out with specific guidelines and rules that keep everyone focused on the lesson's objectives. Practice Activities often generate natural circumstances in which to practice individual target behaviors. Be sure to take advantage of these incidents. For example, let's say you choose Practice Activity 2: Eraser Balance (pages 191-192) to practice the skill Giving Encouragement. The purpose of the activity is to practice cheering and encouraging teammates through a relay. One of Matina's target behaviors is Being a Good Sport. Her team loses the relay, and she has the opportunity to practice her target behavior. Marcos is learning to deal with mistakes. When he drops the eraser and has to start over, he has the chance to deal with his mistake.

Usually the lessons include several activities to choose from to offer flexibility to the leader. Always read them in advance to familiarize yourself with their content and prepare the necessary supplies. In general, plan for more activities than might be necessary. If, for some reason, one activity ends quickly or does not go as well as planned, move on to the next.

The instructions for each activity are included in each lesson. Begin the activity and then join in to take advantage of every opportunity to reinforce the teaching lesson, supportive skills, and individual target behaviors.

Common Questions

1. *Should I continue an activity longer than intended when everyone is learning, participating and enjoying themselves?*

There is no right or wrong answer to this question. Sometimes it is good just to "go with the flow" and let an activity continue on its own, especially if there are many opportunities to reinforce new social skills. However, if it means abandoning a more challenging activity and you will not have another opportunity to carry it out, it may be better to change activities.

Let's assume the focus of the lesson is Asking for Help (6-6) and the children are engaged in Practice Activity 1: Stumped, using the game *Go to the Head of the Class* as described in the directions to the activity. The activity is going well for everyone, and you must decide whether to end the game and move on to Practice Activity 2 or to continue playing. Although everyone is having fun, you decide to end the activity because the child who is winning *Go to the Head of the Class* has not asked for help. He usually knows the answers to the questions and, in fact, others are asking him for help. You decide to move on to Practice Activity 2: Hide and Seek, and give him the bag with the list of items you know are very well hidden. He will likely have trouble finding all of the items in time and will therefore have an opportunity to ask for help.

If you know from previous experience that the children usually lose interest after 10 minutes of an activity, move on to the next activity after 10 minutes, regardless of how much fun the group is having. On the other hand, if you know that once an activity captures everyone's interest they will sustain attention for quite a while, keep on with the activity until it is finished.

It is best to end the group on a positive note, so if you think the experience will deteriorate and become negative by changing activities, continue with the current activity, especially if the time is almost up.

2. Should I repeat a favorite activity in a subsequent session?

This is where knowing children's current interests can be invaluable. If the entire group likes building with building blocks, building blocks can be used in numerous ways in subsequent lessons.

A group of younger elementary students enthusiastically likes the game *Hot Potato*. Because the game is short, gives multiple opportunities to practice Being a Good Sport – the target behavior of many of the students – it is repeated frequently during the weeks to follow.

3. What should I do when an activity fails?

End it quickly and move on to something else. In addition, think about what went wrong and make notes for future groups.

SUPPORTIVE SKILLS TO PROMPT AND REINFORCE

Supportive skills are listed to help identify the associated skills to reinforce during the session.

SUPPLIES

This list, in alphabetical order, includes materials needed to conduct the lesson. Collect and prepare them in advance so you do not waste time getting things together after the children arrive. If you plan to substitute games, be sure they are ready to play.

EXTENDING SKILL DEVELOPMENT

The goal of Super Skills is to make lasting changes in children's personal interaction skills. This goes beyond being able to use the skill in the group setting. The child must also be able to use it in real life. For many children, the acquisition of social skills is a lifelong challenge. For others, it is easier. However, all children, must transfer their learning and generalize it to their home, school and community. This is the purpose of including the section on extending skill development. The strategies are to be used by others involved with the child, including parents, teachers, support staff, neighbors, extended family, siblings and peers. All of these individuals are potential facilitators of successful acquisition of appropriate social behavior by the child with ASD. All of them can be recruited to help transfer learning from Super Skills to real-life circumstances.

To help train parents and others who are actively involved with a child, encourage them to observe the group whenever possible. By watching the group, parents learn strategies for helping their children. Often parents volunteer as helpers and, under the direction of the leader, assume a designated role in the session. This gives the leader the opportunity to coach parents to improve their skills. The suggestions for ***Extending Skill Development*** may be copied for distribution to parent, teachers and others.

In general, ***Extending Skill Development*** includes:

1. Using the Steps to Success Rating Form (Table 5.1; see also the blank form in the Appendix, page 343), adapted from McGinnis and Goldstein (1997) and modified for Super Skills. This form is used to report skill use between sessions. It encourages others to actively practice the skill with the child and gives helpful feedback to the group leader.

2. Posting the Steps to Success in the classroom and at home. This serves as a written prompt or reminder to the child of the way to perform a skill. More important, it reminds those who are working with a child to "be on the same page" and to teach consistently, using the same language and same procedures. Repetition is extremely important for children with ASD.

3. Modeling the skill for the child in natural circumstances.

4. Actively searching for opportunities to use the skill, reminding the child to use the skill and rehearsing with the child in advance if necessary. The more situations in which a child practices a designated skill, the greater the likelihood it will be added to her permanent repertoire of skills.

5. Offering incentives to motivate the child to try the skill, perhaps by earning points or

Table 5.1: Steps to Success Rating Form

Date: 11/13 _____

Margo _____ is learning the skill of: __Introducing_____

The steps involved in this skill are:

1. Smile.

2. Look at the person.

3. Say: "Hi, my name is_____. What's your name?"

4. Listen to the answer and say: "Hi, ____, it's nice to meet you."

1. Did he or she demonstrate this skill in your presence?
   - ☒ Yes
   - ☐ No

2. How well did he or she do in performing the skill? (Check one)
   - ☐ Poor
   - ☐ Below average
   - ☐ Average
   - ☒ Above average
   - ☐ Excellent

3. How difficult was it for him or her to perform the skill? (Check one)
   - ☐ Very difficult
   - ☐ Difficult
   - ☒ Somewhat difficult
   - ☐ Neither difficult nor easy
   - ☐ Somewhat easy
   - ☐ Easy
   - ☐ Very easy

4. Does he or she need continued practice with this skill?
   - ☒ Yes
   - ☐ No

Comments: Margo introduced herself to a substitute teacher at school and did a great job. Earlier in the week I tried to get her to introduce herself to one of my colleagues, and she refused. If you ask Margo what do you do when you meet someone new, she can tell you. It will take continued practice in real-life situations to have her do it consistently.

Please sign and return this form to Super Skills at the next session.

Signature: _____ Mrs. Z _____ Date: 11/14 _____

Adapted from McGinnis, E., & Goldstein, A. P. (1997). *Skillstreaming the elementary school child.* Champaign, IL: Research Press.

tokens that can be exchanged for small prizes. The Target Behavior Practice Chart shown on page 16 (see blank form in the Appendix, page 350) is one way to monitor a child's efforts to practice skills, especially target behaviors, and to reward his efforts. The child (or adult) simply records when a child practices a target behavior and how well the child thinks he did at following the Steps to Success. The child receives "credit" even if he did poorly. The purpose is to reinforce effort, not perfection. Once the entire chart is completed, the child earns a bonus prize.

HOMEWORK

Homework activities can be a positive support to learning. Sometimes homework is a joint project between parent and child and results in a valuable learning experience. This is the ideal. At other times homework can become a power struggle or conflict, because the child does not wish to complete it. When this happens, you can make homework simpler or forego it altogether. It is acceptable to have some students complete homework while others do not. Be sure to reward those who make an effort to finish it, using points, tokens or extra prizes.

Choosing homework assignments can be challenging because of the varied reading and writing skills of group members. Sometimes homework activities are selected from Social Skills Activities for Special Children (Mannix, 1993). The language is simple, writing requirements are minimal and the drawings help children to understand what is happening. Homework can also include practicing the Steps to Success and recording the child's efforts on the Target Behavior Practice Chart (see page 16 and the Appendix, page 350). Additional homework ideas are offered in the homework coupons in the Appendix (page 297).

ENDING THE SESSION

To end each session:

1. Conclude the practice activity and clean up.

2. Quickly review the skill.

3. Return folders to students.

4. Pass out two copies of Steps to Success (see the Appendix, pages 303-333), the Skill Rating Form (see the Appendix, page 343), Extending Skill Development ideas (optional) and any homework activities and notes to parents. Direct students to place these papers in their folders and take them home.

5. Distribute rewards.

6. Say good-bye.

PARENT MEETING

In some settings, establishing a regularly scheduled, postsession parent meeting can help facilitate skill practice between sessions. Parent meetings are usually brief (10-15 minutes). Such meetings can be effectively arranged in a clinic setting, but also in an after-school group. When parents are able to observe and even participate in a group, they learn strategies to help their children become more competent and confident in their social skill abilities. The parent meeting is a chance for parents to ask questions or comment on what they have observed. It also helps them to establish a network of parent peers who are facing issues similar to their own and creates a natural opportunity to share information. Homework and special issues can also be addressed at this time.

Often parents and the leader exchange phone numbers and email addresses at the first meeting so they can maintain contact between sessions. Also, parents who are unable to attend the meeting can then receive needed information via telephone or email directly from the leader. Parents can take turns attending, send an older sibling, or grandparent to the session if they must be absent.

When regular parent meetings are not feasible, leaders can invite parents to the first meeting, to a conference midway through the sessions and again at the end to discuss the child's individual progress. A final evaluation form is a helpful tool for the leader to use to plan future groups. Two examples to be completed by parents are included in the Appendix, pages 300-301; they may be modified for use by a classroom teacher.

IN CLOSING . . .
LIFE AFTER SUPER SKILLS

Although Super Skills has not undergone rigid tests of research, its value to the children with ASD and their families is worth reporting. In their final evaluations and comments, parents and children had this to say:

> *I feel that your entire program is extremely well done. When B. told me after a session that you had said you'd be carrying on Super Skills next year, I was so happy and relieved to hear it. I think the teaching of specific skills, broken into specific steps, is a real plus for the children. And it is clear that you are investing real time and thought in terms of preparation: Materials and activities are clear, simple, varied and pertinent to kids' needs. This is a very valuable experience that is not easily found.*

> *I know that this work is effective. Just last night S. said (upon finding his bed unmade when retiring), "Oh, I forgot to make my bed today. Well, that was a*

mistake, and everybody makes mistakes. I'm doing like we practiced at Mrs. J's, mama." This is so significant because the development of that self-talk has been very challenging, and it is crucial. S.V.

Well-planned and well-focused topics each week – nicely targeted the problem areas. The expanded class – 90 minutes – was a big improvement, time for games (strategically selected!) made it fun and beneficial for the boys. R.T.

In general, I think the exercises are good and relevant. Basing activities on specific target behaviors is effective. I like the fact that I learn from the sessions as well as A. A. has made progress by repeating social skills and covering the topics over and over. L.S.

The group of girls who are true (well-matched) peers provide a safe place to practice skills that are difficult for them. They learn from each other. P.R.

She has begun to initiate conversation at the dinner table and can contribute with prompts. F.T.

SOCIAL INITIATION SKILLS

SKILLS 6-1: GREETINGS

STEPS TO SUCCESS

To greet someone, you:
1. **Smile.**
2. **Use a friendly voice.**
3. **Look at the person.**
4. **Say "Hi" and the person's name.**

THOUGHTS BEFORE STARTING

Greeting is a daily activity that is essential to all of us. It is relatively easy because there are few rules to remember and the rules do not change with the circumstances. Once a child learns to say "hi," he can use this simple greeting over and over. However, this can be troublesome for children who learn the word "hi" but do not know what else to say to begin a conversation, therefore, repeating "hi" ad nauseum.

For most children with ASD, learning to say "hi" is not the issue. The problem is that they do not recognize that greeting is a welcoming behavior that is important for initiating and maintaining social relationships. Some children forget to greet and begin an interaction by asking an inappropriate question such as "Have you ever had a speeding ticket?" "How old are you?" (to an unknown adult), "What is wrong with your face/nose/forehead?" (to a teen who has acne). These children must be taught to greet in addition to the skill of starting a conversation.

Note: Nametags can help the leader and the children who read to learn and remember the names of everyone in the group. Use them for this skill if the majority of children can read and/or you are unfamiliar with the children's names. Pass the nametags out as children arrive.

INTRODUCING THE SKILL

When you see someone you know, it is polite to say hi. This is called a greeting. Today we are going to practice greetings.

Discussion Questions

☐ *What words can we use to greet people?* List suggestions on a flipchart or board ("Good morning," "Hello," "Hey," "How are you doing?").

☐ *Why is it important to greet people?* (We want to be friendly. It's polite. It welcomes people.)

☐ *How can we greet people without using words?* Direct the discussion to behaviors such as high five, wave or a handshake. Provide visual cues or model when needed.

☐ *When someone greets you first, it is friendly to greet her in return. We all want to be friendly.* Greet each group member by name and wait for them to greet you in return, prompting as needed with a phrase or picture card. Use a puppet or stuffed animal to help engage younger children.

☐ *Why is it important to greet people by name?* (Helps them know whom we are talking to.)

☐ *Who is it O.K. to greet? Who is it not O.K. to greet?* List suggestions on a T-chart labeled "O.K." on one side and "Not O.K." on the other as illustrated below. The category O.K. includes parents and other family members, teachers, friends, relatives, classmates, etc. "Not O.K." includes strangers. If needed, discuss how to decide who is a stranger.

GREETING T-CHART

O.K.	NOT O.K.
Mom/Dad	Stranger
Teacher	
Friend	

READ AND REVIEW STEPS TO SUCCESS

WARM-UP ACTIVITY

Direct the children to exit the room one at a time and re-enter with a greeting to the group. Peers respond with a return greeting.

ROLE-PLAYS

Review the role-play format presented in Chapter 5.

 Alternative School Scenarios

1. You get on the bus. Greet the bus driver and the student you sit next to.

2. You enter the classroom. Greet your teacher and the child who sits behind you.

3. You see your older sister in the hall.

4. The principal greets you at recess.

 Alternative Home Scenarios

1. Your grandmother comes to visit.

2. Your mother/father comes home.

3. The doorbell rings and you answer the door.

4. You are mowing the lawn and a neighbor walks by with her baby in a stroller.

 Alternative Community Scenarios

1. You see a neighbor in the supermarket while shopping with your dad.

2. You are in line at the movies when a classmate approaches you.

3. You enter a restaurant and see the school secretary eating there.

4. You see the mail carrier walk up to your house.

PRACTICE ACTIVITIES

Practice Activity 1: Treats

Hold a box of crackers or some other treat and direct the children to line up in front of you.

Instructions

◆ Instruct the first child to greet you using your name and the Steps to Success.

◆ If the child correctly completes all the steps, greet the child in return and give her a treat.

◆ The child now becomes the leader and holds the treats.

◆ If the child misses a Step to Success, the child goes to the back of the line and has a chance to try again.

◆ The next child in line greets the child leader using his or her name.

◆ If successful, the child receives a treat and now becomes the leader.

◆ Proceed in the same manner until all children have had a chance to be the leader.

Practice Activity 2: Music Box

Group the children in a circle.

Instructions

◆ Wind up a music box and begin to pass a ball or beanbag around the circle.

- When the music stops, the child holding the ball/beanbag correctly greets any other student.

- The greeted student responds.

- If either "forgets" one of the Steps to Success, he sits out the next round.

- Proceed in the same manner until everyone has greeted and responded successfully.

Note: The commercial game *Hot Potato* also works well in this activity.

Practice Activity 3: Game Fun

Set up a commercial game such as *Hungry Hungry Hippos; Lucky Ducks;* or *Mr. Mouth.* Choose four participants to begin playing the game by either asking for volunteers, or by selecting students by drawing names from a container or choosing numbers.

Instructions

- Direct the remaining children to approach those who are playing and greet them by name using the Steps to Success.

- A greeted child responds correctly. If she does not, she loses her seat to the child who approached her.

- Prompt as needed. Praise good sportsmanship in addition to successful greetings.

- Switch roles once the game is over, if needed for further practice.

Practice Activity 4: Go *Fish*

Follow the rules for the *Go Fish* card game.

Instructions

- Each participant must greet correctly when asking for a card. For example, "Hi, Sally, do you have a blue fish?"

- If the child forgets to do so, play proceeds to the left without the child completing his turn.

- Remind respondents to use names, such as "Hi, John, go fish."

SUPPLIES

- ◆ Ball, beanbag or *Hot Potato* game
- ◆ Box of crackers or other treats
- ◆ Flipchart or blackboard
- ◆ Games

- ◆ *Go Fish* card game
- ◆ Music box
- ◆ Nametags (optional)

SUPPORTIVE SKILLS TO PROMPT AND REINFORCE

1. Using Kind Talk (page 217)
2. Being a Good Sport (page 247)
3. Following Directions (page 148)

EXTENDING SKILL DEVELOPMENT

Explain the goal of the skill to others and ask them to:

1. Post the Steps to Success in the classroom and at home.

2. Greet the child at least once a day and wait/prompt for an appropriate response.

3. Encourage the child to greet others and practice with the child when needed in advance.

4. Offer incentives to motivate the child to greet others, perhaps by earning a reward for greeting three people a day without prompts. Keep track by placing initials on a card.

5. Encourage peers to greet the child and wait for a response.

SKILLS 6-2: INTRODUCING

STEPS TO SUCCESS

To introduce yourself:

1. **Smile.**
2. **Look at the person.**
3. **Say: "Hi, my name is ___. What's your name?"**
4. **Listen to the answer and say: "Hi, ____, it's nice to meet you."**

THOUGHTS BEFORE STARTING

Introducing oneself is anxiety-provoking for many adults and children alike. However, all of us are regularly called upon to identify ourselves and make "small talk." Some children with ASD easily accomplish the mechanics of this skill due to great imitative abilities but need to work on judgment (who is it appropriate to introduce oneself to and when). Some children fail to recognize the significance of learning and remembering proper names. For others, introducing oneself seems purposeless; after all, you know who you are, so, according to their thinking, others should too.

Note: Nametags can help the leader and the children who read to learn and remember the names of everyone in the group. Use them for this skill if the majority of children can read and/or you are unfamiliar with the children's names. Pass the nametags out as children arrive.

INTRODUCING THE SKILL

Greet each student and encourage students to greet each other. *Today we are going to practice Introducing.*

☐ *Who knows what introducing means?* (Letting others know who you are, finding out who others are.)

- ☐ *When is it important to introduce yourself?* (When you meet someone new.)
- ☐ *Why is it important to know someone's name and to give your name?* (Then you know who they are and they know who you are.)
- ☐ *Why smile?* (It's friendly, polite.)
- ☐ *Where is it O.K. to introduce yourself?* (School, home, church, friend's houses, neighbors, etc.)
- ☐ *When is it not O.K. to introduce yourself?* (Shoppers in stores, strangers on the street, etc.)

READ AND REVIEW STEPS TO SUCCESS

WARM-UP ACTIVITIES

One at a time, greet every group member by saying: *Hi, my name is ___, what's your name?* Wait for each response, and say *Hi ___, it's nice to meet you.*

Ask for a volunteer to introduce himself to the person on his right using the Steps to Success. That person then introduces himself to the person on his right. Continue in this manner until all the children have introduced themselves to somebody in the group. If someone misses a step, ask her to try again.

ROLE-PLAYS

Review the role-play format presented in Chapter 5.

 Alternative School Scenarios

1. You have a substitute teacher.

2. There is a new student in art class.

3. You have a new bus driver.

4. There is a new secretary in the school office.

 Alternative Home Scenarios

1. A friend of your sister's is spending the night at your house.

2. Two people you don't know come to your brother's birthday party.

3. Your dad brings a guest home for dinner.

4. Your aunt brings her boyfriend to Thanksgiving dinner.

Alternative Community Scenarios

1. You go swimming with your dad. There is a boy your age at the pool.

2. You are playing in a park and a girl approaches you.

3. You are walking home and a neighbor you have seen but don't know walks up to you.

4. You are at the movies and see a kid from another class in your school.

PRACTICE ACTIVITIES

Practice Activity 1: Catch

Direct the children to form a circle.

Instructions

◆ Hold a foam ball, look at one of the students and say *Hi, my name is ___, what's your name?*

◆ Throw the ball to the student. The student replies with his name and repeats to another player, *Hi, my name is ___, what's your name?*, throwing the ball.

◆ Continue until everyone has had a turn.

Practice Activity 2: Team Baskets

Divide the group into two teams, A and B. Instruct one member from Team A to sit in a chair and line up Team A behind her. Line up Team B behind a wastebasket situated 8-10 feet in front of Team A.

Instructions

◆ The student in the chair from Team A holds a foam ball and introduces herself to the first student from Team B behind the wastebasket.

◆ If she correctly follows the Steps to Success, she receives one point for her team and tries to make a basket.

◆ If she is successful throwing a basket, Team A tallies two more points.

◆ If she forgets one of the steps, she goes to the back of the line without trying to make a basket and does not earn any points.

◆ If the student from Team B replies appropriately to the introduction, Team B receives one point.

◆ Keep track of points on a flipchart or board.

◆ When a turn is completed, both players move to the back of their team lines. Proceed through all players on a team and then "switch sides."

Practice Activity 3: *Mr. Potato Head Pals*

Distribute one *Mr. Potato Head Pal* card from the game to each student. Distribute the pieces of the game in the following manner: One person receives all of the eyes, one receives all the potatoes, one receives all the hats, etc. No one should have all the parts necessary to complete a potato head. Position the children about the room and tell them they have to complete their potato head.

Instructions

◆ Direct students to move close to the person who has the part they need to complete their potato head.

◆ Have students carry out introductions using the Steps to Success.

◆ If introductions are correct, children can ask for the potato head piece they need.

◆ Monitor and prompt as needed.

Note: This activity can also be played with puzzles, Lego blocks, lotto card pieces or other construction games.

SUPPLIES

◆ Flipchart or blackboard

◆ Foam ball

◆ *Mr. Potato Head Pals*

◆ Nametags (optional)

◆ Wastebasket

SUPPORTIVE SKILLS TO PROMPT AND REINFORCE

1. Following Directions (page 148)

2. Being a Good Sport (page 247)

3. Giving Encouragement (page 188)

4. Starting a Conversation (page 107)

5. Showing Interest in Others (page 225)

EXTENDING SKILL DEVELOPMENT

Explain the goal of this skill to others and ask them to:

1. Post the Steps to Success in the classroom and at home.

2. Encourage the child to introduce himself to others.

3. Rehearse with the child in advance of potential opportunities to use the skill, such as immediately prior to attending a birthday party where there may be people he does not know.

4. Set up opportunities for the child to meet new people, such as office staff, coworkers and students in other classes.

SKILLS 6-3: JOINING IN

STEPS TO SUCCESS

To join others, you:

1. **Move close.**
2. **Watch.**
3. **Wait.**
4. **Ask.**
5. **If "yes," join in.**
6. **If "no," do something else.**

THOUGHTS BEFORE STARTING

For children with ASD, successfully joining others in play or in a group activity is personally challenging (Wing, 1972). Some are intrusive and "butt in" rather than join in. Learning how to join in without disrupting the group is most often difficult for children with AS, who frequently want to direct the activities of others (Attwood, 1998). For more passive children with ASD, moving close and entering at the best opportunity is challenging. They feel ill at ease joining in; therefore, if they try at all, their attempts are usually clumsy and awkward. In addition to knowing the mechanics of what to say and do, correctly judging the timing of an entry is crucial to success.

Although asking to join is not the only way to join a group, it is one of the most direct approaches. Other options include giving encouragement to those playing, offering a suggestion for how to proceed, asking a question about what the group is doing or entering with a greeting. These options may be suitable for children who require an alternative to asking. The final component of this skill is learning what to do when a request to join in is rejected.

INTRODUCING THE SKILL

Hold a bag of M&M's or some other treat. *Today we are going to practice joining in. I have a bag of M&M's. If you wanted one, how could you get one?* When someone responds with some form of "ask," enthusiastically reply with *Yes! You can ASK me. Let's try it.* Have each child who wants an M&M ask for one. *This is one of the steps to joining in. When we want to join what others are doing, we ask them, just as we do if we want an M&M.*

Discussion Questions

- ☐ *What activities are fun to join in?* List suggestions on a flipchart or board.

- ☐ *What does butting in mean?* (Butting in is pushing your way in without asking.)

- ☐ *What is the difference between joining in and butting in?* (When you join in, you ask first.)

- ☐ *How does butting in make people feel?* (It upsets the people who are playing.)

- ☐ *What can you do if you ask to join in and the other kids ignore you?* (Try again. Ask in a different way. Watch them play and wait for a better time. Do something else.)

READ AND REVIEW
STEPS TO SUCCESS

WARM-UP ACTIVITY

Scatter Lego blocks in front of you and begin to build a house. *I am making a house with Lego blocks.* Continue to silently make the house. Wait to see what happens. Someone may ask to join in, offer to help, suggest something to make, etc. Respond affirmatively to each appropriate effort to join in and praise with: *Nice joining in.* Offer a suggestion of what to build if necessary. *You can make the (garage, car, roof, etc.).* Continue to build with the Legos until everyone has joined in correctly.

Problems

✖ Taking Legos without asking to join in.

✖ Taking over what another child is doing without asking.

✖ Taking Legos from another child without asking.

✖ Becoming "bossy."

Solution

☺ Respond with the child's name and say: *It's great that you'd like to join in. What is a different way you can join in?* Prompt the child to look at the Steps to Success if needed. If the child continues to take Legos, or to build without responding to your prompts, repeat the child's name and say: *You are butting in. Stop! Think of a better way to join in.* Wait for the child's response. Place your hands over the child's hands to stop her from building if necessary. *Try again.* Praise her efforts and emphasize her success. *Yes, that's the right way to join in! Nice job.*

ROLE-PLAYS

Review the role-play format presented in Chapter 5.

Alternative School Scenarios

1. You see a group from your class playing tag at recess.

2. You see students from your class hanging Halloween decorations in the hall.

3. A group of kids you know are going to the computer lab during lunch.

4. Some friends are playing catch while waiting for the bus after school.

Alternative Home Scenarios

1. Your sister is starting to make your favorite dessert.

2. Your mom is going shopping at the mall.

3. You see your dad playing a game on the computer.

4. Your brother is riding his scooter in the driveway.

Alternative Community Scenarios

1. You see a group of boys from your neighborhood playing soccer in the park.

2. You see a neighbor boy playing in his front yard.

3. You see a friend ahead of you in line at the movies.

4. You see a group of friends watching a ball game.

PRACTICE ACTIVITIES

Practice Activity 1: Call a Number

Have available an assortment of multiplayer games (*Hungry, Hungry Hippos; Cat Nip; Mr. Mouth; Trouble; Uno; Jenga,* etc.). Instruct each child to throw a die as a way to assign the student a number (no two students should have the same number). Write down the numbers if necessary to remember them.

Instructions

◆ Call out a number. The child who has the number chooses a game and begins to set it up.

◆ Depending upon the total number of children, call out more numbers to signify other children who each choose a game to play. Ideally, arrange to have 3-4 players per game.

◆ Direct the remaining children to ask to join in one of the two (or three, or four) groups. No one should play alone. Consequently, children may have to ask to join in a game that is not their first choice.

◆ Be sure to praise good timing (while game is being set up).

◆ Allow about 5 minutes to play the game and then start over. Call out different numbers to indicate who can choose a game; the others must join in.

Practice Activity 2: Attributes

This alternative to Practice Activity 1 works best with relatively large groups (15-20 children). Have available an assortment of multiplayer games (*Hungry, Hungry Hippos; Cat Nip; Mr. Mouth; Trouble; Uno; Jenga*, etc.). In this activity, each child with an identified attribute (e.g., red shirt) chooses a game. Several children should be selecting a game at the same time.

Instructions

◆ Select children by the color of their clothing, eyes or hair, etc. For example, *Each of you wearing a red shirt, choose one game each* (or each of you with blue eyes, or brown hair and wearing green, etc.).

◆ Continue to call attributes until there are enough games available for all children to join in. Try to set it up so that there will be close to the maximum number of players per game. Direct the remaining children to ask to join in one of the games.

◆ Allow the groups to play the games for a few minutes. Call out an attribute and say *switch*. For example, *All those wearing yellow, switch and join in a different game.* This unpredictability will cause considerable confusion for a few minutes as the children leave a game and hurry to join in a different one. This makes the activity fun and removes the tension and worry of joining in.

◆ Prompt, and guide as needed. Lavish praise when you see kids joining in correctly.

SUPPORTIVE SKILLS TO PROMPT AND REINFORCE

1. Using Kind Talk (page 217)

2. Greetings (page 71)

3. Following Directions (page 148)

4. Being a Good Sport (page 247)

SUPPLIES

- ◆ Assorted multiplayer board games

- ◆ Flipchart or blackboard

- ◆ Lego blocks (or other types of building block)

- ◆ M&M's (or some other desirable treat or item)

EXTENDING SKILL DEVELOPMENT

Explain the goal of the skill to others and ask them to:

1. Post the Steps to Success in the classroom and at home as appropriate.

2. Encourage the child to join in with others and praise her efforts.

3. Rehearse with the child in advance of potential opportunities to use the skill, such as immediately before recess.

4. Set up opportunities for the child to ask to join in.

5. Begin a preferred activity (e.g., making cookies, riding bikes, playing a favorite game) and wait for the child to ask to join in, prompting only if necessary.

6. Require that the child ask to join in with others (instead of butting in) and reward his successes with small treats or tokens.

SKILL 6-4: INVITING SOMEONE TO PLAY

STEPS TO SUCCESS

To invite someone to play, you:

1. **Choose someone.**
2. **Walk close.**
3. **Smile.**
4. **Ask.**
5. **If "yes," go play.**
6. **If "no," ask someone else.**

To answer someone who wants to play, you:

1. **Smile.**
2. **Look.**
3. **Answer.**

THOUGHTS BEFORE STARTING

Many children with ASD prefer to play alone and therefore see no purpose in asking another child to play with them. The challenge for the leader is to create experiences that demonstrate the enjoyment of playing and being with others. So even though the primary intent of this skill is to help children with ASD begin to understand how to invite someone to join in an activity as well as how to respond to such a request, it is also essential to teach that playing with others can be fun.

INTRODUCING THE SKILL

Hold a foam ball. *Today we are going to practice asking someone to play. It can be fun to play with others rather than playing alone. It's not much fun to play ball by myself so I can ask one of you to play with me. I have lots of choices. I could choose* (list children's names). *I am going to ask (Name). (Name), will you play catch with me?* If the child says "yes," proceed to throw the foam ball back and forth for a few turns. If the child says "no," ask someone else. If the child does not answer, ask him again.

Let's list other games that are fun to play with others. Write suggestions on a board or a flipchart.

Discussion Questions

☐ *Besides playing games, what else is fun to do with someone else?* List suggestions: eating out, going to a movie, seeing a ball game, etc.

☐ *When we ask someone to play with us, or join us in an activity, they might say yes or they might say no. What can we do when someone says no?* Discuss the options: ask someone else, play by yourself, do something different, etc.

☐ *Why is it important to answer when someone asks us to play?* (So they know our decision, to be polite, etc.)

READ AND REVIEW STEPS TO SUCCESS

WARM-UP ACTIVITY

Ask a child to play ball. *(Name), will you play ball with me?* Play catch for a few turns using the foam ball. *(Name), ask someone to join us.* Briefly play ball with the two students. *(2nd Name), ask someone to join us.* Continue playing. *(3rd Name), ask someone to join us.* Continue until everyone has joined in and the entire group is playing catch. If a child says "no," ask someone else.

ROLE-PLAYS

Review the role-play format presented in Chapter 5.

 **Alternative School Scenarios**

1. You really want to play ball at recess.

2. You really want to sit with your friend at lunch.

3. You need a partner in gym class.

4. You see a new kid on your street walking home.

Alternative Home Scenarios

1. You want your brother to watch a TV show with you.

2. You want your dad to play a game with you.

3. You want your neighbor to ride bikes with you.

4. You want your brother to eat a pizza with you.

Alternative Community Scenarios

1. Your mom says you can invite a friend to the movies with you.

2. You are skating at the park and see someone you know from school.

3. You dad says you can take a friend to the mall with you.

4. You're going swimming and wonder if the new kid in class would like to come.

PRACTICE ACTIVITIES

Practice Activity 1: One-Game Choice

Place a selection of games on a nearby table.

Instructions

◆ Direct one child to select a game and to ask another child to play with him. (You may need to set a time limit for choosing the game.)

◆ If a child refuses an invitation to play, ask the child with the game to follow the Steps to Success and ask someone else.

◆ Once the first child has a play partner, continue directing children one at a time to choose a game and ask a partner to play.

◆ After all the children have a play partner, set a timer for 3-5 minutes to allow time to play the game.

◆ When the timer rings, stop the games and start over. One by one, direct the play partners to choose a game and ask someone to play. Once everyone is paired, set the timer again to allow time for play.

Practice Activity 2: Half and Half

Place an assortment of games on a table.

Instructions

◆ Select half of the students to choose a game (one game per child).

◆ Direct the students with games to approach the remaining peers and ask someone to play the game using the Steps to Success.

◆ Peers may say yes or no. Prompt and guide as needed.

◆ After partners are chosen, set a timer for 5 minutes to play.

◆ Once the timer rings, stop the game, reverse roles and start over. The second half of the group now chooses a game per child and asks someone from the first half to play.

◆ Set a timer to allow 5 minutes to play.

Problem

✖ Students disagree over who first selected a game. For example, Jane and Mike disagree over who selected *Hungry, Hungry Hippos* first.

Solution

☺ Take advantage of the opportunity to problem solve and say: *Jane and Mike, you have a problem. Only one of you can take the game from the table. How can you solve this problem?* Facilitate a quick discussion of options (pick a number, flip a coin, leave the game on the table, etc.) and then follow through.

Problem

✖ Peer refuses an invitation to play. For example, Zachary refused Devon's invitation to play because he did not want to play the game Devon selected. Now all the other group members have chosen partners.

Solution

☺ Say to Devon: *What should you do? Zachary doesn't want to play with you.* Prompt responses if needed (choose a different game and ask Zachary to play it. Ask to join in a different group). Follow through.

Practice Activity 3: Partners

Choose a question-and-answer game that requires knowledge of a subject to play. Suggestions: *Go to the Head of the Class, Trivial Pursuit for Juniors, Jeopardy,* etc.

Instructions

◆ Set the game up as directed by the game's instructions.

◆ Before each player's turn, tell him that he has the option of inviting someone to be his partner.

◆ He must ask a peer to be his partner before he receives the question. Partners discuss the answer; however, ultimately the player decides what to say.

◆ A peer can be a partner as often as he is asked. A peer can also refuse to be a partner.

Problem

✖ Sometimes the child chooses to answer alone and he can answer the question by himself. Sometimes he may not know or be sure of the answer, and therefore asking someone to join in might have been a better idea. Sometimes a player may decide to ignore a partner's suggestion and this ends up being a mistake, as the partner did indeed have the correct answer.

Solution

☺ Let these situations resolve naturally and do not interfere. Once the player's turn is finished, a quick discussion can occur if necessary that focuses upon something like: *Sometimes, "two heads are better than one."* It is not uncommon for a child with AS to have trouble believing someone else might have a better or right answer, so more teaching may be needed in this area.

SUPPORTIVE SKILLS TO PROMPT AND REINFORCE

1. Dealing with a Problem (page 274)

2. Being a Good Sport (page 247)

3. Joining In (page 82)

4. Dealing with Anger (page 208)

SUPPLIES

◆ Assorted board games

◆ Foam ball

◆ Question-and-answer game

EXTENDING SKILL DEVELOPMENT

Explain the goal of this skill to others and ask them to:

1. Post the Steps to Success in the classroom and at home.

2. Encourage the child to ask others to play with her.

3. Rehearse with the child in advance of potential opportunities to use the skill, such as immediately prior to playing in the park or visiting a friend.

4. Require that the child ask a friend to join in a favorite activity, such as eating at a favorite restaurant or going to the zoo.

5. Set up opportunities for the child to pair with a partner and prompt choosing a partner when needed (lunch, recess).

6. Regularly guide play with the child and peers to build knowledge of rules and foster an interest in playing with others. Gradually remove the adult participation.

SKILL 6-5: GIVING AND RECEIVING COMPLIMENTS

STEPS TO SUCCESS

To give a compliment, you:
1. **Look.**
2. **Use a friendly face.**
3. **Use a sincere voice.**
4. **Say what you like about what the person did.**

To receive a compliment, you:
1. **Smile.**
2. **Look.**
3. **Say, "thank you."**

THOUGHTS BEFORE STARTING

People who give sincere compliments are usually recognized as friendly and positive. Some compliments are directed at a person's appearance, personal possessions, or talents and skills, whereas others are directed at personal traits or aspects of a person's personality. Part of the challenge for children with ASD is recognizing that giving compliments pleases people and is, therefore, a relatively successful friendship strategy. As a rule, receiving a compliment is a positive experience. Most of us like receiving compliments. They help us to feel good about what we do and who we are. Children with ASD frequently like to be on the receiving end of compliments, but often fail to understand that the friendliest response to a compliment is "Thank you," rather than "I know that."

INTRODUCING THE SKILL

Begin by giving each child a compliment. Suggestions:

> *I like the way you smiled when you greeted your friends today.*
>
> *I like the way you are sitting quietly in you seat.*
>
> *You are a great storyteller.*
>
> *You are really talented at drawing. Your figures are so clever.*
>
> *I like the way you help me clean up every week.*
>
> *I like the way you helped me set up the room today. You are so thoughtful.*

Some of the children may say "thank you." If so, respond appropriately. If a child says nothing, simply move on to the next. Once you have given everyone a compliment, say: *I have given each of you a compliment. Giving a compliment is like giving a gift because it usually makes the receiver smile and feel good inside. We give compliments to our friends because we want them to feel good. For example, one of my friends is a really good cook. I could tell her that by saying: "Your cooking is fantastic." She probably knows she is a good cook, but she doesn't know that I think she is a good cook until I tell her. When I give her the compliment, she knows that I think she is a good cook too.*

Discussion Questions

☐ *Who would like to receive a compliment?* List on a flipchart or board (family members, teachers, relatives, classmates, neighbors, just about anyone).

☐ *Let's think of some qualities you can compliment. For example, I complimented my friend's great cooking. What ideas do you have?* Write suggestions on a flipchart or board.

☐ *When you receive a compliment, just as when you receive a gift, you say "thank you." Even when you feel embarrassed or when you already know you did a good job, it is rude to say "I know" or "I know that." Why is it rude?* (It makes the giver of the compliment feel bad, it makes us seem unfriendly.)

☐ *Let's practice saying thank you. I am going to give each of you a compliment again, and this time please say "thank you" after you receive the compliment.* Repeat the same compliments or give new ones.

READ AND REVIEW
STEPS TO SUCCESS

WARM-UP ACTIVITY

Write compliments such as those suggested below on wooden craft sticks and place them in a jar or other container. Label the jar "smileys." Have each child pick a smiley from the container and choose a peer to give it to. Direct the child to read the smiley to the peer and the peer to respond with "thank you." Each child should receive at least one smiley. If a child cannot read, whisper the smiley into his ear.

Smileys

I'm glad you are here today.	I like it when you . . .	You are fun to be with.
You have good ideas.	I'm glad you're here.	You make me smile.
You are a good friend.	It's fun knowing you.	I'm glad we're together.
It is good to see you.	You are nice.	I like to work with you.
I like the way you . . .	I like you.	I like how you . . .
I like knowing you.	Thank you for . . .	I like the way you . . .
You are friendly.	You are great.	You are really good at . . .
I like playing with you.	It's fun being together.	You are awesome!

Note: It is good practice to end all group sessions with compliment sharing. Each member must give one compliment to a peer. Offer the smiley jar to those who have trouble thinking of something to say.

ROLE-PLAYS

Review the role-play format presented in Chapter 5.

 Alternative School Scenarios

1. A classmate is a terrific artist and made a wonderful witch for the classroom window for Halloween.

2. A classmate won a prize in the all-school music contest.

3. A friend has a new Red Wings t-shirt. You think it's really cool.

4. A friend makes a difficult catch in gym class.

 Alternative Home Scenarios

1. Your mom has cooked your favorite meal.

2. A friend of your brother's has a new haircut.

3. Your dad helped you figure out a new computer game.

4. Your grandma made a special dessert for Sunday dinner.

Alternative Community Scenarios

1. A neighbor had a part in a local play. She did really well.

2. Your soccer team won their game. You see the goalie at a restaurant after the game.

3. You go bowling with a friend who scores higher than you.

4. You go skiing with a friend and see she is really good.

PRACTICE ACTIVITIES

Practice Activity 1: Compliment Cards

Prepare enough colored card stock for each child to have two 4x6 cards. At the top of each card write: A Compliment For ____. Leaving the rest blank, at the bottom of each card, write From____.

◆ Distribute two small pieces of paper to each child. *Write your name on each of these pieces of paper. Put your papers into the container* (e.g., a coffee can or envelope).

◆ Instruct the children to draw two names from the container. If children draw their own name, they must put it back and draw another.

◆ *Think of a compliment to give each person you picked. On the corresponding card, write the person's name, the compliment and your name.*

◆ Distribute the cards. If children have trouble writing, write out their compliments for them.

◆ Once the cards are completed, have the children take turns reading the compliments to each other. Prompt the recipient to respond with "thank you" if necessary.

◆ Children can take their personal compliments home.

Practice Activity 2: Seasonal Picture

Determine the theme or subject of a seasonal picture and prepare suitable colored markers and craft supplies. Suggestions include a winter scene, spring picnic, summer vacation, Halloween or Thanksgiving.

Instructions

◆ Divide children into small groups and instruct them to plan the scene. Give each group the materials to make the picture and a very large piece of drawing paper or poster board.

◆ Everyone must have a job. For example, children who cannot draw might glue cotton balls on the paper to make ghosts or a snow-covered mountain. Wooden craft sticks may be used to make people when covered with bits of fabric. Dried leaves may be glued onto trees drawn by another child, or glitter sprinkled onto an ice-skating pond. (Sometimes it is preferable to pass out the supplies after the children have made a preliminary plan to ensure everyone's participation.)

◆ Once the groups have a plan, they can begin to create their picture.

◆ Remind the children to compliment each other on their individual contributions. Praise spontaneous compliments.

◆ Remind the children to ask the group for permission before making any additions or changes to the group picture.

◆ As leader it is often helpful to directly participate in this activity and model giving compliments and guide any problem solving that might be needed.

Problem

✖ A student makes additions to the picture without consulting the group. For example, the students are creating a winter scene. Dimitrius has finished making his snowman and begins to make a pond.

Solution

☺ *Dimitrius, that might be a good idea, but it is up to the whole group to decide what is on the picture and where. How can you ask them?* Do not let him proceed with the pond until he asks for permission from the group. Praise Dimitrius when he does.

SUPPORTIVE SKILLS TO PROMPT AND REINFORCE

1. Using Kind Talk (page 217)

2. Cooperating (page 255)

3. Following Directions (page 148)

4. Giving a Suggestion (page 263)

5. Showing Interest in Others (page 225)

SUPPLIES

◆ Card stock

◆ Craft supplies

◆ Flipchart or blackboard

◆ Markers

◆ Posterboard or large drawing paper

◆ Small jar or can

◆ Small pieces of paper

◆ Wooden craft sticks

☑ EXTENDING SKILL DEVELOPMENT

Explain the goal of this skill to others and ask them to:

1. Post the Steps to Success in the classroom and at home.

2. Encourage the child to offer a compliment to somebody else and to say "thank you" when she receives a compliment herself.

3. Write the names of family members or classmates on pieces of paper and put them in a container. Ask each family member or student to choose a name at meal or snack time. Think of a compliment to give the person. If there are too many students in a classroom, draw 3-5 names out each day of 3-5 different children. Once a name is drawn, it is removed until all names are drawn. If children have trouble thinking of compliments, have a "smiley" container available with suggestions.

4. Write out compliments on 3x5 cards. Instruct the child to choose a compliment and then decide whom to give it to.

5. Offer incentives to motivate the child to compliment others, perhaps by earning a reward for complimenting two people a day without prompts. Keep track by placing initials on a card.

SKILLS 6-6: ASKING FOR HELP

STEPS TO SUCCESS

To ask for help, you:
1. **Recognize you need help.**
2. **Think of who can help.**
3. **Move close to the person.**
4. **Say the person's name.**
5. **Ask in a friendly voice.**
6. **Say, "thank you."**

THOUGHTS BEFORE STARTING

There are many reasons why children with ASD have difficulty asking for help. Some of them seem to prefer to figure things out for themselves and may view asking for help as personal failure. Others are frequently self-absorbed perfectionists and simply do not consider asking for help as an option. They do not understand that another person might have information or skills distinct from their own and therefore useful to them. Others focus on the wrong detail of an assignment or social situation, and consequently miss the main point (Stewart, 2002). They might not recognize the need to ask for help. Finally, it is often difficult for these children to accept mistakes, both in themselves and in others, so asking for help becomes more difficult because you, or the other person, might be wrong.

The emphasis in teaching this skill is on helping children recognize when help is needed, knowing that it is permissible to ask for help and figuring out whom to ask.

☑

INTRODUCING THE SKILL

Today we are going to practice asking for help. Hold a puzzle and put the pieces in wrong. *I can't seem to make these pieces fit together. I keep trying and trying, but it is not working. What should I do? I could keep trying, but then it might take me all day. I know I'm not stupid. I'll be smart and ask for help. Who can help me?* Look around the group. *Well, (Name) is free. I'll ask her.* Move close. *(Name), I'm having trouble. Can you help me with this puzzle? Thank you.*

Discussion Questions

☐ *Everyone has ideas; if I don't know the answer or how to do something, someone else might. Is it O.K. to ask for help?* (Yes.)

☐ *How do you know when you need help?* (When something is too hard, when you don't understand the directions, when you can't do something alone, when you don't know what to do, when there is too much to do and you might not finish on time.)

☐ *Who can help?* (Usually anyone; look for someone who is not busy.)

☐ *What can you say to ask for help?* (Write suggestions on the board: "I need help." "Would you help me, please?" "I would appreciate help with this." "I have a problem and I think you can help.")

☐ *When you don't know how to do something or can't do it by yourself, does it mean you are stupid? Does it mean you are a failure?* (No.)

☐ *What should you do if the first person you ask cannot help you?* (Ask someone else.)

☑

READ AND REVIEW STEPS TO SUCCESS

WARM-UP ACTIVITY

Use riddles from riddle books or commercial riddle cards. Ask for a volunteer. Choose a difficult riddle and read it to the volunteer. The volunteer might reply with "I don't know." Point to the Steps to Success and praise Asking for Help. Reward with bonus points or tokens if desired. Move on to the next volunteer and read a different riddle. Take turns solving riddles until everyone has had a chance to ask for help.

Problem

✖ Invariably someone in the group will know the answer to the riddle and may blurt out the answer or raise his hand. Choose whether or not to allow such "offers to help."

Solution

☹ If not allowed, the child whose turn it is must ask someone else for help.

☺ If allowed, prompt the child to follow the Steps to Success for Offering Help.

ROLE-PLAYS

Review the role-play format presented in Chapter 5.

🎬 Alternative School Scenarios

1. You are working on a math problem and you cannot figure out how to do it.

2. You can't find your book bag and the bus is coming.

3. You are working at the computer and it keeps freezing up.

4. You have lost your lunch ticket.

🎬 Alternative Home Scenarios

1. You are having trouble with your homework. You are home with your older sister.

2. You can't get your boots on and your ride to school is coming.

3. You are trying to get your bike out of the garage but the car is in the way.

4. You are wrapping a birthday present for your mom and you can't get the wrapping paper folded right.

 **Alternative Community Scenarios**

1. You are recycling cans at the grocery store and the machine stops working.

2. You are at the library and can't find the book you need for a report.

3. You and your friend are at the mall. You can't find your mom.

4. You are in the grocery store shopping for your favorite cereal. You can't reach it.

PRACTICE ACTIVITIES

Practice Activity 1: Stumped

Set up a game such as *Go to the Head of the Class* or *Trivial Pursuit for Juniors*. Each child begins play as the game directs.

Instructions

◆ On each turn, the player can ask for help if she does not know the answer to the question.

◆ Each player must ask one person at a time for help until someone (or no one) can help.

◆ A player who raises his hand to offer help or blurts out the answer misses his turn.

Practice Activity 2: Hide-and-Seek

Hide assorted items, such as pieces of candy, colored erasers, little toys, colored thread, etc., about the room. Write the names of several very specific items on a note card and put each card in a small bag. (Use a picture list for those who cannot read.) Make sure that the number of times an item is written matches the number of that item hidden in the room. Pass out bags to one half of the group, one to each. Review lists to ensure everyone knows the items they are searching for. Direct the remaining members to sit at the table and chat or simply watch. Set a timer for 1-2 minutes.

Instructions

◆ The players with cards must find the items on the card before the time is up.

◆ Players may ask for help from someone at the table by following the Steps to Success.

◆ Players may not tell other players where items are located. If a child tells where items are located, he must sit out the remainder of the turn.

◆ Players who find all their items in time receive a treat, token or bonus point.

◆ Repeat with the second half of the group. Continue to play until everyone has asked for help successfully and has earned a reward.

SUPPORTIVE SKILLS TO PROMPT AND REINFORCE

1. Listening (page 143)

2. Offering Help (page 194)

3. Receiving a Suggestion (page 268)

4. Being a Good Sport (page 247)

SUPPLIES

◆ Flipchart or blackboard

◆ *Go to the Head of the Class, Trivial Pursuit for Juniors*

◆ Note cards

◆ Puzzle

◆ Riddles

◆ Small bags

◆ Small items to hide

EXTENDING SKILL DEVELOPMENT

Explain the goal of this skill to others and ask them to:

1. Post the Steps to Success in the classroom and at home.

2. Observe and identify specific situations where asking for help is needed.

3. Model asking for help.

4. Specifically ask the child to help with tasks. Explain to the child why her help is needed, such as the task will get done faster, the task takes two people, the task is too hard, etc.

5. Review and rehearse with the child in advance of potential opportunities to ask for help.

6. Point out to the child instances where people are helping each other, such as holding a door open, carrying packages, looking for a lost item, etc.

7. Set up situations where the child will likely need help from others and prompt the child to ask for help when necessary.

8. Help the child understand that others may have different information that may be useful to the child.

9. Set up a formal "helping time," perhaps when cleaning up is required. Emphasize "helping" rather than chores.

10. Use natural situations to foster asking for help.

11. Praise the child for asking for help.

12. Offer incentives to motivate the child to ask for help if needed, perhaps by earning a token. Tokens can be exchanged for special privileges or treats.

SKILLS 6-7: STARTING A CONVERSATION

STEPS TO SUCCESS

To start a conversation, you:
1. **Look friendly (relax) and smile.**
2. **Choose a common, shared topic.**
3. **Begin with a greeting.**
4. **Ask a polite question or make a polite comment.**

THOUGHTS BEFORE STARTING

One of the difficult aspects of this skill is determining an appropriate topic of conversation. Topics that might fascinate an individual student with ASD, such as shipwrecks, train engines or mountain peaks, might have little attraction to his peer group. Often children with ASD are not interested in the same topics as their peers (Atwood, 1998).

Helping students to recognize the need to converse on topics of shared appeal is one of the biggest challenges in teaching this skill. One does not start a conversation by asking inappropriate personal questions or by lecturing about factual information. The Steps to Success are guidelines and may have to be individualized to emphasize a particular component. For example, a child who usually monopolizes the conversation may need a time limit, such as "make a polite comment in less than 10 seconds."

INTRODUCING THE SKILL

Today we are going to practice starting a conversation.

Discussion Questions

☐ *What is a topic?* (The subject of the conversation.)

☐ *What are some common topics of conversation?* (Home, school, pets, vacations, etc.)

☐ *What does shared topic mean?* (A subject that interests both people.)

☐ *Why do you think it is important to choose a shared topic to talk about?* (It's more interesting to everyone and everybody can participate in the conversation.)

☐ *If I want to start a conversation with you about my summer vacation, I could start by saying: "Hi, guys. This summer I went to the seashore with my family." What other ideas do you have for how I could start the conversation?* List possible alternatives. (You know what? Can I tell you something? I had a great time at the sea. What did you do for summer vacation? etc.). *There are lots of ways to start a conversation. Conversations can start with a question or with a comment.*

READ AND REVIEW STEPS TO SUCCESS

WARM-UP ACTIVITY

This activity requires answering a question and then directing the same question to some one else. I'll start: I like to eat pizza. (Child's name), what is your favorite food? The child replies: *I like to eat ____. (Second child's name), what is your favorite food?* Second child replies: *I like to eat ____. (Third child's name), what is your favorite food?* Continue like this until all children have had a chance to answer and ask the question. Then proceed in the same manner with the following practice topics: favorite movie, favorite color and favorite game.

ROLE-PLAYS

Review the role-play format presented in Chapter 5.

 Alternative School Scenarios

1. You have a substitute teacher in art class.

2. You see someone you like on the playground. You haven't seen him for a few days.

3. A friend has a new Detroit Lions jacket. You think it's really nice.

4. You saw your favorite hockey team play the last game of the season. You want to tell your friend.

Alternative Home Scenarios

1. Your mom has just walked into the house after work. You want to tell her you got an "A" on your science test.

2. A friend of your brother's is visiting. Your brother has to answer the phone and you are left alone with the friend.

3. You want to tell your dad about your bowling score.

4. Your sister saw a movie last night with her friends. You want to hear all about it.

Alternative Community Scenarios

1. A new family moved in next door. You see a boy standing in the yard.

2. You are shopping at the mall and see one of your classmates in the music store.

3. You walk into the video store with your sister and see your neighbor looking at videos.

4. You are walking home from school and see someone you know from recess.

PRACTICE ACTIVITIES

Practice Activity 1: Conversation Coupons

Copy and cut apart the Conversation coupons on pages 113-114. Prepare four envelopes, each containing all of one type of coupon. For example, one envelope contains the "what topic" coupons; a second contains the "who" coupons, etc. Add and delete coupons as needed to fit the individual circumstances of the children in the group. Label each envelope with its contents and give them out to students.

Instructions

◆ One member begins the activity by choosing a coupon from her envelope. For example, she might choose "friend" from the "Who" envelope.

◆ One at a time, the other members select coupons from their envelopes that "match" the first coupon. The student with "Where" coupons might choose "mall," the student with "When" coupons might choose "shopping" and the final student with "What Topic" coupons might choose "birthday party."

◆ Copy the choices onto a flipchart or board.

◆ Students who do not have envelopes act as judges. The judges determine whether or not a chosen coupon matches the other selections.

◆ If a coupon does not match, the student must make another choice. Briefly discuss why a coupon is not suitable for a given situation.

◆ Give one point to each member for successful choices. No point is awarded for unaccepted matches.

◆ Pass the envelopes to the right and start again.

Additional suggestion: Instead of receiving points for success, play *Oreo Matchin' Middles*. When a group successfully defines the context of the conversation, each player quickly chooses a pair of cookies and tries to make a match. *Memory* played with a deck of playing cards may be used also.

Note: It is possible to give each participant all four envelopes and have each one make personal selections in all categories. However, one of the functions of Super Skills is to encourage children to work together, not alone. Therefore, as often as possible, ask children to complete activities with a partner or as a group, not individually.

Practice Activity 2: Conversation Hunt

Prepare a list of 3-5 common topics of conversation for each student. (The list may be a picture list for children who have trouble reading.) Pass out a different-colored marker to everyone in the room (including adults or older siblings who might be observing).

Instructions

◆ Direct each child to approach someone in the room and start a conversation on one of the topics on his or her list. The children must follow the Steps to Success and converse for 2-3 exchanges.

◆ The conversation partner judges whether or the not the Steps to Success were followed and signs her name on the list next to the topic discussed.

◆ Once a signature has been obtained, the student is free to approach someone else to begin a conversation on a different topic and receive another signature.

◆ No topics can have the same colored signature. The goal is to receive signatures next to as many topics as possible from different people.

Suggested Topics: Pizza, television shows, pets, birthdays, toys, movies, weekend activities, holidays, vacation plans, class trips, homework.

Practice Activity 3: Conversation Starters

Using topics from Practice Activity 1, suggested topics from Practice Activity 2, or topics that are unique to your group, make a "deck" of topic cards by writing each topic on a note card. Include a few "blank" cards. Set up any board or card game of your choice, such as *UNO, Chutes and Ladders, Mr. Potato Head Pals,* etc.

Instructions

◆ Define the parameters of the conversation, such as the conversation should be acceptable in the classroom with students you know, or the conversation should be acceptable at home with your parents.

◆ At the beginning of a turn, one player draws a card from the deck of topic cards and presents a conversation starter to the group on that topic. For example, if the chosen topic is pizza, he might respond, "What is your favorite brand of pizza?" or "I like pizza with mushrooms, do you?"

◆ When a student draws a blank card, he determines the topic and the conversation starter.

◆ Judge whether or not a given starter is acceptable for the specified situation. If your group is small, ask peers for their opinions.

◆ When the starter is accepted, the player assumes his turn at the board or card game. When the starter is not accepted, he does not take his turn at the game.

◆ Ask peers to explain why a given starter is unacceptable if possible, and discuss what makes a topic or question inappropriate. For example, a student draws a blank card and replies, "Do you know how many people died on the Titanic?" Ask peers to give their opinions of this conversation starter. Some of them might reply "that's boring" or "you always talk about the Titanic." Help the student to understand that conversations should interest both communication partners, not just one person. A better opener might be "One of my favorite movies is the *Titanic*. Have you seen it?"

SUPPORTIVE SKILLS TO PROMPT AND REINFORCE

1. Using Kind Talk (page 217)

2. Exchanging Conversation (page 124)

3. Following Directions (page 148)

4. Showing Interest in Others (page 225)

SUPPLIES

◆ Board/card game(s)

◆ Conversation coupons (pages 113-114)

◆ Deck of topic cards

◆ Different-colored markers

◆ Envelopes

◆ Flipcharts or blackboard

◆ Topic lists

EXTENDING SKILL DEVELOPMENT

Explain the goal of this skill to others and ask them to:

1. Post the Steps to Success in the classroom and at home.

2. Place written "conversation starter" comments or questions near the child.

3. Require that the child start one conversation daily with a peer. If necessary, rehearse beforehand with an adult. Gradually expand expectations for the number of exchanges and the number of peers required.

4. Play guessing games to encourage students to ask questions.

5. Try to limit the number of questions directed towards the child, but expand upon comments made in the child's presence. For example, instead of asking "Did you see that pass?" say, "That was a great pass!" This models possible conversation starters for the child.

6. Offer incentives to motivate the child to try and start conversations, perhaps by earning a reward for starting two conversations a day without prompts. Keep track by placing initials on a card.

7. Offer incentives to peers to start conversations with the child with ASD.

Practice Activity 1: Conversation Coupons

What Topic	What Topic	Where	Where
Weather	Vacation Plans	Classroom	Bus
School Subject	Holiday Event	Home	Park
New Movie	Home Problem	Place of Worship	School Yard
Favorite Movie	School Problem	Store	Neighbor's Home
TV Show	Food	Relative's House	Sidewalk
Video Game	Favorite Activity	Movie Theater	Street
School Event	Birthday Party	Restaurant	Lunchroom
Family Event	Music	Car	Office
Current Event	Pets	Public Library	Lesson
Sporting Event	Favorite Topic	Skating Rink	Scouts
Religious Event	None: Be Quiet	Mall	Special Event
Book Report	Personal Problem	Therapy Appointment	Friend's House

Practice Activity 1: Conversation Coupons

Who	Who	When	When
Teacher	Police Officer	Teacher Talking	Parents Talking
Parent	Friend of Parent	Meal/Snack Time	Doing a Chore
Clergy	Aunt	Free Time	Reading
Friend	Adult Stranger	Parent on Phone	Helping
Cousin	Doctor	Studying	Watching TV
Salesclerk	Cashier	Waiting	Watching a Movie
Classmate	Uncle	Class Time	Shopping
Sibling	Grandparent	Traveling	Doing Homework
Librarian	Nurse	Getting Ready	Visiting
Principal	Adult Leader	Playing	Camping
Office Worker	Child Stranger	Walking	Introducing
Neighbor	Babysitter	Adult Driving	Resting

SKILL 6-8: ENTERING A CONVERSATION

STEPS TO SUCCESS

To enter a conversation, you:
1. **Listen.**
2. **Watch.**
3. **Wait for a pause.**
4. **Smile.**
5. **Speak for a short time on the topic.**

THOUGHTS BEFORE STARTING

Similar to starting a conversation, entering a conversation includes several strategic challenges for children with ASD. For example, for children who are not particularly interested in the same topics as their peers, joining a conversation has little meaning or social value. They prefer to remain on the fringe of social interaction, or talk to adults who are attentive to their factual monologues about peculiar subjects (Atwood, 1998). For others, particularly those with AS, waiting for a pause or speaking on the topic is difficult. Interrupting, introducing an entirely unrelated topic or arguing inappropriately is common with this group. They are interested in dominating the interaction and often cause significant disruption to the conversation. For both groups, the Steps to Success are identical; however, the emphasis will be different. Practicing the distinctive reciprocal structure of conversation should be a valuable part of every Super Skills session.

INTRODUCING THE SKILL

Today we are going to practice entering a conversation.

Discussion Questions

☐ *Who remembers what a conversation is?* Accept and praise responses.

☐ *When we want to join in a conversation, we wait and listen for a pause. A pause is a short gap in the conversation when the people having the conversation stop talking. A pause is a signal, like a green light, to enter the conversation. What would happen if we did not wait for a pause?* (We would be interrupting. We would be impolite.)

☐ *Who remembers what a topic is?* Accept and praise responses.

☐ *When we enter a conversation the right way, we talk on the same topic that the others are talking about, not something different. We can ask a question or make a comment.* Show the question starters on page 122. *When you ask a question, you can start the question with one of these words.*

☐ Show the comments on page 123. *When you make a comment, it can start with one of these phrases or words.*

☐ *Let's practice asking questions and making comments on the topic. These puppets are Max and Donnie.* Max speaks first: *"I went trick or treating for Halloween."* Donnie replies: *"Me too, I got lots of candy."* O.K., what is the topic of their conversation? (Halloween, trick-or-treating.)

If you wanted to join in this conversation what questions or comments could you make? Who wants to start? Go around the group and ask every child to make a comment or ask a question.

READ AND REVIEW STEPS TO SUCCESS

WARM-UP ACTIVITY

Prepare a small paper sack with 3-4 items, such as Beanie Baby, postcard or photograph of a vacation place, photograph of your family, favorite CD or video, candy bar, etc. *I have several items in this paper sack. I will draw one out and start the conversation. Take turns entering the conversation by asking a question or making a comment. You can get help from the Question and Comment starters. Everyone gets one turn for each item in the bag.* Proceed to remove an item from the sack and make a comment about it such as: *This is my favorite Beanie Baby.* One at a time each member must make a comment or ask a question. Proceed through 2-3 items.

ROLE-PLAYS

Review the role-play format presented in Chapter 5.

 ## Alternative School Scenarios

1. Your teacher is explaining the spelling homework for this week to a student. You have a question about the homework, too.

2. Some classmates are talking about seeing a movie. You already saw it and thought it was pretty good.

3. The principal is telling your teacher there will be a fire drill today. You hate fire drills because the alarm is so loud.

4. Some kids at lunch are talking about their summer vacations. You want to share what you did over the summer.

 ## Alternative Home Scenarios

1. Your dad and brother are talking about what pizza to order for dinner. You have an idea.

2. Your parents are talking about limiting the amount of time you spend watching TV. You want to suggest an alternative.

3. Your brother and sister are arguing about the rules to a computer game. You know the game really well.

4 Your parents are talking about visiting your grandparents this weekend. You have a soccer game.

 ## Alternative Community Scenarios

1. Your neighbor is going to pay your brother to do some yard work. You know how to water the flowers.

2. Some neighbors are planning a yard sale. You'd like to help at the sale.

3. Your Scout troop is planning a camp-out. You would like to suggest what to take along.

4. Some kids from your neighborhood went to a new water park. You want to know more about it.

PRACTICE ACTIVITIES

Practice Activity 1: Join a Conversation Bingo

Copy and distribute the Join a Conversation bingo card (page 121). Distribute one card per player and sufficient tokens to play.

Instructions

◆ Decide on a topic for the conversation. Sometimes it is helpful to start with a written phrase such as, *This week I went to . . . My favorite movie is . . . Have you ever been to . . .?*

◆ Ask for a volunteer to begin the conversation.

◆ Give players a token every time they join in the conversation correctly using the Steps to Success and one of the Question Starters or Comments on their bingo card.

◆ Once a child has a "bingo," start a new conversation on a different topic.

Problem

✖ Some students need help joining in.

Solutions

☺ Write a prompt.

☺ Point to an appropriate cue on their bingo card.

☺ Whisper what to say.

Practice Activity 2: Trivial Pursuit

Use *Trivial Pursuit* or *Trivial Pursuit for Juniors*, or choose another question-and answer-game. Divide the group into two teams. Do this by counting off, taking names from an envelope or designating team leaders, who then take turns choosing members for their team.

Instructions

◆ Present one question per team.

◆ Each team has 1 minute to discuss the question and present you with their answer.

◆ Remind them you will be watching to see who joins in the conversation. Give bonus points when you see the team including everyone in the discussion.

◆ Tally points on a flipchart or board.

Problem

✖ Invariably one person on the team raises a hand to answer the question without consulting with his team members first.

Solution

☺ Ignore the the player that raised her hand and remind the group to "talk about the answer together."

Note: If you have enough space to separate the teams so they can talk without being overheard, present the same question to both teams simultaneously. This reduces idle time.

Alternative: This activity can be played successfully using riddles. Teams have 1 minute to solve the riddle.

Practice Activity 3: Topic Conversation

If the students are having difficulty determining what to say to join in a conversation, give each of them a piece of paper and instruct them to write or dictate the conversation topic at the top of the paper. Suggestions include holiday plans, weekend plans, collections, etc.

Instructions

◆ Direct the children to write/dictate four things they know or could ask on the topic. Assist those who need help writing.

◆ Give each child three tokens.

◆ Ask for a volunteer to begin the conversation.

◆ Remove a token each time a child joins the conversation using the Steps to Success. When a child has joined in three times, he is to stop talking and let the others have a turn to join in.

◆ Repeat with new topics.

SUPPORTIVE SKILLS TO PROMPT AND REINFORCE

1. Using Kind Talk (page 217)

2. Starting a Conversation (page 107)

3. Exchanging Conversation (page 124)

4. Showing Interest in Others (page 225)

SUPPLIES

- ◆ 2 puppets
- ◆ Bingo card (page 121)
- ◆ Blank paper
- ◆ Flipchart or blackboard
- ◆ Miscellaneous objects

- ◆ Paper sack
- ◆ Question Starters and Comments (pages 122-123)
- ◆ Tokens
- ◆ *Trivial Pursuit for Juniors*

EXTENDING SKILL DEVELOPMENT

Explain the goal of this skill to others and ask them to:

1. Post the Steps to Success in the classroom and at home.

2. Place written comments or question starters near the child.

3. Require that the child enter one conversation daily with a peer. If needed, rehearse beforehand with an adult. Gradually expand the expectations for the number of exchanges and the number of peers.

4. Play guessing games to encourage the child to ask questions.

5. Remind the child of the conversation topic when the child joins in off the topic.

6. Use the "15-second rule" if the child has a tendency to monopolize conversations. This means the child must finish talking within 15 seconds.

7. Offer incentives to motivate the child to try entering conversations, perhaps by earning a reward for joining two conversations a day without prompts. Keep track by placing initials on a card.

8. Offer incentives to peers to start conversations with the child with ASD.

Practice Activity 1: Bingo Card

Who	**I like**	**Where**
When	**FREE SPACE**	**Where**
Which	**Do/Did**	**How**

Practice Activity 1: Question Starters

Who	**What**	**Where**
Why	**?**	**Do/Did**
When	**Which**	**How**

Practice Activity 1: Comments

I ...	*I think ...*	*I like ...*
That is ...	You sure ...	Awesome
I wonder ...	Cool	*I know ...*

6:9 EXCHANGING CONVERSATION

STEPS TO SUCCESS

To exchange conversation, you:

1. **Look.**
2. **Listen.**
3. **Talk about yourself.**
4. **Ask about others.**
5. **Take turns talking and listening.**

THOUGHTS BEFORE STARTING

Children with ASD have difficulty chatting on mainstream topics such as movies, TV shows, family or school events (unless verbatim dialogue from the movie is needed). They can be quite fluent when reciting facts but unable to talk about their thoughts or feelings in a situation (Stewart, 2002). It is difficult for them to recognize any purpose in finding out the experiences, thoughts, or feelings of others. Learning the art of reciprocal conversation requires hours of practice. Initial efforts will likely be stilted and mechanical. Extensive guidance by conversation partners or others will be necessary.

INTRODUCING THE SKILL

Today we are going to practice exchanging conversation.

☐ *What is a conversation?* Accept responses and praise volunteering. At some point in the discussion, point out that a conversation occurs when people take turns talking and listening.

☐ Begin a monologue on a topic you can talk about for several minutes. Ignore any questions or comments. Keep talking for a few minutes and then ask: *Is this a conversation?* (No.) *Why not?* (The leader is the only one talking; the leader is not giving anyone a turn to talk.)

❑ *How did you feel when I didn't give you a turn to talk?* (Bored, left out, frustrated, didn't care, etc.)

❑ *When one person does all the talking, it makes others feel left out, hurt and even bored. You do not want other people to feel bad, so you include them in the conversation. You do this by asking a question about them or pausing so they can join in the conversation. Exchanging conversation means you take turns talking and listening.*

❑ *In school, there is a time when teachers do all of the talking, who knows when this is?* (Lecture or other suitable answer.) *This is not a conversation. Teachers are lecturing. They are giving information. The students' job is to listen and ask questions if they do not understand. Lecturing is different from exchanging conversation.*

❑ *If I want to have a conversation with you about my trip to the museum yesterday, I can start by saying: "Yesterday I saw the Egyptian exhibit at the history museum." Then I can stop talking and give you a chance to make a comment or ask a question, or I can ask you: "Have you seen the exhibit?" Let's try it.* Repeat the first statement of your monologue and wait for a question or comment from a student. Continue the conversation for a few exchanges if possible. If no one makes a comment or asks a question, prompt with: *What comment could you make or question could you ask?* Praise responses.

READ AND REVIEW STEPS TO SUCCESS

WARM-UP ACTIVITY

Distribute prepared note cards on a topic of conversation, one card per student. Each note card should contain a question or comment appropriate to the topic. Direct the students to keep their questions and comments brief and to the point. They are to join in when they think the question or comment on their card best "fits" into the conversation. Read note cards to students who need help reading. Ask them to repeat the comment or question back to you if necessary.

Topic Suggestion: Favorite pizza.

Note Card Questions and Comments

What is your favorite pizza?

I think _____ pizza is really good.

The best pizza is _____.

We order our pizza from _____.

I don't like _____ on pizza.

Do you like mushrooms?

Do you like thin or thick crust?

My favorite pizza is _____.

Once the exchange is completed, comment on what went well with the conversation.

Problem

✖ One child monopolizes and tries to dominate the conversation

Solution

☺ Remind the children to "take turns talking." Use a watch and limit responses to 15 seconds or less. This helps students learn to pause to give others a chance to join in. Use a stop sign or hold up your palm to signal when 15 seconds are over. If this makes some members of the group too upset, give a 5-second warning by holding up your hand and counting down to zero with your fingers.

ROLE-PLAYS

Review the role-play format presented in Chapter 5.

🎬 Alternative School Scenarios

1. You want to tell your friend about the new puppy you got last night.

2. A classmate has been absent from school all week. He returns on Friday.

3. Your teacher has a new family photo on her desk.

4. You want to tell the music teacher you can help set up for the evening program.

🎬 Alternative Home Scenarios

1. Your dad and you are cleaning the garage. You want to know more about the camping trip planned for next weekend.

2. Your mom says your grandma is coming to visit next week for your birthday.

3. Your mom wants you to help her plan your little brother's birthday party.

4. Your sister just got back from a school trip to Chicago. You want to hear all about it.

Alternative Community Scenarios

1. You go swimming and see a friend you haven't seen all summer.

2. Your neighbor has a new car. You really like cars.

3. You are in the mall and see your aunt shopping with your grandpa.

4. You see your teacher at the video store. You want to tell her your dad will help out with the Halloween party next week.

PRACTICE ACTIVITIES

Practice Activity 1: Conversation Scripts

Select scripts from the Conversation Exchange Scripts on pages 130-132 or develop your own. Each script consists of two parts, A and B. Ask for two volunteers to exchange a conversation using Parts A and B as guides, respectively. Proceed until everyone has had a turn as a conversation partner.

Modified from Freeman, S., & Dake, L. (1997). Movie conversation. In *Teach me language.* Langley, BC: SKF Books.

Practice Activity 2: Family Photo

This activity requires a family photograph from each member of the group.

Instructions

◆ Instruct children to choose a partner and start a conversation about families, using their family photographs to guide the exchange.

◆ They are to ask polite questions, make comments and tell about their families.

◆ After about 2-3 minutes of conversation, call out "switch partners." Pairs must find different partners.

◆ Continue to switch partners every 2-3 minutes until all possible partner combinations have had time to chat about their families. Prompt and guide as needed.

◆ If some members of the group need direct guidance to be able to participate in this activity, prepare question prompts on cue cards ahead of time. Prompts might include the following: Who is in your family? Where do you live? How old is your brother (sister)? When was this picture taken? Distribute the cards as needed.

Note: This activity may also be completed with a special object brought from home or photographs of a favorite vacation.

Practice Activity 3: Envelope Choice

Prepare two envelopes, each with one half of the Conversation Starters on page 133. Divide the group into two teams (A and B) and have them sit facing each other. Give each team an envelope of Conversation Starters.

Instructions

◆ The first participant from Team A draws a conversation starter from her envelope and reads it to the person facing her from Team B.

◆ The opponent from Team B responds with an appropriate conversation exchange. The Team A member responds a second time, followed by the Team B opponent. The goal is three exchanges per team. If three exchanges are too difficult for the group, begin with a single exchange.

◆ Set a timer for 2 minutes (or less if only one exchange is expected).

◆ Each team receives one point per successful exchange made within the 2-minute limit. If a team member has trouble thinking of a response, he can request help from a specific teammate. Otherwise, teammates are not to interrupt.

◆ As leader, judge acceptable responses and tally points. If a team member corrects a response within the 2-minute limit, he receives a point.

◆ Once the first conversation exchange is completed, start again with the next two opponents. This time a member from Team B chooses a Conversation Starter and reads it to the opposing Team A member.

◆ Continue in this manner until all pairs have had a turn.

◆ To begin a second round, have one team "slide" down a chair and start with a new opposing partner.

SUPPORTIVE SKILLS TO PROMPT AND REINFORCE

1. Using Kind Talk (page 217)

2. Starting a Conversation (page 107)

3. Entering a Conversation (page 115)

4. Showing Interest in Others (page 225)

5. Asking for Help (page 101)

SUPPLIES

◆ Conversation Exchange Scripts (pages 130-132)

◆ Conversation Starters (page 133)

◆ Envelopes

◆ Family photos

◆ Flipchart or blackboard

◆ Note cards

EXTENDING SKILL DEVELOPMENT

Explain the goal of this skill to others and ask them to:

1. Post the Steps to Success in the classroom and at home.

2. Place written comments or question starters near the child.

3. Develop a conversation library. Using note cards, write a topic on the card and list questions or comments suitable to the topic. Practice exchanging conversation using the cards as a guide.

4. Require that the child exchange one conversation daily with a peer. If needed, rehearse beforehand with an adult. Gradually expand expectations for the number of exchanges and the number of peers.

5. Praise with "good comment" or "good question" when the child spontaneously and appropriately enters a conversation.

6. Remind the child of the conversation topic when the child is off topic.

7. If the child has a tendency to monopolize conversations, use the "15-second rule" – the child must finish talking within 15 seconds. He may also need a reminder to "get to the point."

8. Offer incentives to motivate the child to try exchanging conversation, perhaps by earning a reward. Keep track by placing initials on a card.

9. Offer incentives to peers to exchange conversation with the child with ASD.

Practice Activity 1: Conversation Scripts: Script 1

MY WEEK: PART A	MY WEEK: PART B
How was your week?	**My week was . . .**
What did you do?	**I went . . .** **What did you do?**
I went . . . **Who did you . . . ?**	**I . . .**
I was with . . .	**How did you . . .?**
I . . . The best part was . . .	**The best part was . . .**
I think . . . **What do you think?**	**I think . . .**
Next week I will . . . **What about you?**	**Next week I will . . .**

Practice Activity 1: Conversation Scripts: Script 2

WINTER BREAK: PART A	WINTER BREAK: PART B
How was your winter break?	My break was . . . How was yours?
Mine was . . . What did you do?	I . . . What did you do?
I . . . Who did you . . .?	I . . . What about you?
I was with . . .	How did you . . .?
The best part was . . .	Cool. The best part for me was . . .
I think . . . What do you think?	I think . . .
I'm glad to . . . Winter break was . . .	Yeah, winter break was . . .

Practice Activity 1: Conversation Scripts: Script 3

HALLOWEEN: PART A	HALLOWEEN: PART B
What did you do on Halloween?	**I went trick or treating. Did you?**
Yeah. Who did you go with?	**I went with . . .** **What about you?**
I . . . **Isn't it cool when . . . ?**	**Yeah. I was a . . .** **What about you?**
I was a . . . The best costume **I saw was . . .**	**Where did you . . .?**
The best part was . . .	**Cool. The best part for me** **was . . .**
I think . . . **What do you think?**	**I think . . .**
I'm glad to . . . **Halloween is . . .**	**Yeah. Halloween is . . .**

Practice Activity 3: Conversation Starters

My grandpa was in a car accident.	I saw a good movie last night.
This pizza is really bad.	I had a test in math today.
I went skiing this weekend.	Science class was really fun today. We saw a movie.
I really like to ice skate.	My sister broke her arm yesterday.
What do you like to do after school?	What is your favorite subject in school?
I really like to play video games.	I went to Disney World for spring break.
This class is really hard.	I think the Red Wings are a great hockey team.
My mom works at the hospital.	I really like to play soccer.
Mrs. Johnson is my English teacher.	I think a failed the history test.
My bike was stolen last night.	I don't know what to get my mom for her birthday.
Jason is having a birthday party on Saturday.	I'm going shopping this weekend.
I'm going to visit my brother this weekend.	I've got a test tomorrow.

SKILL 6-10: ENDING A CONVERSATION

STEPS TO SUCCESS

To end a conversation, you:

1. **Wait for a pause.**
2. **Look.**
3. **Give a short, simple explanation.**
4. **End with a friendly farewell.**

THOUGHTS BEFORE STARTING

Ending a conversation, whether the exchange is brief or lengthy, is by and large straightforward and uncomplicated. It requires determining a reason why the exchange is over (usually because one of the parties must do something else), making a simple statement to that effect and closing with a farewell. One common explanation is, "I have to go now," followed by "see you later" or "bye."

Children with ASD often fail to recognize the need for this simple closure strategy. Sometimes they simply turn away and walk off, or abruptly stop talking and ignore the other person. At other times they continue talking, oblivious to the other person's attempts to end the conversation. That is, they fail to pick up on the facial expressions, body language and comments typically used to terminate an interaction. Difficulties terminating conversation, just like many other skill deficits among students with ASD, may relate to the inability to understand another's perspective.

INTRODUCING THE SKILL

Today we are going to practice ending a conversation.

Discussion Questions

☐ *You know a movie is over when you come to the end, or a race is over when one person crosses the finish line, but how do you know when a conversation is over?* (When you don't have any more to say, when you have to do something else, etc.)

☐ *When you need to end a conversation, it is polite to tell the person you are talking with. Then he or she can finish talking. You do this by giving a simple explanation. I am talking to you after school and my mom comes to pick me up. The reason I have to end our conversation is that my ride is here. So I say that. "My ride is here." I've got to go now." If you have any more to say to me, you can quickly say it; like, "O.K. I'll call you tonight," or "I'll see you at lunch tomorrow." Then I use a friendly farewell. I might say, "O.K. bye," or "See you tomorrow."*

☐ *How might you feel if I just stopped talking, turned my back to you and got into the car without saying good-bye?* (Hurt, insulted, offended.)

☐ *Even though you can see that my ride is here, it is <u>always</u> rude to walk away from a friend or family member when they are still talking without an explanation.*

☐ *How can you tell when someone else wants to end the conversation?* (Facial expression, words, body language.)

☐ *What should you do when the other person wants to end the conversation?* (Quickly wrap up what you want to say and use a friendly farewell.) *It is rude to keep on talking.*

READ AND REVIEW STEPS TO SUCCESS

WARM-UP ACTIVITY

Place the Short Explanations/Friendly Farewells (page 140) on the table in front of the children. Using a flashlight and timer, tell the children that you are going to quickly move the flashlight beam from one child to another. When the beam is directed at them, they are to choose and read aloud any Short Explanation and any Friendly Farewell of their choice. Set the timer for 1 minute and tell the students you are going to count how many turns they can complete in 1 minute.

Begin by pointing the flashlight beam at yourself and promptly read your choices, such as, *I need to go. See you tomorrow.* Rapidly move the light beam to a child and wait for his reply. Swiftly progress through all the children, randomly selecting "targets" to read selections. Repeat again if necessary, or challenge the students to see how many different explanation and farewell combinations they can come up with.

Note: Tell any non-readers exactly what to say on their turn before you set the timer.

ROLE-PLAYS

Review the role-play format presented in Chapter 5.

Alternative School Scenarios

1. You are working on a project after school with a partner in the library. You have to leave to go to a music lesson.

2. You are talking to the classroom assistant before school. A friend is waiting for you.

3. You are sitting on the school bus with a friend. Your bus stop is next.

4. You are playing with a friend from another class during recess. The whistle blows and recess is over.

Alternative Home Scenarios

1. You are talking to your mom about your day at school. You have to get started on your homework.

2. Your sister is telling you about her trip to the zoo. You have to get ready for bed.

3. You and your grandmother are planning a shopping trip. You have to set the table for dinner.

4. You are talking to your dad about a new video game. Your friend comes over to play.

Alternative Community Scenarios

1. You are playing in the park with a friend when it is time for you to go home.

2. You and your friend are doing math homework at his house. Your mom comes to pick you up.

3. You meet a friend while waiting for a carry-out pizza with your dad. The pizza is done and your dad is ready to go.

4. You are telling the receptionist in the dentist's waiting room about your plans for spring break. It's time for your appointment.

PRACTICE ACTIVITIES

Practice Activity 1: Forest Partners

Copy the conversation topics below on to note cards, one topic per card.

Instructions

◆ Direct the children to think of the name of a tree (oak, elm, cherry, walnut, hickory, pine, redwood, maple, orange, lemon, etc.).

◆ List the choices on a board or flipchart. Have each child select a different name.

◆ Proceed to call out pairs of trees to be conversation partners and give each pair a note card labeled with a conversation topic (or have children draw a card from an envelope).

◆ Direct the children to converse on the topic written on their note card until you instruct them to end the conversation.

◆ At the end of about 2 minutes, announce a reason to finish the conversation, such as your bus is coming, and have them end the conversation.

◆ Collect the topic cards, call out different pairs of trees and begin again. Continue for at least three conversation exchanges.

Note: If required, write pertinent questions on the cards ahead of time to aid conversation exchange.

Conversation Topics: Favorite ice cream, pets, birthday parties, favorite movie, unusual toy, brothers and sisters, birthday gift for dad, Mother's Day.

Practice Activity 2: *Farewell Mr. Potato Head Pal*

Set up the *Mr. Potato Head Pals* game as directed in the instructions.

◆ Before each player takes a turn spinning the spinner to collect a part for her Mr. Potato Head, she must use a short explanation and friendly farewell. (Example: *I've got to go now, see you later.*)

◆ If she forgets, she misses her turn.

◆ Do not give verbal reminders but have Short Explanations/Friendly Farewells (page 140) available for cueing if needed.

Note: This game is designed for four players. Use partners if necessary. If one partner forgets to use a farewell, the other can reply. Alternatively, choose a different game, such as *Oreo Matchin' Middles.*

Practice Activity 3: *Hot Potato*

Play the traditional game of *Hot Potato.* However, change it so that when a child is out of the game, he receives a bonus point for remembering to use a friendly farewell.

Note: You can also play musical chairs with the same requirement.

SUPPORTIVE SKILLS TO PROMPT AND REINFORCE

1. Listening (page 143)

2. Starting a Conversation (page 107)

3. Exchanging a Conversation (page 124)

SUPPLIES

◆ Flashlight

◆ Flipchart or blackboard

◆ *Hot Potato* game

◆ *Mr. Potato Head Pals*

◆ Note cards

◆ Short Explanations/Friendly Farewells (page 140)

◆ Timer

☑ EXTENDING SKILL DEVELOPMENT

Explain the goal of this skill to others and ask them to:

1. Post the Steps to Success in the classroom and at home.

2. Regularly review Short Explanations and Friendly Farewells (page 140) with the child.

3. Model the skill frequently.

4. Prompt the child when he forgets to use the skill.

5. Review and rehearse with the child in advance of opportunities to end conversations.

6. Set up situations where the child must end a conversation.

7. Offer a suggestion of how to end a conversation in situations when the child is unable to think of one.

8. Praise the child for using the Steps to Success and point out that he is being friendly.

Friendly Farewells	Short Explanations
See you later.	I've got to go now.
Bye.	I'd better get going.
See you tomorrow.	My ride is here.
See you.	I've got things to do.
Good-bye.	It's time for me to go.
So long.	I need to go.

CHAPTER 7

SOCIAL RESPONSE SKILLS

SKILL 7-1: LISTENING

STEPS TO SUCCESS

To show you are listening, you:
1. **Look at the speaker.**
2. **Use a friendly face.**
3. **Stay still, quiet and calm.**
4. **Think about what is being said.**

THOUGHTS BEFORE STARTING

The skills of listening and following directions are closely related. Often we tell a child to "listen" when we really mean "listen and do what I say." The ability to "listen," and thus follow directions, is influenced by how information is presented. Telling a child with ASD, "I don't want to see you running in the hall again," may have the unintended effect of encouraging him to run when you are not looking (i.e., you don't see him running). When this happens, we say that the child "doesn't listen" because we have told him not to run in the hall. This is not a listening problem, however, but a communication problem, as the adult failed to speak in a way the child understands, given the child's tendency to interpret language literally. As a result, we must be careful how we construe "listening."

Many years ago I began a discussion about anger with a group of children with ASD using a magazine illustration of a child jumping on his bed. The head and face of the child in the illustration were larger than normal to emphasize his very angry facial expression. When I asked the children to tell me what was happening in the picture, one child noticed a tiny glass on the bedside table that was tipping and spilling liquid. I had not even noticed the glass at all as it was tiny. This illustrated to me first-hand how individuals with ASD tend to focus on parts of information rather than the whole. Their skill lies in focusing on details while they have severe deficits in organizing information (Meyer & Minshew, 2002). Thus, asking a child to listen to a teacher's lengthy directions and to recall the main idea of the assignment may end up frustrating everyone involved. A typical response when the child fails is, "Didn't you listen?" Given that infor-

mation is likely to be jumbled and forgotten somewhere in the child's brain, such a question misses the mark. These children need help in developing a memory "storage system" to be able to access information (Stewart, 2002).

Considering the problems inherent in "listening" for children with ASD, listening is presented here as a separate skill with an emphasis on *showing* one is listening. It assumes that the child is able to comprehend and follow through.

INTRODUCING THE SKILL

Today we are going to practice listening.

Discussion Questions

☐ *What does listen mean?* (To hear, pay attention, etc.)

☐ *How do I know you are listening to me right now?* (Looking at me, smiling, being quiet, sitting still, etc.)

☐ *Sometimes you are listening but it doesn't look that way. Why is it important to show you are listening?* (So the speaker knows you are listening.)

☐ *Sometimes people want to talk to you. They might say your name but sometimes they just start talking. What should you do?* (Look at them and listen to what they are saying.)

☐ *What might happen if you do not look or listen?* (They might get upset, think you are unfriendly, repeat what they said, etc.)

☐ *When is it important to listen even if you are not interested in what the person is saying?* (When receiving directions from someone, when a friend, parent, teacher or other adult is talking to you.)

☐ *What can you do if the person is talking too much and you don't understand any more?* (Say "I don't understand." Raise your hand if you are in class and tell the teacher. Look puzzled/confused.)

READ AND REVIEW
STEPS TO SUCCESS

WARM-UP ACTIVITY

Show me listening.

> *Everyone who is happy today, clap your hands.*
>
> *If you have sisters, blink your eyes.*
>
> *If you have brothers, raise your right hand.*
>
> *If you have a pet dog, raise your left hand.*
>
> *If you have another kind of pet, raise both feet.*
>
> *If your favorite color is red, bark like a dog.*
>
> *If your favorite color is blue, meow like a cat.*
>
> *If you have another favorite color, oink like a pig.*
>
> *If you are in Super Skills today, sit quietly.*

Adapted from Foster, E. S. (1989). All about you. In *Energizers and icebreakers*. Minneapolis, MN: Educational Media Corporation.

ROLE-PLAYS

Review the role-play format presented in Chapter 5.

Alternative School Scenarios

1. A friend is telling you about her weekend.
2. The teacher is explaining the homework assignment.
3. Your science partner is giving her ideas for a joint project.
4. A friend asks to borrow your math book.

Alternative Home Scenarios

1. Your dad is explaining your new allowance system.
2. Your sister is giving you ideas on what to buy your mom for her birthday.
3. Your grandma is telling you about her trip to Florida.
4. Your mom is telling you how to spell the word "people."

Alternative Community Scenarios

1. The librarian is explaining where the resource books were moved to.

2. Your mom is giving you a short list of things to find in the grocery store.

3. Your friend is telling you what happened at the Scout meeting you missed.

4. The guide at the Native American exhibit is explaining the totem pole.

PRACTICE ACTIVITIES

Practice Activity 1: Flashlight

Instructions

◆ Using a flashlight beam, point to one child at a time.

◆ Direct the child targeted with the beam to describe her favorite restaurant (TV program, after-school activity, vacation place).

◆ Direct the remaining children to show they are listening by following the Steps to Success. When the child is finished, the others take turns making a comment or asking a question.

◆ Proceed until everyone has had a turn.

Problem

✖ Some children in the group give lengthy monologues when it is their turn to talk.

Solution

☺ Keep the flashlight beam turned on while each child is talking. Turn it off to signal when the child's turn is finished (after 15-20 seconds).

Practice Activity 2: Yesterday's Story

Make sufficient copies of Yesterday's Story (Appendix, page 351).

Instructions

◆ Distribute one copy to each child and ask the children to complete it. Some children will need help with writing. (To save time, have the children complete the story at home ahead of time.)

◆ Once the stories are written, ask a volunteer to read his story aloud to the group. Other children are to show they are listening and be prepared to take turns asking questions and making comments.

◆ If help is needed to think of questions and comments, use the Question Starters and Comments (pages 122-123).

Practice Activity 3:

Several traditional games may be used to practice listening skills. These include *Simon Says, Bingo, Go Fish* and "musical chairs."

SUPPORTIVE SKILLS TO PROMPT AND REINFORCE

1. Following Directions (page 148)

2. Entering a Conversation (page 115)

3. Staying on Task (page 156)

SUPPLIES

◆ Flashlight

◆ Flipcharts and blackboard

◆ Miscellaneous games
  (pages 122-123)

◆ Question Starters and Comments
  (Appendix, page 299)

◆ Yesterday's Story (Appendix, page 351)

EXTENDING SKILL DEVELOPMENT

Explain the goal of these skills to others and ask them to:

1. Post the Steps to Success in the classroom and at home.

2. Praise the child for "good listening."

3. Use the cue "Show me listening," when a child needs prompting in this area.

4. Look for opportunities to model listening and point them out to the child.

5. Set up a reward system that reinforces listening if needed.

SKILL 7-2: FOLLOWING DIRECTIONS

STEPS TO SUCCESS

To follow directions, you:
1. **Look.**
2. **Listen.**
3. **Ask questions if necessary.**
4. **Do it now.**

THOUGHTS BEFORE STARTING

On the surface, following a direction appears to be fairly simple. However, for children with ASD, such a request presents numerous challenges. They must pay attention to what is happening in the surrounding environment, comprehend the information when it is given and often be able to recall it several moments later. They must also recognize the main objective of the direction, and not focus on some minute detail that, although related, is not the main point. In addition, they must learn to differentiate when directions are given to a group (which includes the child) and when directions are given to individuals (which might or might not include the child). Recognizing the need for help with directions and being able to access help is another challenge for youngsters with ASD. The best way to receive help is to ask the right questions.

Some children feel pressured by time constraints, while others misjudge how long an activity might take, how long they have taken already, or how much time is left. These children must learn to notice time in order to successfully follow the direction. Timers or time-keeping systems can help.

A problem for many children, including some with ASD, is that they have learned to avoid or escape when adults do not press compliance. Adults inadvertently reinforce noncompliance by not following through. For example, a parent would like the child to put away his toys before bedtime. After repeated unsuccessful requests to the child, who is watching television, the parent gives up. The child thereby escapes the task and goes to bed without cleaning up. Over time, the child learns he can escape this unpleasant task by ignoring the parent's direction. Such children need compliance training coupled with a reinforcement system to "relearn" how to follow directions.

A typical problem for children with AS is "bossiness"– telling both adults and peers what to do by blurting out unwelcome advice that often gets them into trouble. Considering that a suggestion might not be welcome is outside of the child's customary way of thinking. Therefore, these children have to learn to ask if their advice is wanted.

A related problem is a child's inability to see and to understand another's point-of-view in the situation, sometimes referred to as "perspective-taking" (Twachtman-Cullen, 2000). He cannot separate individually distinct roles and responsibilities, such as between adult and child. The child might say, "You are not the boss," usually when he is being told to do something he does not want to do. One strategy to help address this problem is to define individual roles and list them on a sheet of paper. For example, "In the classroom it is the teacher's responsibility to give directions. It is the student's responsibility to ask questions if he does not understand the directions and then to follow them."

Some final thoughts concern the way directions are given. Directions should be clear, precise and to the point. Visual supports may be necessary such as gestures, pictures, lists or charts. Directions should not include a choice unless the child truly has a choice. A common mistake is to use a question such as "Can you put your coat away?" Another mistake is to offer explanations such as "Put your coat on because it is cold outside." Some children (particularly those with AS) argue with the explanation rather than comply ("It's not cold outside"). Further, multistep and complex instructions are usually overwhelming and confusing, and frequently repeating directions only teaches the child that the adult does not mean the direction the first time. Instead, make sure you have the child's attention before giving the direction. Ask her to repeat the direction, tell or show her exactly what to do and praise compliance (see Chapters 3 and 4).

INTRODUCING THE SKILL

Today we are going to practice following directions.

Discussion Questions

☐ *What is a direction?* Accept responses that might include: tell how to do something, tell what to do.

☐ *Who gives directions?* (Parents, teachers, other adults.)

☐ *Should kids give directions? In what situations?* (Yes, when asked by others.) List examples such as how to play a game, how to make a toy work, how to make something.

☐ Pass out *Oreo Matchin' Middles* game pieces, one per child. *Let's practice following directions. Listen carefully.* Give the following directions one at a time. *Keep your cookie closed. Put your cookie on your head. Put your cookie under your chair. Hold it high. Hold it low. Open it. Trade it with a friend. Put it in the box.* Praise compliance.

Note: You can use real cookies, puzzle pieces or cards in place of the plastic cookies from the game. For added fun, use real cookies and a final direction of "Eat it or put it in the box."

READ AND REVIEW STEPS TO SUCCESS

WARM-UP ACTIVITY

1. Prepare an envelope with "direction" phrases such as those suggested on page 155.

2. Complete this activity in one of two ways:

   • One at a time, choose a child to select a direction from the envelope. The child singles out a peer by name and gives the direction. The peer must comply. Praise compliance.

   • Pick a direction from the envelope and single out children individually, in pairs, in small groups or the entire group to comply. Praise compliance.

ROLE-PLAYS

Review the role-play format presented in Chapter 5.

Alternative School Scenarios

1. Your teacher tells the class to put away spelling words and to get out your math books.

2. Your teacher tells you to take a note to the office.

3. Your teacher tells you to read the lunch menu to the class.

4. Your teacher tells you to correct your spelling test.

 ### Alternative Home Scenarios

1. Your mom tells you to put away your toys.

2. Your dad tells you to turn off the computer and get ready for bed.

3. Your dad tells you to come inside and get ready for dinner.

4. Your mom tells you to take out the garbage.

 ### Alternative Community Scenarios

1. At the city library, the librarian tells you to please whisper.

2. Your neighbor asks you to water her flowers while she is on vacation.

3. Your mom asks you to get out of the swimming pool and get ready to go home.

4. A stranger in the elevator asks you to push the button for floor 3.

PRACTICE ACTIVITIES

Practice Activity 1: Sponge Painting

Prepare in advance: Plastic containers filled with paint, sponges cut into shapes.

Instructions

◆ *(Name), Please pass out one piece of paper to each person.*

◆ *(Name), Please pass out the paint and sponges, one color to each person.*

◆ *Please sit down and wait for the directions.*

◆ *Everyone, pick up your sponge and make one shape in the middle of your paper.*

◆ *Put the sponge in the container. Pass the container to the person on your left.*

◆ *Pick up the sponge and make three shapes on the bottom of your paper.*

◆ *Put the sponge in the container. Pass the container to the person sitting on your left.*

◆ Proceed to give directions for all paint colors.

◆ Praise compliance. Give directions for clean-up.

Note: Art and craft activities of any sort are good practice for following directions. Making holiday decorations, sand art, bead art or origami paper folding can also be enjoyable. Keep the activity simple and make it fun. Be aware of students who have difficulties with fine-motor skills, and choose activities accordingly.

Practice Activity 2: Scavenger Hunt

Prepare a list of items to find. Suggestions include things found out-of-doors, in the classroom, at home or in the community. Choose items that best fit the location of your group. Suggested items for a classroom scavenger hunt include:

◆ Something that writes

◆ Something that rolls

◆ Something white

◆ Something made of plastic

◆ Something that makes a noise

◆ Something red

◆ Something old

◆ Something smooth

◆ Something shiny

◆ Something that erases

◆ Something made of wood

◆ Something quiet

◆ Something that cuts

◆ Something written

Instructions

◆ Direct the children to choose a partner and give each pair of students a list of items and a bag to place the items in once they have found them.

◆ Direct pairs to locate the items and place them in their bag. Give a time limit in which to find as many of the items as possible.

Note: For students who cannot read, make a picture list.

Problem

✖ One student takes the bag and the list and begins the scavenger hunt without his or her partner.

Solutions

☺ Wait a few minutes for the uninvolved child to approach his partner and ask to join in. If the child does not do so, coach him to remind his partner that they are supposed to hunt for the objects together.

☺ Stop the student who took the bag and the list. Say something like, "We have a problem. Please tell me the directions for the scavenger hunt." Review the directions and emphasize that he has a partner to work with. Problem solve how they can complete the task together (divide the list in half, one partner holds the bag and the other holds the list, talk about each item on the list and decide what to find, etc.).

Additional Practice Activities

1. For some groups, board games that require following directions while playing the game are good choices. Some of my favorites are the games of *Allowance* and *Talking, Feeling, Doing*.

2. Food preparation activities are also good choices. Reading a recipe and following the directions can be excellent practice. Assign one step in the recipe to each child or to a pair of children. Drawing numbers from an envelope is an alternate way to assign steps. The number drawn corresponds to a step in the recipe. If there are six or more children in the group, divide the group in half and prepare two recipes.

3. Another fun activity is a treasure hunt. Prepare numbered clues and hide the "treasure." Use partners.

SUPPORTIVE SKILLS TO PROMPT AND REINFORCE

1. Using Kind Talk (page 217)

2. Listening (page 143)

3. Staying on Task (page 156)

SUPPLIES

- *Allowance*

- Bags

- Envelope with written directions

- List of items for scavenger hunt

- Newspaper

- *Oreo Matchin' Middles*

- Paper

- Paper towels or wipes

- Plastic containers with paint

- Sponges cut into shapes

- *Talking, Feeling, Doing*

- Timer

EXTENDING SKILL DEVELOPMENT

Explain the goal of this skill to others and ask them to:

1. Post the Steps to Success in the classroom and at home.

2. Be sure they are giving directions that the child understands and can easily follow.

3. Simplify directions when necessary and present visual prompts if appropriate.

4. Use the cue "This is a direction," when the child has trouble complying.

5. Praise initial efforts to follow directions as well as satisfactory completion of the task.

6. Encourage the child to ask questions about the directions and offer guidance and explanations when needed.

7. Follow through with the child and persist in carrying out as much of the task as possible.

8. Set up a reward system that reinforces compliance for the child who has otherwise learned noncompliance.

Warm-Up Activity: "Direction" Phrases

Sit on the floor.	Tap your head with your hand.
Stand in front of your chair.	Clap your hands three times.
Stand behind your chair.	Smile.
Stand next to (Name).	Open your mouth and say: "Ahhhh."
Hop around the table one time.	Stamp your feet five times.
Wave your hands in the air.	Put your hand on your knee.
Cross your legs.	Put your hand on your elbow.
Touch the floor with your hand.	Fold your hands in your lap.

SKILL 7-3: STAYING ON TASK

STEPS TO SUCCESS

To stay on task, you:
1. **Listen carefully to the directions.**
2. **Ask questions when you do not understand.**
3. **Look at the task.**
4. **Show you are working.**

THOUGHTS BEFORE STARTING

Many children with ASD find it is easy to focus and complete preferred activities but difficult to remain focused on nonpreferred tasks. Their attention often wanders when tasks are uninteresting or difficult, and it is not uncommon for them to retreat to an inner world of movie dialogue, a favorite subject matter or simply to daydream.

One of the crucial issues when working with children who have problems staying on task, is what expectation to set for task completion. Is the child to complete a specific number of problems? Is he to work for a specific length of time? When is he finished with the task? This parameter should be decided in advance and clarified for the child by stating how many problems to complete, setting a time limit, or showing a finished product (Dalrymple, 1995).

Distractions also cause problems in concentration. For example, others moving about the room, unusual sounds, action viewed through a window, or even uncomfortable clothing can all contribute to problems staying on task. It is important to assess and attempt to control the environmental variables that contribute to any child's attention difficulties. However, it is also important to create self-awareness in the child. This session focuses on increasing self-awareness and begins to teach the child how to stay on task until an activity is completed.

INTRODUCING THE SKILL

Today we are going to practice staying on task.

Discussion Questions

☐ *What does staying on task mean?* (Doing what you are supposed to, following directions, fulfilling an assignment.)

☐ *If you got a new video game for your birthday and worked really hard at mastering the first level, and finally did it, how would you feel?* (Happy, excited, proud, etc.)

☐ *What happens when people stay on task?* (They finish the job, get paid, accomplish a goal, might get good marks, etc.)

☐ *The boss asks your dad to write a report for a big meeting tomorrow and he spends all day working on it to get it finished. He gives it to the boss at the end of the day. What will the boss think of your dad?* (Will be pleased, will think he is a hard worker, dependable, etc.)

☐ *Your teacher gives you a history assignment. You are to read pages 25-30 and answer questions 1-3 at the end of the chapter. How does your teacher know that you are reading the pages?* (Looking at the book.)

What should you do if you don't understand one of the questions? (Ask.)

How does your teacher know that you are answering the questions? (Writing.)

You keep working and finish. How does your teacher feel? (Happy.)

How do you feel? (Happy, proud, relieved, etc.)

READ AND REVIEW
STEPS TO SUCCESS

WARM-UP ACTIVITY

Divide the children into small groups of 2-3 and distribute the pieces of a large floor puzzle to each small group. Direct the children to divide up the pieces in their small group so that each person has the same number of pieces. Instruct them not to ask for or take pieces from each other. They can give one or more of their pieces to someone else if they choose. They must work together to complete the puzzle without talking. Remind them to look at the pieces and show they are working.

ROLE-PLAYS

Review the role-play format presented in Chapter 5.

Alternative School Scenarios

1. Your teacher tells the class to read library books for 5 minutes.
2. Your teacher tells the class to clean out their desks.
3. Your science teacher tells you to feed the gerbils.
4. Your gym teacher tells the class to run three laps around the gym.

Alternative Home Scenarios

1. Your mom tells you to put away your toys.
2. Your dad tells you to get ready for bed.
3. Your dad tells you to finish your homework.
4. Your mom tells you to bring in the mail.

Alternative Community Scenarios

1. Your music teacher asks you to watch and listen carefully while she plays a short song on the piano.
2 Your neighbor asks you to stay with her daughter in the yard while she runs inside to answer the phone.
3. You are in the church at your uncle's wedding service. A soloist is singing.
4. You are in the grocery store with your mom and she asks you to help her bag the groceries.

PRACTICE ACTIVITIES

Practice Activity 1: Word Find

Divide the children into pairs and place them at separate tables if possible to minimize distractions. Pass out markers and one piece of paper to each pair. Each paper should have the word "FRIENDSHIP" written at the top.

Instructions

◆ Pairs are to see how many words they can create using the letters in the word "friendship."

◆ Direct the pair to choose one person to write their answers.

◆ Praise those who are looking at the task and who show they are working. Compare results when the partners are finished.

Note: Hidden pictures, mazes, crossword puzzles and word searches may also be used.

Practice Activity 2: Assorted Games

Many commercially available games help practice staying on task. Some of my favorites are:

◆ *Mr. Mouth:* Children must concentrate and pay attention in order to try to get their colored chips into the mouth that is rotating. The first one to do so is the winner.

◆ *Light Bright:* This activity requires placing colored pegs into holes to create a picture. Assign colors to each participant or a specific area to work on. This works best with three participants or fewer.

◆ *Oreo Matchin' Middles:* This matching game requires children to choose cookies to create a match. The one with the most pairs is the winner. This works best with 2-4 players.

◆ *Allowance:* This advanced game requires reading, counting and making change. A player travels around the board earning an allowance and then spends it on various fees and items. Extra money is earned through special jobs.

◆ *Lego Creator:* This game is great for those who like to build with Legos. Participants choose a card and then attempt to make the object depicted by traveling around the board. Significant self-control is required as players lose pieces to other players, so it is not always the best choice for a group focused on staying on task.

◆ *Bingo:* This favorite is known to most everyone and is easy to play unless you have students who do not recognize numbers and letters. In that case, use *Colors and Shapes Bingo.*

Practice Activity 3: Craft Project

Art and craft activities of any sort are good practice for staying on task. Making holiday decorations, sand art, bead art, or origami paper folding can also be enjoyable. Visit a craft store for other project ideas. Keep the activity simple and make it fun. Be aware of difficulties with fine-motor skills and choose activities accordingly. As a general principle, use partners to complete a project whenever feasible. This promotes working together and cooperating.

SUPPORTIVE SKILLS TO PROMPT AND REINFORCE

1. Listening (page 143)

2. Following Directions (page 148)

3. Being a Good Sport (page 247)

4. Cooperating (page 255)

SUPPLIES

◆ Assortment of games

◆ Craft project supplies

◆ Flipchart or blackboard

◆ Floor puzzles

◆ Markers

◆ Paper

◆ Pencils

✓ EXTENDING SKILL DEVELOPMENT

Explain the goal of this skill to others and ask them to:

1. Post the Steps to Success in the classroom and at home.

2. Be sure they are assigning tasks that the child is capable of carrying out.

3. Minimize distractions and attempt to control any environmental variables that reduce on-task behavior.

4. Clarify for the child the expectations for task completion.

5. Simplify directions and present visual prompts when necessary.

6. Use a cue card designating "off task" and "on task" when the child has difficulty staying on task.

7. Praise initial efforts to stay on task as well as satisfactory completion of the task.

8. Encourage the child to ask questions about task directions when necessary, and offer guidance and explanations accordingly.

9. Persist in guiding the child to finish the task when possible.

10. Set up a reward system that reinforces task completion.

SKILL 7-4: WAITING

STEPS TO SUCCESS

To wait, you:
1. **Stay still, quiet and calm.**
2. **Think: "It's hard to wait but I can do it."**
3. **Make a waiting plan.**
4. **Do it.**

THOUGHTS BEFORE STARTING

Waiting is difficult for all of us, but necessary almost every day. Children spend time waiting in lines, in traffic, for a meal, to talk to someone, to see a health professional, to use an object, to ask for help, to be called upon in class, to use a computer, to play with a friend and on numerous other occasions. As difficult as waiting can be, many of us find things to do to pass the time. We might sing, write, draw, listen to music, make mental lists, look at a magazine, etc. Being able to wait appropriately is an important survival strategy and one that is necessary for children with ASD to learn.

The emphasis of this skill is on recognizing and accepting the need to wait and doing so patiently, perhaps finding something to do if the wait is lengthy. Predicting the length of the wait is especially difficult. If you know the wait will be 5 minutes, you can bring something to do while waiting. But if you don't know how long the wait will be, it can be hard to prepare. In my experience, it is this unknown feature that makes waiting challenging. Guiding children to make a waiting plan is crucial to minimizing problems.

INTRODUCING THE SKILL

Today we are going to practice waiting.

Discussion Questions

☐ *What does to wait mean?* (Delay, stop, pause.)

☐ *Sometimes you have to wait. Let's list examples of when you might have to wait.* (To talk to the teacher, for the computer, in line, to take a turn at a game, to play, to eat, etc.)

☐ *Is waiting easy or hard?* Briefly discuss when waiting is easy and hard.

☐ *Whether waiting is easy or hard, it is important to stay still, quiet and calm. Why?* Lead a short discussion of the possible consequences of being restless, loud and upset. If necessary, point out that waiting quietly does not mean telling someone to "hurry up," pushing, interrupting or otherwise bothering others.

☐ *When waiting is hard, it's helpful to think to ourselves: "It's hard to wait but I can do it." Let's say it together: "It's hard to wait but I can do it." Good job.*

☐ *When you have a long wait, you make a waiting plan. This means you do something while you are waiting. Let's think of what you can do when you have to wait.* List suggestions that might include read, play something else, draw, listen to music, etc.

Note: Some groups are ready for a discussion of the following terms related to waiting: "hold your horses," "hang on," "kill time" and "pass the time." Discuss when these phrases might be used and what they mean.

READ AND REVIEW STEPS TO SUCCESS

WARM-UP ACTIVITY

Distribute the pieces of an alphabet floor puzzle to the group. (Other puzzles may also be used.) Direct the children to assemble the pieces in the correct order, demonstrating for you how to wait quietly and calmly for their turn. Praise "good waiting."

With an older group (ages 8-10), play a quick game of *Jenga*. Praise waiting quietly and calmly for a turn. If this game is unavailable, substitute any short card game, such as *Uno, Go Fish,* or *Crazy Eights.*

ROLE-PLAYS

Review the role-play format presented in Chapter 5.

 Alternative School Scenarios

1. You need help with your math. The teacher is helping someone else.

2. You are ready to go out for recess. Your friend is getting his boots on.

3. You are standing in the cafeteria lunch line and it is really long.

4. You want to swing on the swings at recess. Someone else is already there.

 Alternative Home Scenarios

1. Your dad is preparing dinner. You are really hungry.

2. Your mom is helping your sister with her homework. You have a question about a history project.

3. Your sister is taking a shower. Your favorite TV show starts soon and you have to take a shower too before it starts.

4. Your dad is talking to a neighbor. You have a question about cutting the grass.

Alternative Community Scenarios

1. You are in line at McDonald's waiting to order your food.

2. You went grocery shopping with your mom and are in the checkout line.

3. You are in line to buy a ticket to the movies with your dad and brother.

4. You are in the video store with your mom and she asks you to wait while she chooses a movie for your sister.

PRACTICE ACTIVITIES

Practice Activity 1: Decorative Bags

Give each child a small paper bag. Provide one pair of scissors, one glue stick or bottle, and one set of markers for every four students.

Instructions

◆ Direct the children to decorate their bag with assorted fabric, sequins, drawings, construction paper cut-outs, or stickers. (Provide whatever decorative materials you choose.)

◆ Ask the children to share and take turns using the basic supplies.

◆ Coach the children to develop individual waiting plans and to use them. Praise their efforts.

Problem

✖ Some youngsters take supplies and do not relinquish them for others to use.

Solutions

☺ Praise those who are waiting patiently. (You can also give bonus points.)

☺ Encourage passive children to ask to use the supplies.

☺ Set a timer for a specific time length, such as 1 minute. When the timer goes off, everyone is to put down what they are using and give someone else a turn to use the items. Set the timer again. This is most helpful if the group has to learn turn-taking skills.

☺ Let the situation play out without interference from you. The children who finish first have to come up with waiting plans while they wait for their peers to finish.

Practice Activity 2: Roll a Story

Provide a roll of business machine paper and one pencil. Arrange the children side by side in a line. Write on the beginning of the roll of paper "Once upon a time" and roll it out like a ribbon in front of the group.

Instructions

◆ One at a time, ask players to add three to four words to the story, connecting them to the words the last player wrote. The word flow does not have to be logical. Children who cannot write may dictate their words to a peer.

◆ Remind the students to wait calmly and quietly for their turn. Be sure to praise their efforts. It's up to you how long the story is and how many turns a player has.

◆ Read the story aloud after it is finished.

Note: If the group is getting too excited and silly, regain control by inserting yourself into the line and writing: The End. Read the story aloud.

Adapted from: Gregson, B. (1982). A long story. In *The incredible indoor games book*. Carthage, IL: Fearon Teacher Aids.

Practice Activity 3: Build a Gas Station

This activity is similar to Practice Activity 1, except that it uses building blocks instead of craft supplies. Provide a box of building blocks such as Legos.

Instructions

◆ Direct the group to build a gas station (or skyscraper, airplane, cathedral or sports arena). Each member connects three blocks per turn. They can be as creative as they like.

◆ Children are NOT to build something else while waiting their turn. Instead, they might think about what blocks they can add when it is their turn.

◆ They may not remove someone else's blocks once they are placed.

◆ Model giving compliments and praise waiting quietly and calmly.

Problem

✖ Someone is bossy and directs where and how others are to place the building blocks.

Solution

☺ Remind the group that there is no one way to build a gas station, just as there is no one way to write a story. Everyone's ideas are welcome. Sometimes when you combine your imaginations and ideas you create something much more interesting than you could alone. Remind the group that they are to wait quietly, not be bossy and see how the gas station develops.

SUPPORTIVE SKILLS TO PROMPT AND REINFORCE

1. Following Directions (page 148)

2. Being a Good Sport (page 247)

3. Staying on Task (page 156)

SUPPLIES

- Building blocks
- Craft supplies (glue, scissors, markers, misc. decorative materials)
- Flipchart or blackboard
- Floor puzzle

- *Jenga*
- Paper bags
- Pencils
- Roll of business machine paper

EXTENDING SKILL DEVELOPMENT

Explain the goal of this skill to others and ask them to:

1. Post the Steps to Success in the classroom and at home.

2. Clarify for the child the expectations for waiting, especially the length of the wait, if possible.

3. Praise the child for waiting calmly and quietly.

4. Use the cue "Show me waiting," when a child needs prompting.

5. Praise initial efforts to wait as well as satisfactory completion of the waiting interval.

6. Look for opportunities to model waiting and point them out to the child.

7. Guide the child in creating a waiting plan for long waits.

8. Set up a reward system that reinforces waiting when needed.

SKILL 7-5: READING BODY LANGUAGE

STEPS TO SUCCESS

To read body language, you:

1. **Look for clues:**
   a. **the face**
   b. **gestures**
   c. **what the body does**
2. **Recognize the clue.**
3. **Understand the clue.**
4. **Respond to the clue.**

THOUGHTS BEFORE STARTING

Correctly reading the nonverbal cues that are common in social interaction is fundamental to social competence. It is a complex skill that requires noticing and understanding facial expression, body posture and gestures (Nowicki & Duke, 1992). Most of us automatically regulate our personal interactions by instinctively looking at people with whom we are communicating. The information we collect and process cues us about where to stand, where to look, when to join in, when to joke, etc. For children with ASD, learning these cues is similar to learning a complex foreign language. It takes intensive practice for them to figure out how to recognize and interpret the cues and, finally, how to react appropriately.

INTRODUCING THE SKILL

Today we are going to practice reading body language. What is body language? Can bodies talk?

Discussion Questions

☐ *A person's face and body give clues about what he or she is thinking and feeling. These thoughts and feelings may be different from what you are thinking and feeling. The clues are silent, sometimes called nonverbal cues. They are just as important as the words people use to communicate. When you understand the clue, you can decide what to do.*

☐ *See if you can guess what I am saying with my body by reading my silent clues.*

Use facial expression and gestures to demonstrate the following.

Hello. (Wave and smile.)	Look at that. (Point and turn head.)
Come here. (Gesture.)	Talk louder. (Cup hand to ear, lean closer.)
I don't know. (Shrug shoulders.)	I'm confused. (Look confused.)
No. (Shake head.)	I'm bored. (Turn away.)
Go away. (Gesture.)	Yes. (Nod head.)

☐ *Reading bodies is like reading books. Once you know where to look, you can get all kinds of information about what is happening. If you want to know what is happening in a book, you look at the cover, read the title or look at the pictures. If you want to know what is happening inside a person, you look at his or her face, gestures and body.*

☐ *But just looking at the clues isn't enough. You have to understand the clues and know what to do with them once you find them. Let's look at some pictures.* Show pictures of people engaged in typical activities, such as eating dinner, playing at a party, watching a movie, etc. It should be obvious from looking at the picture what is happening and how the people in the picture might be feeling or what they might be thinking. Pictures may be found in magazines or purchased from one of the many commercial sources, such as the Photo Emotion Cards (Living and Learning, Salem, Oregon).

Show each picture to the group and ask questions similar to the following:

- *What is happening here?*

- *What is this person saying with his body?*

- *How do you know?*

- *What might happen next?*

Note: Excellent photographs of facial expressions are depicted in the poster *Emotions* (Carson-Dellosa Publ.; www.carsondellosa.com).

READ AND REVIEW STEPS TO SUCCESS

WARM-UP ACTIVITY

Direct one child to stand up. *Put your shoulders back. Stand up straight. Put a big smile on your face. Great job. Group, what is (Name)___'s body telling us?* (Happy, excited, proud.)

Direct another child to stand, or ask for a volunteer. *Hang your head. Slouch your shoulders. Move slowly. Close your eyes a little. Great job. Group, what is (Name)___'s body telling us?* (Tired, sad.)

Direct a third child to stand, or ask for a volunteer. *Tense your body. Clench your fists. Put a scowl on your face. Pace about the room. Great job. Group, what is (Name)___'s body telling us?* (Angry, furious.)

ROLE-PLAYS

Review the role-play format presented in Chapter 5.

Alternative School Scenarios

1. You are talking to your partner about your ideas for the science project. Your partner looks away, rolls his eyes and starts to play with his pencil.

2. You enter class and see your friend looking at her spelling test. She looks upset. When she sees you coming, she quickly turns the test paper over.

3. You get on the school bus and sit with a friend. He is smiling when he greets you.

4. You bring a ball over to your friend at recess. He motions you to get away from him. He looks like he is about to cry.

Alternative Home Scenarios

1. When you come home from school, you notice your mom has made a special dessert and she is smiling.

2. Your brother comes home from football practice. His head is down and his shoulders are slumped. He goes straight to his room.

3. Your mom is helping you with your math homework. It is hard and you don't want to do it. You say, "This is stupid." Your mom sighs and puts her head in her hands.

4. A friend comes to your birthday party. He's smiling, carrying a gift and waves hello from across the room.

 ## Alternative Community Scenarios

1. Your friend has come to play at your house. You sit together at the computer and he watches you play. Pretty soon he shrugs his shoulders, gets up and walks away.

2. You are at the mall with your cousin. You have been looking at video games for a long time. Your cousin is wandering about the store not really looking at anything. He is not smiling.

3. You and a friend are at a movie. It is really scary. Your friend closes his eyes, puts his hands over his ears and bends his face down to his knees.

4. You and a friend are sledding at a park. You have gone first the last two times down the hill and are insisting that you be first again. Your friend sighs, clenches her fists and turns her face away from you.

PRACTICE ACTIVITIES

Practice Activity 1: Silent Actors

Copy and cut apart the scenarios on page 174. Attach each scenario to a 3x5 card. Add a few blank cards and put all the cards into a shoebox or other container. Ask for a volunteer to go first.

Instructions

◆ The child draws a card from the box and, using gestures and facial expressions only, proceeds to act out the feeling noted on the card. Assist any child who needs help reading. (If the card is blank, the child acts out a feeling of his choice.)

◆ The group tries to guess what feeling is portrayed.

◆ The first child to guess correctly takes the next turn.

◆ Offer suggestions to actors if needed. Praise participation.

Practice Activity 2: Draw a Card

Copy and cut apart the Draw-a-Card statements on page 175. Attach each statement to a 3x5 card and put them in a box. Divide the group into teams and have them sit facing each other.

Instructions

◆ The first player on a team chooses a card, reads it and approaches any player from the opposing team. Assist any child who needs help reading.

◆ The first player repeats the statement from the card using body language and voice tone congruent with the feeling word on the card.

◆ The opposing player gives a response that indicates an understanding of the emotion and the body language conveyed by the first player.

◆ Each player receives one point for effort, another point if the language and corresponding body language match up, and a third point if the response indicates an understanding of the emotion conveyed.

◆ When body language and voice tone do not match the designated emotion, ask the player to repeat his performance, taking the player aside and offering suggestions if needed.

◆ Continue taking turns between teams. Tally points on a board.

Note: The same language is deliberately used in several statements. This compels students to use as well as notice body language and voice tone in order to figure out how to convey the emotion as well as how to interpret it.

SUPPORTIVE SKILLS TO PROMPT AND REINFORCE

1. Listening (page 143)

2. Exchanging a Conversation (page 124)

3. Reading the Feelings of Others (page 176)

SUPPLIES

- ◆ Draw-a-Card Statements (page 175)
- ◆ Flipchart or blackboard
- ◆ Glue or tape
- ◆ Note cards

- ◆ Pictures of daily scenes
- ◆ Scenarios (page 174)
- ◆ Shoebox

EXTENDING SKILL DEVELOPMENT

Explain the goal of this skill to others and ask them to:

1. Post the Steps to Success in the classroom and at home.

2. Observe and identify specific situations where reading body language can help the child communicate with others.

3. Use exaggerated facial expressions and gestures to help communicate body language. Ask the child to interpret what she sees.

4. Ask the child to watch others and identify what is happening in a given situation. Ask the child to notice where others in the situation are looking.

5. Watch a television show or movie with the sound off with the child. Focus on the actors' facial expressions and body language and attempt to follow the plot. Stop the show at random and ask the child what is likely to happen next.

6. Point out what emotions or thoughts the child's body language demonstrates to others and ask the child if this is the effect she intends to communicate.

Practice Activity 1: Silent Actors Scenarios

You have a bad stomachache: Hold your stomach, bend over, and look like you are in **pain**.

You have lost your book report. Look **worried**.

You hear a loud noise behind you. Turn around and look **afraid**.

Your team won. Jump up and down. Clap your hands and look **excited**.

Your homework is too hard. Look **frustrated**.

Your dad brought you a present when he returned from a business trip. Look **surprised**.

The movie is boring. Turn away and look **bored**.

Your team lost the race. Hang your head and look **sad**.

Your teacher has given you two spelling lists. You don't know which one to study. Look **confused**.

You won a prize. Stand up straight and look **proud**.

You tore your favorite sweatshirt. Look **upset**.

You cannot play on the computer. Look **angry**.

Practice Activity 2: Draw-a-Card Statements

"I had a test in math today." **Happy**
"I had a test in math today." **Worried**
"I had a test in math today." **Angry**
"I had a test in math today." **Distressed**
"Mrs. Smith is my art teacher." **Happy**
"Mrs. Smith is my art teacher." **Anxious**
"Mrs. Smith is my art teacher." **Confused**
"Joe is having a birthday party on Sunday." **Disappointed**
"Joe is having a birthday party on Sunday." **Excited**
"Joe is having a birthday party on Sunday." **Upset**
"I went shopping last Saturday." **Bored**
"I went shopping last Saturday." **Delighted**
"I got jeans for my birthday." **Disappointed**
"I got jeans for my birthday." **Happy**

SKILL 7-6: READING THE FEELINGS OF OTHERS

STEPS TO SUCCESS

To read the feelings of others, you:
1. **Look for clues.**
   a. **Read body language.**
   b. **Listen to the tone of voice.**
   c. **Listen to the words.**
2. **Recognize the feeling.**
3. **Understand the feeling.**
4. **Respond to the feeling.**

THOUGHTS BEFORE STARTING

Reading body language and reading the feelings of others go hand in hand; however, it is easier to teach them in two separate lessons. The primary emphasis for both skills is on recognizing what is happening in a given situation and responding appropriately. Therefore, some of the same activities may be used for both skills.

INTRODUCING THE SKILL

Today we are going to begin with a story. Read *A to Z – Do you ever feel like me?* (Hausman & Fellman, 1999). This is an excellent book that depicts convincing situations with photographs of children in the illustrations, as opposed to cartoon characters or drawings. As you read about each emotion, have the children guess what it is, then lead a discussion of situations where the children have experienced the same or similar feelings.

Discussion Questions

☐ *Why is it important to recognize what people are feeling?* (Show concern, compassion, comfort, happiness, etc.)

☐ *When the same thing happens to different people, will they feel the same way?* (Not always.)

☐ *If school is canceled because of a snow storm, I might be disappointed because I can't see my friends, but my teacher might be happy because she can catch up on her lesson plans, the janitor might be irritated because he knows it will be more work to clean the sidewalks and the principal might be worried because he knows there are no more snow days left so he will have to schedule a make-up day. It's the same event, but everyone does not think and react the same way. Every reaction is O.K., but you need to figure out what the feeling is so you can show you understand. It is very important that you are sensitive to how other people are feeling.*

☐ *What can you say to me to show you understand that I am disappointed because I can't see my friends?* (I'll miss my friends too, that's a bummer, maybe you can talk on the phone, etc.)

☐ *What should your body language look like?* (Sympathetic, no smile, calm.)

☐ *What might you say to show you understand that the teacher is happy?* (That's great, have fun, I'm happy for you, etc.)

☐ *What should your body language look like?* (Smile, friendly.)

☐ *What might you say to the janitor?* (That's a lot of work, I'm sorry for you, etc.)

☐ *What should your body language look like?* (Sympathetic, no smile, calm.)

☐ *What might you say to the principal?* (Gee, that's a problem isn't it?)

☐ *What should your body language look like?* (Sympathetic, no smile, calm.)

READ AND REVIEW STEPS TO SUCCESS

WARM-UP ACTIVITY

Open the book *A to Z – Do you ever feel like me?* to a letter page and act out the depicted emotion without identifying what it is. Ask the children to name the feeling. Ask a volunteer to choose a different letter, look it up in the book and act it out for the group to guess. Continue through all the children in the group. If there is enough time, ask the children to think of generic responses to some of the emotions demonstrated. For example, *what might you say to someone who is (afraid, confused, angry) to show you understand how he or she feels?*

ROLE-PLAYS

Review the role-play format presented in Chapter 5.

Alternative School Scenarios

1. A friend comes to school after a short absence and tells you his grandfather died.

2. You are working on a class project with a partner. She cuts her finger on a piece of paper.

3. A friend is scowling and tells you he is grounded because he didn't do his homework.

4. A friend tells you she won the art contest for best drawing.

Alternative Home Scenarios

1. A friend comes to your house to play and calls your sister by the wrong name. She corrects him. He looks embarrassed.

2. Your younger brother comes home from school and trips on the stairs.

3. Your mom enters the kitchen with a big smile and says she got a new job.

4. Your dad comes in the house frustrated because the lawn mower won't start.

Alternative Community Scenarios

1. A friend has come to play at your house. He tells you his aunt was in a car accident and is in the hospital.

2. While walking to the store with your mom you see a child lying on the sidewalk crying. His bicycle is lying next to him.

3. You receive an invitation to a birthday party. When you see another friend at the mall, you find out he wasn't invited.

4. You and a friend are at the video store. He says he's afraid of scary movies.

PRACTICE ACTIVITIES

Practice Activity 1: Emotional Collage

Instruct group members to find a partner, or divide the group into pairs.

◆ Give each set of partners a stack of magazines, pair of scissors, glue, paper and a list of eight emotion words such as those listed on page 182. The list can be the same for everyone, or you can develop different lists from the word choices on page 182.

◆ Direct the partners to locate and cut out pictures of people in the magazines that demonstrate the emotions on the list. Glue the pictures to the paper and label them.

Practice Activity 2: Emotional Bingo 1

Duplicate the bingo cards on pages 183-184 and pass out one to each player.

Instructions

◆ Read one of the scenarios on page 187. Ask the children to decide what emotion(s) the person might be feeling and to place a token on that emotion on their bingo card. Encourage discussion as there may be more than one choice to a scenario. However, there is usually one best choice.

Practice Activity 3: Emotional Bingo 2

Duplicate the bingo cards on pages 184-185 and pass out one to each player.

Instructions

◆ Read one of the scenarios on page 187. Ask the group to decide what emotion(s) the person might be feeling and to place a token on the best response on their bingo card. Encourage discussion, as there will be more than one choice to a scenario. However, there is usually one best choice.

Note: If the group members can manage two bingo cards at the same time, pass out two bingo cards at the end of this skill and play them simultaneously. The first person with a bingo on both cards is the winner.

SUPPORTIVE SKILLS TO PROMPT AND REINFORCE

1. Listening (page 143)

2. Reading Body Language (page 168)

3. Using Kind Talk (page 217)

4. Exchanging Conversation (page 124)

SUPPLIES

- Bingo cards (pages 183-186)
- Book: *A to Z – Do you ever feel like me?*
- Flipchart or blackboard
- Glue
- List of emotions (page 182)
- Magazines
- Paper
- Scenarios (page 187)
- Scissors
- Tokens

EXTENDING SKILL DEVELOPMENT

Explain the goal of this skill to others and ask them to:

1. Post the Steps to Success in the classroom and at home.

2. Observe and identify specific situations where responding to another's emotional state demonstrates sensitivity and concern for others. Offer appropriate language suggestions to the child as required.

3. Use exaggerated facial expressions and gestures to help communicate emotions. Ask the child to interpret what he sees.

4. Ask the child to watch others and identify what is happening in a given situation. Ask the child to identify what others in the situation might be feeling.

5. Watch a television program or movie with the child. Focus on the actors' facial expressions, body language and voice tone. Stop the show at random and ask the child what the actors are feeling.

6. Point out what emotions the child's body language and voice tone demonstrate to others. Ask the child if this is the effect he intends to communicate.

Practice Activity 1: Emotions List

List 1	List 2	List 3
Happy	Depressed	Worried
Enraged	Bored	Tired
Frustrated	Delighted	Elated
Overwhelmed	Jealous	Distressed
Calm	Upset	Afraid
Sad	Confused	Angry
Anxious	Nervous	Envious
Excited	Surprised	Loving

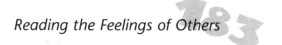

Practice Activity 2: Emotional Bingo 1

Bingo Cards

CONFUSED	**DISTRESSED**	**SORRY**
EXCITED	**FREE SPACE**	**WORRIED**
SAD	**EMBARRASSED**	**PROUD**

DISTRESSED	**SORRY**	**WORRIED**
EXCITED	**FREE SPACE**	**PROUD**
EMBARRASSED	**SAD**	**CONFUSED**

Practice Activity 2: Emotional Bingo 1 (Cont.)

Bingo Cards

EMBARRASSED	WORRIED	SAD
DISTRESSED	FREE SPACE	PROUD
EXCITED	CONFUSED	SORRY

EXCITED	SAD	PROUD
EMBARRASSED	FREE SPACE	WORRIED
CONFUSED	SORRY	DISTRESSED

Practice Activity 3: Emotional Bingo 2

Response Bingo Cards

I'm sorry to hear that.	*Are you O.K.?*	*That is great!*
Maybe I can help?	*FREE SPACE*	*What is the matter?*
That is too bad.	*Awesome!*	*That's O.K.*

That is great!	*That is too bad.*	*What is the matter?*
Are you O.K.?	*FREE SPACE*	*Awesome!*
Maybe I can help?	*That's O.K.!*	*I'm sorry to hear that.*

Practice Activity 3: Emotional Bingo 2 (Cont.)

Response Bingo Cards

Awesome!	That is too bad.	Are you O.K.?
What is the matter?	FREE SPACE	Maybe I can help?
I'm sorry to hear that.	That's O.K.	That is great!

What is the matter?	Maybe I can help?	That's O.K.
That is great!	FREE SPACE	I'm sorry to hear that.
Are you O.K.?	That is too bad.	Awesome!

Practice Activity 3: Scenarios

A friend . . .

tells you he is moving away.
is crying in the school bathroom.
trips and falls while running on the playground.
tells you he is going to Disney World for spring vacation
tells you she doesn't know how to figure out a math problem.
tells you his sister is in the hospital.
shows you his diorama for an American history project.
apologizes for cutting in front of you.

SKILL 7-7: GIVING ENCOURAGEMENT

STEPS TO SUCCESS

To give encouragement, you:

1. **Read the person's feelings.**
2. **Look.**
3. **Use a friendly face and voice.**
4. **Make a hopeful comment such as,**
   a. **"Nice try."**
   b. **"You can do it."**
   c. **"It'll be O.K."**
   d. **"You'll get it."**

THOUGHTS BEFORE STARTING

Giving encouragement to those who are feeling hopeless or discouraged is another skill that is often foreign for children who are prone to self-absorption (Attwood, 1998). Many students do not realize that encouraging others, although relatively simple to do, shows caring, sensitivity and support, and that it may help the other person feel more confident, or simply a little better, to know that a friend is concerned about them. Children with ASD require practice recognizing when others need encouragement and following through with a suitable remark.

INTRODUCING THE SKILL

Begin with one of the following tongue twisters: "She sells seashells by the seashore," or "The bootblack brought the black boot back." Ask for a volunteer. *I want you to repeat what I am going to say. It might be hard, but I think you can do it.* Repeat one of the tongue twisters. If the volunteer succeeds in repeating it correctly, praise her efforts. If she is incorrect, give some encouragement to try again. If other students want to try repeating the tongue twister, give them encouragement as well.

Today we are going to practice giving encouragement.

Discussion Questions

☐ *What is encouragement?* (When you say something to someone to help them feel hopeful, such as "keep trying.")

☐ *When should you give encouragement?* (When another person looks discouraged, when someone did poorly in something like a test, performance or game, when you want someone to keep trying.)

☐ *Why do you give encouragement?* (To cheer up another person when they feel discouraged, to let the person know you support them, to let the person know you care about them, that you are a friend.)

☐ *How does it feel to receive encouragement?* (Good, better.)

READ AND REVIEW STEPS TO SUCCESS

WARM-UP ACTIVITY

Place a wastebasket some distance (8-10 feet) from the group and explain that they are going to take turns shooting baskets using a foam ball.

◆ Give each player three tries to make a basket.

◆ Model giving encouragement and prompt students as necessary to use the Steps to Success.

◆ Praise those who encourage their peers and reward with bonus points.

ROLE-PLAYS

Review the role-play format presented in Chapter 5.

Alternative School Scenarios

1. Your teacher returns spelling tests to the class. You see your neighbor look at his test and then throw it away. He looks at you and shrugs his shoulders.

2. You enter music class with a friend. She tells you she wants to try out for the school orchestra. She doesn't think she is good enough.

3. You are in gym class playing kickball. It is one of your teammates' turn to kick the ball.

4. Your classmate tells you he is afraid to give his book report in front of the class.

Alternative Home Scenarios

1. Your brother has a piano recital tomorrow. He is really nervous.

2. Your sister is learning to play a new video game. She's been trying for a long time but hasn't quite mastered it yet.

3. Your brother is learning to ride his bicycle without training wheels. He keeps falling.

4. Your babysitter made hamburgers for dinner. They didn't turn out very good.

Alternative Community Scenarios

1. Your friend has come to visit. He tells you he is in a swim meet tomorrow. Last week his team lost.

2. Your neighbor's dog is lost. He has been searching for the dog for two days without success.

3. You and your friend are playing games at his house. He keeps losing.

4. Your mom is trying to find a parking space at the mall. It is really crowded.

PRACTICE ACTIVITIES

Practice Activity 1: Missing Object

Place an assortment of items on a tray, such as a pencil, key, small candle, eraser, paper clip, watch, coin, etc. The activity will be more difficult the more items there are on the tray.

Instructions

◆ Give the group about 1 minute to study the items on the tray and try to remember them.

◆ Ask a volunteer to leave the room.

◆ While the child is out of the room, remove one item from the tray and remind the others to think of ways to encourage their friend to do well when he returns.

◆ When the child returns to the room, he has 30 seconds to decide which item is missing.

◆ Praise and give bonus points to children who offer encouraging remarks (without giving the answer).

◆ Continue playing until everyone has had a turn.

Variations

1. Remove two or more items rather than just one.

2. Pair children with a partner. Partners confer and make a decision together.

3. Divide the children into two teams. One member from each team leaves the room and has 30 seconds to decide what item is missing upon returning. Teammates encourage players. Tally points for correct responses.

Practice Activity 2: Eraser Balance

Determine a relay course through which team members must travel (such as to a wall and back). The course may be easy or more difficult through the use of obstacles such as a piece of furniture, large box, etc. Draw names of two team captains. Team captains take turns choosing team members. The captain's job is to lead the team in encouraging players, so although they are positioned at the head of each line, they play last. Line up each team behind a piece of tape on the floor and give the first player on each team a chalkboard eraser.

Instructions

◆ At the start signal the first player on each team to balance the eraser on her head and walk as quickly as possible to the destination and back to the second team member. The player may not touch the eraser.

◆ Should the player drop the eraser, she must return to the front of the line and start again.

◆ When the player returns to the team, she gives the eraser to the next person.

◆ The next player travels the course transferring the eraser to the third person and so on.

◆ The winner is the first team that can move the eraser through all the team members and the course without dropping it.

◆ Frequently praise evidence of good sportsmanship and offer bonus points when you hear encouragement given.

◆ Make sure the losing team congratulates the winning team at the end of the game and that the winning team responds with "good game."

SUPPORTIVE SKILLS TO PROMPT AND REINFORCE

1. Listening (page 143)

2. Reading the Feelings of Others (page 176)

3. Reading Body Language (page 168)

4. Using Kind Talk (page 217)

5. Dealing with Mistakes (page 200)

SUPPLIES

◆ Chalkboard eraser (2)

◆ Flipchart or blackboard

◆ Foam ball

◆ Tape

◆ Tray of assorted objects

◆ Wastebasket

EXTENDING SKILL DEVELOPMENT

Explain the goal of this skill to others and ask them to:

1. Post the Steps to Success in the classroom and at home.

2. Observe and identify specific situations where others need encouragement.

3. Review and rehearse with the child in advance of potential opportunities to give encouragement.

4. Set up situations where the child must give encouragement to others.

5. Offer a suggestion of how to give encouragement when the child is unable to think of one.

6. Use natural situations to foster giving encouragement.

7. Praise the child for giving encouragement and point out that he is being friendly.

8. Offer incentives to motivate the child to give encouragement if needed, perhaps by earning a token. Tokens can be exchanged for special privileges or treats.

SKILL 7-8: OFFERING HELP

STEPS TO SUCCESS

To offer help, you:
1. **Notice if someone needs help.**
   a. **Look at what they are doing.**
   b. **Look at their body language.**
   c. **Listen to their words and voice tone.**
2. **Use a friendly voice.**
3. **Ask if you can help.**
4. **If the person says "yes," then help.**
5. **If the person says "no," do not help.**

THOUGHTS BEFORE STARTING

Children who fail to notice what is happening around them tend to miss opportunities to demonstrate kindness by offering to help. Most children with ASD are happy to help with a task if asked. However, they do not typically notice when they might be of assistance. This skill requires paying attention to the environment, recognizing situations where help is needed and following through.

A related problem for some children with AS is that they often intrude into situations where their assistance and advice is unwelcome. For example, they may insist upon "helping" even though their offer has been refused. Similarly, in situations where their help has been accepted, they may end up dominating the interaction and alienating those around them.

INTRODUCING THE SKILL

Before the children arrive, strew books and papers about the room. Overturn a few chairs, generally making a mess. As the children arrive, make comments such as, *What a mess, I don't think I can get this room ready in time for our group. This chair is so heavy. Look at all these books.* Sigh and look frustrated. Wait for the children's responses. If anyone offers to help, respond with a warm *Thank you, I sure can use your help,* or something similar. Others may take the cue and offer to help, too. Praise their efforts. If no one offers to help, give a more direct prompt such as *I sure could use some help here,* and, if necessary, *(Name), please give me some help with these books.* When the room has been returned to normal, say something like, *Thank you for your help. You have shown me the skill for today, which is Offering Help.*

Discussion Questions

☐ *How can you tell when someone might need your help?* (Look at what is happening, facial expression, body language, tone of voice, etc.)

☐ *What words can you use to offer help?* (Can I help you? Do you need help? Do you want help? What can I do to help?)

☐ *Sometimes you notice someone is doing something fun, like baking cookies, and you might offer to help because you want to bake, too. At other times you might notice someone is doing something that is not much fun, like cleaning up. You don't really like to clean so you don't want to help. Remember, offering to help shows you are concerned about others. It is being kind.*

☐ *Sometimes when you help, it is easy to take over the job and become bossy. Why is this not a good thing?* (The other person might feel hurt or offended.)

How can you tell if you are becoming bossy? (Watch the other person's body language and facial expression. Check yourself.)

☐ *Is it O.K. to accept someone's offer to help?* (Usually, yes.)

☐ *Does accepting help mean you are stupid?* (No.)

☐ *What should you do if the other person refuses your help and you really want to help?* (Do something else. Do not insist on helping.)

**READ AND REVIEW
STEPS TO SUCCESS**

WARM-UP ACTIVITY

Secretly hide a piece of hard candy somewhere in the room. Ask for a volunteer.

◆ Direct the volunteer to search the room and find the piece of candy you have hidden.

◆ Direct the remaining group members to watch the search. They may begin to call out places for the volunteer to look. If they do, ask, *Are you offering help?* The children will probably agree.

◆ Prompt them to follow the Steps to Success and ask the volunteer if he wants help. Initially, the volunteer may elect help or not. Eventually, the volunteer may get frustrated or run out of places to search and may want to give up looking. If he has refused previous offers of help, ask him if he wants to rethink his decision.

◆ If peers have not offered to help, wait as long as possible for them to offer to help search. Prompt them when necessary with an indirect prompt such as *(Name) is having trouble finding the candy, what could you do?* Once everyone has offered to help and is searching, offer to help find the candy. Give it to the volunteer and praise participation.

ROLE-PLAYS

Review the role-play format presented in Chapter 5.

🎬 Alternative School Scenarios

1. Your friend is working at the class computer. She is scowling.

2. A teacher is trying to open the door while carrying a stack of books, her purse and briefcase into the school.

3. Your friend is looking for his book bag. He can't find it and the bus is coming. He looks upset.

4. Your friend slips and falls on the icy sidewalk. He drops his book bag.

🎬 Alternative Home Scenarios

1. Your mom is carrying bags of groceries into the kitchen. They are really heavy. She looks tired.

2. Your dad is making pizza for dinner. He is looking for the cheese but cannot find it.

3. Your brother spills his juice.

4. Your sister is doing her homework. She is frowning and tapping her pencil. Your parents are gone for the evening.

Alternative Community Scenarios

1. Your elderly neighbor is raking the leaves in his yard. He is moving pretty slowly.

2. You and your dad are taking care of errands. When you get to the video store you notice there are several videos on the back seat of the car.

3. Your Scout meeting is over and your leader is cleaning up after snacks. You are waiting for your ride home.

4. You are leaving the mall with your mom. In front of you is an elderly woman trying to push open the heavy door.

PRACTICE ACTIVITIES

Practice Activity 1: Snack Helpers

Bring ingredients for a snack, such as brownie, cookie, pudding, or drink mix, fruit, cheese and crackers, pizza or tacos.

Instructions

◆ Place the ingredients and preparation items for a snack on the table. Do not assign jobs but make a comment such as *I'm not sure I can make this snack in time for us to eat it.* Nonchalantly look at the ingredients, pick them up and put them down again. Look a bit worried.

◆ Wait for children to offer to help prepare the snack before you assign tasks. Plan in such a way that jobs are shared and children must work cooperatively. Do not allow anyone to work alone.

◆ Praise the Super Skills of Cooperating, Using Kind Talk and Staying on Task.

Practice Activity 2: Helping Stations

Prepare two or three helping tasks as suggested below and set them up about the room.

Instructions

◆ Direct children to line up. The first child in line approaches one of the tasks and tries to complete it.

◆ The second child in line moves close to the first child and uses the Steps to Success to offer help.

◆ If the second child offers help correctly, he receives a token or bonus point.

◆ The second child approaches the next task and starts it. The first child goes to the back of the line. The third child approaches the second child and offers help.

◆ Continue until everyone has had one or two turns.

◆ If a child does not use the Steps to Success, guide him until he is successful.

Problem

✖ Invariably a child refuses an offer of help. This is usually because the child does not recognize or understand that offering and accepting help is a reciprocal gesture of friendship. He may view accepting help as personal failure, and therefore try very hard to complete the task on his own.

Solution

☺ Discuss the reciprocal nature of friendship; especially how it feels when an offer of help is rejected. In addition, it may be useful to teach the Super Skill Asking for Help (page 101).

Sample Helping Tasks

◆ Carry a heavy stack of books from one place to another

◆ Sort paper by color

◆ Stuff envelopes

◆ Sort coins

◆ Complete a complicated puzzle

SUPPORTIVE SKILLS TO PROMPT AND REINFORCE

1. Reading Body Language (page 168)

2. Using Kind Talk (page 217)

3. Reading the Feelings of Others (page 176)

4. Cooperating (page 255)

SUPPLIES

◆ Flipchart or blackboard

◆ Items to set up for helping tasks

◆ Small piece of hard candy

◆ Snack ingredients

EXTENDING SKILL DEVELOPMENT

Explain the goal of this skill to others and ask them to:

1. Post the Steps to Success in the classroom and at home.

2. Observe and identify specific situations where offering help is a friendly gesture.

3. Model offering help.

4. Review and rehearse with the child in advance of potential opportunities to offer help.

5. Set up situations where the child can offer help.

6. Use natural situations to foster offering help.

7. Point out to the child instances where people are helping each other, such as holding a door open, carrying packages, looking for a lost item, etc.

8. Praise the child for offering to help and point out that she is being friendly.

9. Offer incentives to motivate the child to offer help if needed, perhaps by earning a token. Tokens can be exchanged for special privileges or treats.

SKILL 7-9: DEALING WITH MISTAKES

STEPS TO SUCCESS

To deal with a mistake, you:

1. **Take a deep breath.**
2. **Keep calm.**
3. **Think, "It's a mistake, but I can handle it."**
4. **Choose:**
   a. **Ask for help.**
   b. **Try again.**
   c. **Admit your mistake, apologize and try to correct it.**
   d. **Accept another's apology.**

THOUGHTS BEFORE STARTING

Many children with ASD are perfectionists and may view mistakes as "failures." They have trouble accepting mistakes they make themselves as well as those made by others. We must help them to realize that everyone makes mistakes and that it is O.K. Sometimes they have difficulty trying something that is hard for fear of making a mistake. It is important to reinforce that many times the only way to learn new things is to try. Children who are used to constant help may need extra encouragement to try tasks independently and cope with their mistakes.

The unpredictable nature of mistakes may also cause problems. It is difficult to know exactly when a mistake might happen. For children who are rule-bound, this can create much anxiety. Finally, some children with AS tend to blame others for their mistakes and look for excuses. They need help learning that the responsible reaction is to admit your mistake and try to correct it. In this lesson many aspects of making mistakes are included, and it can be a bit overwhelming. It may be helpful to divide the lesson into two sessions.

INTRODUCING THE SKILL

Today we are going to practice dealing with mistakes. A mistake is an accident, like spilling grape juice on your shirt, denting your new bicycle, losing your lunch money or forgetting your homework.

Discussion Questions

☐ *What mistakes have you made?* List mistakes.

☐ *How did you handle them?* Discuss children's responses.

☐ *How did you feel when you made mistakes?* (Embarrassed, sad, angry.)

☐ *How can you plan to avoid making the same mistake again?* (Take more time, ask for help, ask a question, work carefully.)

☐ *Have you ever heard the phrase "learn from your mistakes"? What does it mean?* (It is not always a bad thing to make a mistake.)

☐ *Everybody makes mistakes. Sometimes people are afraid to try something because they are afraid of making a mistake. They worry and think they might do it wrong.* Take out a prepared academic worksheet such as math problems copied from a math workbook. Say something like, *Gee, these problems look hard. I'm not sure I will know how to do them. I might make a mistake. Maybe I shouldn't even try. Have any of you ever felt this way about a school assignment or something that seems hard to do?* Discuss responses. Proceed by saying something like, *Well, I guess I'll try the first problem.* Make a deliberate and obvious mistake on the worksheet that is visible to the children sitting next to you. It is likely that someone will point out your mistake. Respond with *Oh, it's a mistake, I can handle it. Can someone help me?*

☐ *What can you do when someone else makes a mistake, such as bumping into you, cutting in line, or borrowing your crayons and breaking one?* (Say, it's O.K. , it was an accident.)

☐ *One quality that most people admire in others is the ability to admit when they are wrong, apologize for a mistake and try to correct it. Why is it important to apologize and try to correct a mistake?* (Accept responsibility.)

☐ *Compare this to someone who believes he never makes a mistake, is never wrong, and never guilty of anything. He always looks for someone to blame and makes excuses for what happens. Do you think this person has a lot of friends?* (Probably not. Others probably think he is rude and thinks only about himself. They might not want to play with him.)

READ AND REVIEW
STEPS TO SUCCESS

WARM-UP ACTIVITY

Copy the statements below (or make up others) onto notecards and pass them out to the members of the group. The first child accuses the student on his left of the act written on the card. The second student (accused) flips a coin and responds accordingly (heads guilty and tails innocent). Each student must follow the Steps to Success. If the accuser has made a false accusation, she must apologize for her mistake.

Adapted from Richardson, R. C. (1996). Someone else made me do it. In *Connecting with others: Lessons for teaching social and emotional competence grades 3-5*. Champaign, IL: Research Press.

Statements

You left my jacket out in the rain and it got all wet.

You forgot to return my library books.

You lost my favorite sweater.

You ate the last of my birthday cake.

You didn't take out the garbage.

You forgot your book report.

You took my CD player from my room and didn't put it back.

You made a mess in the kitchen and didn't clean it up.

ROLE-PLAYS

Review the role-play format presented in Chapter 5.

 **Alternative School Scenarios**

1. You arrive at school late and realize you forgot your homework.

2. Someone walks by your desk and bumps into you.

3. You knocked your teacher's cup off her desk and broke it.

4. You borrowed a book from the library and can't find it.

🎬 Alternative Home Scenarios

1. Your mom checks your homework and finds three spelling errors.

2. You borrow your brother's favorite CD and scratch it.

3. You make popcorn in the microwave and burn it.

4. Your dad puts pickles on your hamburger. You don't like pickles.

🎬 Alternative Community Scenarios

1. Your friend asks you to put his money in your pocket for safe keeping. When you get to the movies, you can't find it.

2. It's your birthday and one of your friends forgets his gift at home.

3. You can't find your jacket and are late to Scouts.

4. You drip ketchup on your aunt's carpet.

PRACTICE ACTIVITIES

Practice Activity 1: Marble Drop

Determine a relay course through which team members must travel (such as to a wall and back). The course may be easy or made more difficult through the use of obstacles such as furniture, cardboard boxes, etc. Place a container at the end of the course. Instruct everyone to write/dictate his or her name on a small piece of paper and place it in an envelope. Draw names from slips of paper for two teams. Line up each team behind a piece of tape on the floor. Give each player a spoon with a marble in it.

Instructions

◆ At the start signal, the first player on each team carries the marble on the spoon to the container and drops it in with one hand while the other hand is behind his back. The player may not touch the marble or cover the spoon with his hand.

◆ If the player drops the marble along the way, she must return to the front of the line and start again.

- When the player successfully deposits the marble in the container and returns to the line, the next player begins the course.

- If the next player starts before the previous player is behind the line, he must start over.

- The winner is the first team that deposits all of their marbles in the container and returns to the line.

- Give bonus points to members who apologize for their mistakes and to those who accept the apologies.

- Praise good sportsmanship and offering encouragement.

- Make sure the losing team congratulates the winning team at the end of the game and that the winning team responds with "good game."

Adapted from Foster, E. S. (1989). Spoon marbles. In *Energizers and icebreakers for all ages and stages.* Minneapolis, MN: Educational Media Corporation.

Practice Activity 2: Card Pair-Up

Copy onto card stock the statements on page 207. Make sufficient copies so each pair of students has a set. Place each set in an envelope. Direct the students to choose a partner and give each pair an envelope.

Instructions

- Direct partners to work together to pair each blaming statement with the correct admitting mistake statement.

- Once the teams are finished, discuss the following:

  - *What is the difference in how blaming and admitting mistakes statements usually begin?* (I …)

  - *What phrase is often included when admitting a mistake?* (I'm sorry.)

  - *Which set of phrases is the most responsible way to deal with mistakes?* (Admitting mistakes.)

Practice Activity 3: Admitting Mistakes

Copy the cards on page 207. Cut them apart and place them in two separate envelopes. One contains Blaming Statements and the other contains Admitting Mistakes. Select a game such as *Wheel of Fortune* or another game of choice.

Instructions

- Set up the game according to the directions.

◆ At the start of each player's turn, he draws a card from the Blaming Statements envelope.

◆ He thinks of a more responsible phrase to replace the Blaming Statement and tells the group. If the group agrees the statement more appropriately deals with the mistake, the player takes his turn at the game.

◆ If the player cannot think of a more suitable phrase, he searches through the Admitting Mistakes envelope until he has found one. Play continues to the next player while he is searching. Once he has located the appropriate response, he can take his turn.

Practice Activity 4: "Oops"

Direct the children to sit in a circle.

Instructions

◆ Read the statements below to the group one at a time and wait for their response.

◆ When they make a mistake, they are to respond with "Oops, I made a mistake."

Statements

1. Clap your hands, if you are sad today.

2. Stomp your feet, if you have red hair.

3. Raise your right hand, if you are wearing jeans.

4. Raise your left hand, if you have a pet.

5. Hoot like an owl, if you are wearing shoes.

6. Cover your eyes, if you are a girl.

7. Touch your head, if you are a boy.

8. Blink your eyes, if you are wearing green.

9. Stand on one leg, if you have blue eyes.

10. Hop on one foot, if you are happy today.

SUPPORTIVE SKILLS TO PROMPT AND REINFORCE

1. Listening (page 143)
2. Giving Encouragement (page 188)
3. Cooperating (page 255)
4. Dealing with a Problem (page 274)

SUPPLIES

- Blaming Statements and Admitting Mistakes (page 207)
- Coin
- Flipchart or blackboard
- Envelopes
- Game, such as *Wheel of Fortune*
- Marbles
- Math worksheet
- Note cards
- Spoons

EXTENDING SKILL DEVELOPMENT

Explain the goal of this skill to others and ask them to:

1. Post the Steps to Success in the classroom and at home.
2. Observe and identify specific situations where the child must deal with a mistake.
3. Review and rehearse with the child before potential mistakes.
4. Set up situations where the child must deal with mistakes.
5. Offer a plan for how to deal with a mistake when the child is unable to think of one.
6. Use natural situations to foster successful dealing with mistakes of others.
7. Praise the child for admitting mistakes and point out that he is being responsible.
8. Offer incentives to motivate the child to admit mistakes if needed, perhaps by earning a token. Tokens can be exchanged for special privileges or treats.

Practice Activity 3: Admitting Mistakes

Blaming Statements	Admitting Mistakes
My sister threw my homework away.	I didn't put my homework away.
You never told me that rule.	I didn't follow the rule.
The teacher kept me in during lunch recess.	I didn't do my work so I missed lunch recess.
I didn't break it, David did.	I'm sorry I broke your toy.
So I spilled the milk . . . Who cares?	I'm sorry I spilled the milk. I'll clean it up.
Spelling is so stupid.	I will study my spelling words so I do well on the test.
It isn't my fault your plant fell off. You shouldn't have put it there.	I'm sorry I knocked your plant over. I'll get the vacuum cleaner.
I didn't push Matthew. He fell down by himself.	I'm sorry I pushed Matthew. I'll apologize to him.
You got out of line. I didn't cut.	I cut in front of you, I'm sorry.

SKILL 7-10: DEALING WITH ANGER

STEPS TO SUCCESS

To deal with anger, you:

1. **Stop.**
2. **Take a deep breath.**
3. **Let it go.**
4. **Think: "What is happening here?"**
5. **Make a plan.**
   a. **Wait it out.**
   b. **Talk it out.**
   c. **Walk it out.**
   d. **Apologize if necessary.**
6. **Do it.**

THOUGHTS BEFORE STARTING

Learning to deal with their own anger and the anger of others is important for all children. Everyone must learn to cope with broken promises, false accusations, surprises, refusals, teasing, changes, frustration, disappointment and confusion without losing control. Being told "no," making a mistake, losing or forgetting something, confronting a "surprise," such as a change in routine or schedule, and struggling with difficult or overwhelming tasks are frequently triggers of intense emotional reactions in children with ASD. Other triggers might be misunderstanding directions, sensory overload, increased stress, and lack of control over the environment (Myles & Southwick, 2005). In many children, the reaction may be excessive anger, but in some children it is intense anxiety or sadness.

Often children have difficulty recognizing these emotions in themselves and in others. Irritation may quickly escalate to rage, or mild anxiety turn to panic. We must help these children to recognize their personal triggers and teach them how to deal effectively with the situation.

INTRODUCING THE SKILL

Begin to blow up a balloon and keep blowing air into it until it is about ready to pop. *What will happen to this balloon if I keep blowing air into it?* (It will pop.) *This balloon is like anger. Anger can build and build and eventually blow up. But you can learn ways to deal with anger so that your anger shrinks* (slowly let the air out of the balloon). *Today we are going to practice dealing with anger.*

Modified from: Gajewski, N., Hirn, P., & Mayo, P. (1996). Taking charge of anger. In *Social star: Conflict resolution and community interaction skills (Book 3)*. Eau Claire, WI: Thinking Publications.

Discussion Questions

☐ *What makes you angry?* List events or feelings that sometimes lead to anger, including being left out, broken promises, false accusations, surprises, refusals, teasing, changes and frustration. *These events are called anger triggers. They are not the same for everyone. What makes one person angry might make another person sad. For example, if Nick is not invited to Sally's birthday party, he might feel sad. But if Allen is not invited, he might feel angry because he thought Sally was his friend. It's important to know and recognize your anger triggers so you can figure out how to deal with them.*

☐ *Some people get angry very quickly while others are slow to anger. Let's talk about your anger response.* Take a quick poll of who is slow to anger and who is quick to anger.

☐ *How do you know you are getting angry?* Discuss body cues, internal thoughts.

☐ *When you are getting angry, the first thing to do is stop what you are doing. Let's practice. Hop around the room until I tell you to stop.* Let the children hop for a bit and then call out "Stop." Praise good control.

Next, take a deep breath and let it out. Stand up and take a deep breath. Let it go. Taking a deep breath is also a good thing to do when someone else is angry with you. By calming down you can stay in control and hear what the person has to say.

Now you have to figure out what is happening, what is making you or the other person angry. Look at this picture. (Show a picture of an anger situation from a magazine or other source.) *What is happening here? Why is the person angry?*

Then you make a plan to let the air out of your anger, to shrink your angry feelings or to help the other person deal with the problem. Let's talk about your choices. What does "wait it out" mean? (Wait until the other person stops talking, wait until later to deal with the problem, wait until you feel calm, etc.)

What does "talk it out" mean? (Talk about the problem, find out why the other person is angry, get help with a problem, etc.)

What does "walk it out" mean? (Walk away for now, take a break, do something else, etc.)

When would you need to apologize? (If you made a mistake, did something wrong, etc.)

☐ *What is not O.K. to do when you are angry?* (Push, hit, break, throw, kick, spit, etc.)

READ AND REVIEW
STEPS TO SUCCESS

WARM-UP ACTIVITY

Pass out markers and drawing paper or building blocks to everyone. *I want you to draw something on your paper (or make something with your blocks). I am going to surprise you and do something unexpected. When that happens, I want you to stop what you are doing and take a deep breath.* Approach children one at a time and deliberately provoke anger by taking a marker or block, bumping an arm, taking a paper, etc. Give bonus points to those who stop and take a deep breath. Discuss the best plan for dealing with anger in this situation (tell the person to stop, move away, ignore, etc.).

ROLE-PLAYS

Review the role-play format presented in Chapter 5.

Alternative School Scenarios

1. You are drawing a picture when someone walks by and bumps your desk.

2. You enter your classroom and find the desks have been moved.

3. You bring a favorite toy to school and can't find it when it is time to go home.

4. Your teacher says you have to rewrite your report because she can't read it.

Alternative Home Scenarios

1. You didn't do your chores after school. Your mother is angry with you.

2. Your parents won't let you go to the movies because you didn't do your home-work.

3. You want to stay up and play with your new game but your dad says you have to go to bed.

4. Your dad promised to take you to a ball game but he forgot to buy the tickets and now it's too late.

Alternative Community Scenarios

1. You want to stay and play longer at a friend's house. You call your mom and she tells you to come home now.

2. A friend accuses you of taking money from his room.

3. While at the park you are teased for playing on the "baby swings."

4. Your mom is driving to your grandma's and is taking a new route. You want to go the old way.

PRACTICE ACTIVITIES

Practice Activity 1: Degrees of Anger

Place a long piece of masking tape on the floor to make a thermometer. Mark the tape and place notecards next to it as follows:

- ◆ 0 degrees: Calm

- ◆ 20 degrees: Annoyed

- ◆ 40 degrees: Frustrated

- ◆ 60 degrees: Angry

- ◆ 80 degrees: Furious

- ◆ 100 degrees: Enraged

Direct the children to stand at 0 degrees and move along on the thermometer according to how angry they would feel at each statement you read.

Instructions

◆ Read the following statements one at a time and wait for the children to move on the thermometer.

- School is out and you are waiting on the sidewalk for your mom to pick you up.

- Your mom is late.

- You are missing your favorite TV show.

- The principal comes out and says your mom has a flat tire and will be late.

- He invites you to play on the computer in his office while you wait.

◆ Read the following statements one at a time and wait for the children to move on the thermometer.

- You notice your dog is not in the house.

- You look in the yard and the garage and can't find her.

- You see cars going by on the road.

- Your mom comes outside and tells you a neighbor called to say that your dog is in his garage.

◆ Read the following statements one at a time and wait for the children to move on the thermometer.

- You can't find your favorite CD.

- Your brother took it to school without your permission.

- He forgot to bring it home.

- Your mom calls his teacher who finds it and puts it away.

◆ Discuss the following:

- Do all of you have the same degree of anger?

- What influences your degree of anger?

Practice Activity 2: Board Game Anger

Set up one or more of the following games: *Sorry; Trouble; Hungry, Hungry Hippos; Mr. Mouth;* or *Lego Creator.* Each of these games offers multiple opportunities for children to become angry and to subsequently practice dealing with their anger using the Steps to Success.

Instructions

◆ Direct the children to play according to the rules of the game.

◆ Prompt using the Steps to Success. Offer bonus points and praise children who demonstrate coping with their anger appropriately and those who are good sports.

Problem

✖ Someone wants to quit playing because she is not doing well in the game.

Solution

☺ Do not allow anyone to quit. Encourage those who need a break to take one. Do not penalize anyone for taking a break and returning to the game.

SUPPORTIVE SKILLS TO PROMPT AND REINFORCE

1. Being Flexible (page 232)

2. Dealing with a Problem (page 274)

3. Reading the Feelings of Others (page 176)

4. Dealing with Mistakes (page 200)

SUPPLIES

◆ Balloon

◆ Building blocks

◆ Drawing paper

◆ Flipchart or blackboard

◆ Game(s): *Sorry, Trouble, Hungry, Hungry Hippos; Mr. Mouth;* or *Lego Creator*

◆ Markers

◆ Masking tape

◆ Note cards

☑ EXTENDING SKILL DEVELOPMENT

Explain the goal of this skill to others and ask them to:

1. Post the Steps to Success in the classroom and at home.

2. Observe and identify specific anger triggers in the child.

3. Review and rehearse with the child in advance of potential anger triggers.

4. Set up situations where the child must deal with anger.

5. Offer a plan for how to deal with anger when the child is unable to think of one.

6. Use naturally occurring situations to deal with anger (e.g., with difficult tasks, when one is losing at a game, with frustrating experiences). Prompt the child as needed

7. Praise the child whenever she spontaneously handles frustration, disappointment or anger well, such as lets someone else go first, handles losing, says "good game," asks for help, etc.

8. Offer incentives to motivate the child to deal with anger if necessary, perhaps by earning a token. Tokens can be exchanged for special privileges or treats. Consider starting a paper chain using strips of paper (1x6) for demonstrating self-control. Each time the child uses self-control and deals with anger, he is congratulated and receives a paper strip to add to the chain. As the chain grows, he is reminded of how well he is doing.

9. Expose the child to more supervised and structured situations where opportunities to practice self-control occur if the child typically loses control by crying, screaming or throwing things.

10. Play games by the rules. Do not allow the child to cheat in order to win. Always play "the right way." Do not allow the child to leave a game because she is losing. Insist that the game be completed. If necessary, take a break.

CHAPTER 8

GETTING ALONG WITH OTHERS

SKILL 8-1: USING KIND TALK

STEPS TO SUCCESS

To use kind talk, you:
1. **Look at the person.**
2. **Use a friendly face.**
3. **Use a calm voice.**
4. **Use nice words.**

THOUGHTS BEFORE STARTING

The skill of Using Kind Talk includes four concurrent elements: eye contact, facial expression, voice tone and language. Often, this skill is especially challenging for children with ASD because of problems regulating voice tone. Acquiring the skill typically requires extensive practice and, for some students, it must be reviewed in every Super Skills session.

The "how" one makes a comment or asks a question often requires as much practice as "what" one says. For example, "I don't want any" is a relatively neutral statement when spoken in a friendly tone of voice. However, the message changes when an irritable or angry voice tone is used. Many children with ASD have difficulty recognizing when their voice tone is inappropriate and adjusting it accordingly. They also fail to recognize that using this skill influences whether others perceive them as friendly or unfriendly.

INTRODUCING THE SKILL

Today we are going to practice Using Kind Talk.

Discussion Questions

☐ *What is kind talk? What does it look like? What does it sound like?* Lead a brief discussion on the skill.

- [ ] *If I say, "That's mine!"* Use an angry facial expression and tone of voice while glaring at a student. *Is it kind or unkind? What about if I say, "That's mine."* Use a neutral facial expression and voice tone. *I'm sure you agree that how I say the words is just as important as what words I say.*

- [ ] *When I use unkind talk, how do you feel?* Elicit feelings of sad, hurt, and angry. *How do you feel when I use kind talk?* Elicit feelings of O.K., good, etc. Present more examples of kind/unkind talk if necessary. It may be helpful to show a photograph or poster of sad and angry faces as well as happy faces to support the discussion of feelings.

- [ ] Show a picture of children arguing or fighting (perhaps from a story or a magazine article). *Are they using kind or unkind talk? How do you know?* Point out facial expressions and body language.

- [ ] Pass around a hand mirror and have students practice making a friendly face into the mirror.

READ AND REVIEW STEPS TO SUCCESS

WARM-UP ACTIVITY

Copy the following statements onto 3x5 cards and place them in an envelope. Have children draw a card from the envelope and make the statement to a peer, first using unkind talk and then using kind talk, adding or changing words if necessary to change unkind to kind talk. If possible, tape record the activity and play the tape after everyone has had a turn. Discuss differences in voice tone.

I need help.	That's not right.	Pass the markers.
You're wrong.	Don't take that.	You can have these.
I don't want any.	That's mine.	I want more juice.
I want to play.	You can't have any.	Don't do that.

ROLE-PLAYS

Review the role-play format presented in Chapter 5.

Alternative School Scenarios

1. You need help with a math assignment and your teacher is helping someone else.

2. Your friend did poorly on a science test.

3. You can't find your scissors and need to borrow your neighbor's.

4. You erased your spelling mistake so hard you made a hole in the paper.

Alternative Home Scenarios

1. You don't like the dinner your mom prepared.

2. You want to watch TV but your sister is watching her show.

3. You need help with your homework.

4. Your brother is on the computer and you need to use it for an assignment.

Alternative Community Scenarios

1. You are at the mall with your mom and you want a new video game.

2. You want to play on the swing at the park but your friend is there first.

3. You are swimming in the pool and someone splashes you.

4. The waitress forgot your drink order.

PRACTICE ACTIVITIES

Practice Activity 1: Shape Box

Draw an equal number of sad and happy faces individually on note paper. Cut them apart and place the faces in an envelope.

Instructions

◆ Direct each child to draw one face from the envelope.

◆ Pass out the pieces of a shape box to the group and give one child the box.

◆ Direct children to take turns asking for the box using kind/unkind talk according to the face they chose from the envelope.

◆ The child who is in possession of the box decides whether or not to grant the request.

◆ Talk about who received the shape box, who did not and why.

◆ Repeat the activity using a puzzle if desired.

Practice Activity 2: *Don't Break the Ice*

Copy and cut apart the phrases on page 223-224. Place them in an envelope or small paper bag. Choose a simple game such as *Don't Break the Ice* for the children to play.

Instructions

◆ Ask for a volunteer judge. The judge decides whether or not the Steps to Success are followed.

◆ The first player begins by choosing a phrase from the envelope.

◆ The player repeats the phrase using kind talk to the player on her right.

◆ If the judge decides the Steps to Success were followed, the player strikes one ice cube in the tray until it has fallen.

◆ If the judge decides the Steps to Success were not followed, he explains his decision and the player has one more chance to say the phrase.

◆ Proceed around the table until the ice has broken.

◆ The player who breaks the ice becomes the judge.

Practice Activity 3: "What If"

Prepare a set of "what if" situations such as those listed on page 221 or others that are suitable to the children in the group. Ask students to choose a partner.

Instructions

◆ Give a "what if" situation to each pair. Tell the children that they are to act out a 1-minute (or less) skit for the group using their "what if" situation. The partners must choose roles.

◆ Set a timer for 3 minutes of practice (more if needed).

◆ At the end of 3 minutes, each pair takes turns presenting their skit to the entire group.

◆ Group members who are not acting at the moment judge each skit and assign it a numerical rating from 1-10, with 1 being poor and 10 being outstanding.

◆ Each judge records the score on a small piece of paper. Collect the scores and total them.

◆ Proceed through all the skits, judging and scoring them as they are completed.

◆ Share the final scores with the group.

◆ If time permits, assign new situations using the same partners; however, have partners reverse roles this time. For example, in the first situation the child who was the sister becomes the "you" in the subsequent skit.

What if . . .

1. You borrowed a book from the library for your science project and then gave it to your sister who left it on the bus? Your assignment is due Monday. What can you say to your sister?

2. You got an "A" on your spelling test but your neighbor got a "D"? What can you say to your neighbor?

3. Your mom went to a lot of trouble to make a special dessert but you don't like it? What can you say to your mom?

4. It's your birthday and your grandma bought you a new pair of pajamas that you don't like? What can you say to your grandma?

5. You are supposed to do a report about desert animals with a friend but he hasn't done any work? What can you say to your friend?

6. Your dad was on a business trip and was late getting home for your soccer game? What can you say to your dad?

7. Your friend borrows and then breaks your new video game? What can you say to your friend?

8. Your little brother smears chocolate all over your new pants? What can you say to your brother?

9. It really bothers you that recess is at a different time every day? What can you say to your teacher?

10. Your teacher forgets to tell the class about an assembly? Suddenly the principal announces that all classes are to report to the gym. What can you say to your teacher?

SUPPORTIVE SKILLS TO PROMPT AND REINFORCE

1. Showing Interest in Others (page 225)

2. Reading the Feelings of Others (page 176)

3. Listening (page 143)

4. Cooperating (page 255)

SUPPLIES

- ◆ 3x5 note cards
- ◆ *Don't Break the Ice* game
- ◆ Drawn sad and happy faces
- ◆ Envelopes
- ◆ Flipchart or blackboard

- ◆ Picture of children arguing/fighting
- ◆ Shape box (e.g., from magazines)
- ◆ Timer
- ◆ Using Kind Talk phrases (page 223-224)

EXTENDING SKILL DEVELOPMENT

Explain the goal of this skill to others and ask them to:

1. Post the Steps to Success in the classroom and at home.

2. Look for opportunities to prompt and model using kind talk.

3. Talk about how people use friendly voices daily and ask the child to identify when others are using friendly or unfriendly talk and facial expressions.

4. Support the child's efforts to use kind talk and praise his successes.

5. Matter-of-factly identify unkind talk used by the child by saying quietly: "That's unkind talk" (unfriendly face), etc., and calmly prompt the child to "Show me a friendly face" (calm voice).

Practice Activity 2: *Don't Break the Ice* – **Using Kind Talk Phrases**

Please pass the potatoes.	May I have some, please?	Please, don't take my markers
Excuse me. Those are mine.	Hi, Jack. Will you play with me?	I can't play. I have to go home.
Mary, do you have a pencil?	Will you share, please?	Can I go to Michael's house?
Can I help you?	I need help.	Please help me.
What time do we have to leave?	How old are you?	Can I have some?
Those are mine. Put them down.	Would you like a cookie?	Would you come to my house?
Let's play together.	Can we trade books?	Can I play too?
That hurts.	I don't want any.	I don't want to go.

Practice Activity 2: *Don't Break the Ice* – Using Kind Talk Phrases

This is a bad day.	Let's go to the park.	Please stay here.
Where are my shoes?	How many more do I have to do?	I don't like that.
How do you know that?	Leave me alone.	This doesn't work.
I don't have any.	I can't do this.	That's too bad.
What are you doing?	I don't want your help.	Do I have to?
I want to watch my TV show.	This is too hard.	My pencil broke.
Let's play with my trains.	You are teasing me.	That's not funny.
You are cutting in line.	What kind of ice cream is that?	It's my turn.
Can I have a turn?	What do you want to play?	Do I have to go?

SKILL 8-2: SHOWING INTEREST IN OTHERS

STEPS TO SUCCESS

To show interest in others, you:

1. **Use a friendly face and voice.**
2. **Look.**
3. **Ask a question, or comment about:**
   a. **What the person is doing**
   b. **What the person is thinking**
   c. **How the person is feeling**

THOUGHTS BEFORE STARTING

Showing interest in others is a basic strategy used to initiate relationships and friend-ships. People show caring, thoughtfulness and sensitivity by the questions they ask and the comments they make. They regulate this communication by observing each other's emotions. Successful friendships are not one-sided, but occur when friends are equal partners in the relationship.

Teaching this aspect of friendship to children with ASD is often challenging. Some chil-dren are too engrossed in their personal interests to show any interest in others; besides, they often do not understand the importance of doing so. They are perfectly content to talk continuously about their favorite topic. Others ask embarrassing person-al questions or make offensive comments about another person's features, activities or habits without any regard for the negative aspects of their behavior. Frequently this interest occurs to satisfy a curiosity or to simply blurt out a thought. Usually the child is not trying to initiate a friendship.

INTRODUCING THE SKILL

Today we are going to practice showing interest in other people.

Discussion Questions

☐ *Why is it important to show people you are interested in them?* (To be polite, make friends, show thoughtfulness.)

☐ *Friends show interest in each other, not just themselves and their own interests. That is, successful friendships are equal. What are some things your friends like to do?* List.

☐ *How can you tell if you are taking too much time talking about yourself and your interests?* (Read body language and feelings of other person.)

☐ *What can you do when you are talking and your friend looks uninterested?* (Change the subject; ask about the other person.)

☐ *What is the difference between being interested in someone and being nosey?* (Being nosey usually means asking a personal or private question that most people do not want to talk about, like their age, personal habits, appearance or personal problems; being interested means taking a genuine interest in somebody by listening, showing care and concern, etc.)

☐ *Let's list some general questions you can ask to show you are interested in someone.* (What are you doing? What is the matter? How are you? How was your vacation?)

READ AND REVIEW STEPS TO SUCCESS

WARM-UP ACTIVITY

Make a copy of the Expedition exercise (page 230) for everyone. Tell the group that they are going on an expedition to learn about the interests and preferences of group members. Pass out pencils. Direct everyone to move about the room asking questions of each other and writing in names as they are revealed. No one may write in his own name, unless it is to write it on another person's paper. Assist those who need help reading. Exchange answers when finished.

ROLE-PLAYS

Review the role-play format presented in Chapter 5.

 Alternative School Scenarios

1. You see a friend painting a picture.

2. Your friend comes to school on crutches.

3. You know your friend had a spelling test today. You see him after school.

4. You see a new boy in your class.

Alternative Home Scenarios

1. You walk into the house and your sister is crying.

2. Your mom comes into the house carrying shopping bags.

3. Your grandmother comes to visit. You haven't seen her for several weeks.

4. Your dad comes home from a fishing trip.

 Alternative Community Scenarios

1. Your neighbor has a new dog. You notice he is playing in the yard with it.

2. You are at a friend's house when his brother comes in carrying a soccer ball.

3. You are visiting your aunt and see photographs on her refrigerator.

4. You are at the movies. After the show you see a classmate in the lobby.

PRACTICE ACTIVITIES

Practice Activity 1: *Jenga*

Set up the game *Jenga*.

Instructions

◆ At each player's turn, the player removes a piece of the Jenga tower after he has asked another player a question about himself. If necessary, provide topic prompts and the Question Starters and Comments on pages 122-123.

Practice Activity 2: Bingo Interest

Make copies of the Bingo Interest cards on page 231 for each child. Pass out the cards and tokens to each player.

Instructions

◆ At each player's turn, he asks a peer a question or makes a comment that shows interest in the other person.

◆ If he is successful, he places a token on his bingo card.

◆ The first person with a bingo is the winner.

◆ Repeat as often as you like.

Practice Activity 3: Yesterday's Story

Make a copy of Yesterday's Story (Appendix, page 351) for each student.

Instructions

◆ Distribute one copy to each child and ask the children to complete it. Some children will need help with writing. (To save time, have the children complete the story at home ahead of time.)

◆ Once the stories are written, begin with a volunteer who reads his story aloud to the group.

◆ Ask other children to show they are interested, taking turns asking questions and making comments related to the story.

◆ Give a token or sticker for every appropriate comment or question.

SUPPORTIVE SKILLS TO PROMPT AND REINFORCE

1. Starting a Conversation (page 107)

2. Exchanging Conversation (page 124)

3. Entering a Conversation (page 115)

4. Listening (page 143)

5. Reading the Feelings of Others (page 176)

SUPPLIES

- ◆ Bingo Interest cards (page 231)
- ◆ Expedition handout (page 230)
- ◆ Flipchart or blackboard
- ◆ *Jenga* game
- ◆ Markers

- ◆ Pencils
- ◆ Question Starters and Comments (pages 122-123)
- ◆ Tokens
- ◆ Yesterday's Story (Appendix, page 351)

EXTENDING SKILL DEVELOPMENT

Explain the goal of this skill to others and ask them to:

1. Post the Steps to Success in the classroom and at home.

2. Observe and identify specific situations where showing interest is being friendly.

3. Review and rehearse with the child in advance of potential opportunities to show interest in others.

4. Set up situations where the child might have an opportunity to show interest in others.

5. Give the child the assignment to find out one thing about another person every day and report what he has discovered.

6. Prompt the child to "ask a different question," if she tends to ask the same question repeatedly.

7. Use natural situations to foster showing interest in others.

8. Praise the child for showing interest in others and point out that he is being friendly.

9. Offer incentives to motivate the child to show interest in others if needed, perhaps by earning a token. Tokens may be exchanged for special privileges or treats.

10. Remind the child to "read body language" when indicated.

Warm-Up Activity: Expedition

Find Someone Who:

1. Plays video games: _____

2. Eats mushroom pizza: _____

3. Lives in a white house: _____

4. Plays a musical instrument: _____

5. Collects something: _____

6. Has been to a foreign country: _____

7. Likes to read: _____

8. Rides a bicycle: _____

9. Likes to swim: _____

10. Has a pet: _____

Practice Activity 2: Bingo Interest

School	**Family**	**Game**
TV Show	**Free Space**	**Snack**
Sport	**Pet**	**Trip**

SKILL 8-3: BEING FLEXIBLE

STEPS TO SUCCESS

To be flexible, you:
1. **Stop.**
2. **Take a deep breath.**
3. **Let it go.**
4. **Think: "What is happening here?"**
5. **Make a plan.**
6. **Remember:**
   a. **There is more than one right way.**
   b. **There is always another way.**

THOUGHTS BEFORE STARTING

Being flexible is unknown and foreign to children who are rigid in their thinking and preferences. Their reliance on rigidity and routine helps them to predict and manage life's daily events. However, life is not rigid, but fluid and spontaneous.

The typical child with ASD has difficulty when the unexpected occurs and in new or unfamiliar situations (Moore, 2002). In such circumstances, being unable to predict what will happen next intensifies the child's growing stress and anxiety and may result in increased rigidity and a possible meltdown. Flexibility is essential in such situations to manage feelings of excitement, uncertainty, or even misunderstanding.

Other children with ASD, particularly those with AS, believe there is only one right way to do things. Their inability to "let go" in an argument, and insistence upon rigidly following specific rules, interferes with their ability to successfully establish peer relationships (Stewart, 2002). Finally, rigid monologues about narrow special-interest topics coupled with an unyielding "know-it-all" attitude frequently annoy and alienate those whom the child is trying to befriend. If they are ever to develop social competence, children with ASD must experience the flexibility that is required when trying to come to some sort of agreement with others, as well as when solving problems. We must show them that flexibility is nothing to be afraid of.

INTRODUCING THE SKILL

Today we are going to practice being flexible.

❑ *Stand on your toes and stretch your hands to the sky. St-r-r-r-re-e-e-t-c-h as far as you can. Now, bend over as far as you can to the floor, then twist your body to the right, now turn it to the left. Move your arms around. Stand up and take a deep breath. Let it go.*

❑ *Our bodies are flexible. They twist and stretch and bend and turn in different directions. If you drop something on the floor, you can bend down to pick it up. Try it. If you want a cookie from the top shelf, you can reach your arms up to get it.*

Discussion Questions

❑ *Is your brain flexible? Do your thoughts adjust, turn and adapt?* Briefly discuss yes or no.

❑ *When do you need to use flexible thinking?* (To solve a problem, come to an agreement with others, cooperate or manage unexpected events.)

❑ *Some people think there is only one right way to do things and that different ways are no good or are wrong. This is called being rigid, or rigid thinking. Rigid is not flexible. It doesn't stretch or adapt. Rigid is straight and unbendable, like this toy soldier* (show toy). *People who have rigid thinking have trouble working with others and have trouble making friends. They always want things to be their way. They can't let go of an argument, because they think they are right. However, there is always more than one right way. Life is not rigid. People who use flexible thinking know this. They try to be flexible so they will get along with others and make friends. Think of being flexible as this Gumby doll. He is flexible and bendable* (show Gumby toy).

❑ *Let's pretend your dad is driving you to school and he misses the turn on the highway. Now you are afraid you will be late for school. How do you feel?* (Nervous, worried, maybe angry.)

What can your dad do? Discuss ideas, emphasizing there is always another way: turn around, take a different route, explain to the teacher why they were late.

What can you say to your dad that shows flexible thinking? (It's O.K., dad; everyone makes mistakes, don't worry, we have time, etc.)

READ AND REVIEW STEPS TO SUCCESS

WARM-UP ACTIVITY

Remind everyone to show flexibility.

☐ 1. Stand up, turn off the lights and announce: *Power failure, now what can we do?* Lead a discussion of options such as get out a flashlight, move to a different room, open the door, etc.

2. Come to an agreement and follow through, moving if necessary.

☐ 1. *Gosh, I'm feeling really sick. My head hurts and my stomach is upset. I might have to sit out for a while. What can we do?* Discuss options such as act out the role-plays without you, ask a different adult to lead the group, take a short break, determine a student leader, etc.

2. Come to an agreement and follow through for several minutes if possible.

ROLE-PLAYS

Review the role-play format presented in Chapter 5.

🎬 Alternative School Scenarios

1. You are in an argument with a partner. You want the title of your joint report to be "Southwestern Native American Tribes." He wants the title to be "Native Americans: Tribes of the Southwest."

2. You enter your classroom with a friend and are surprised to find a substitute teacher.

3. The principal announces indoor recess because the playground is muddy. You were counting on playing outdoors.

4. The math lesson is taking longer than the time scheduled. You are starting to worry that you might miss lunch.

Alternative Home Scenarios

1. You are playing your favorite game on the computer and have made it to the last level when the computer suddenly freezes.

2. You really like to wear your red sweater to school and have worn it every day this week. You put it on today and your mom tells you to put it in the laundry because it is dirty.

3. Your sister has two friends sleeping over. They are watching a movie and it is time for your favorite television show.

4. Your dad is helping you organize information for your dinosaur report. You want to put all the information in a pile. He thinks you should sort it into folders.

 ### Alternative Community Scenarios

1. Your friend's dad is caught in traffic so he is late picking you up for your Scout meeting.

2. You are at a birthday party and the hostess forgets to serve you ice cream.

3. Your dad and you are shopping for a notebook for school. You want a red one but they don't have any. You don't have time to go to another store and you need the notebook tomorrow.

4. You and a friend are going swimming. When you get to the pool, it is closed.

PRACTICE ACTIVITIES

Practice Activity 1: Makeovers

Direct the children to stand up and go to a place where they can move about freely.

Instructions

◆ Call out the name of an object and direct the children to make their entire group into that object, bending, turning, adapting as needed. Suggested objects include helicopter, ship, cathedral, tree, waterfall, bus and skyscraper. The group must work together to decide the component parts and put them together.

◆ Reinforce cooperating and compromising as well as being flexible.

◆ If a child has trouble being flexible, guide her through the Steps to Success.

Adapted from Gregson, B. (1982). *The incredible indoor games book.* Carthage, IL: Fearon Teacher Aids.

Practice Activity 2: Breathing Clay

Ask for a volunteer sculptor. The remaining players are blobs of silent clay.

Instructions

◆ Direct the sculptor to silently mold the breathing clay into a sculpture by arranging arms, legs and body parts. The clay must be flexible to allow the sculptor to create. The clay and sculptor must remain silent while the clay is "molded."

◆ Children take turns being the sculptor.

Adapted from Gregson, B. (1982). *The incredible indoor games book.* Carthage, IL: Fearon Teacher Aids.

Practice Activity 3: Flexible Creations

Ask each child to think of a color and record the choices on a piece of paper. No two colors may be the same. Call out pairs of colors who will be partners for this activity. (You can also put the color choices into a bag and draw them out two at a time.) Prompt children to be flexible if they are not partnered with their favorite friend.

Instructions

◆ Give each pair of students a choice to create a picture from a small sack of craft supplies (show them the supplies) or to build a creation from a small sack of building blocks. They must come to an agreement that is acceptable to both of them before they receive their bag of materials.

◆ Remind them to exchange ideas and plan before starting.

◆ Both of them must participate in making the creation.

Problem

✖ Some partners spend so much time arguing about what materials to choose or what to make that there is little time left to start creating.

Solutions

☹ Let students choose to use both craft supplies and blocks. This is not a good solution in this case because this choice does not insist upon flexibility.

😐 Let the problem play out to its natural end without interfering so the children experience the natural consequences of their rigidity. This is O.K. as long as you are able to manage any escalating anger that might occur.

☺ Point out that this problem shows "rigid thinking" and ask the children to make a plan for being flexible. They may have to compromise. Give them suggestions if needed or ask peers for suggestions.

SUPPORTIVE SKILLS TO PROMPT AND REINFORCE

1. Compromising (page 238)

2. Giving a Suggestion (page 263)

3. Cooperating (page 255)

SUPPLIES

- ◆ Building blocks
- ◆ Flashlight
- ◆ Flipchart or blackboard
- ◆ Gumby doll

- ◆ Paper and pencils
- ◆ Small bags of craft supplies
- ◆ Toy soldier

EXTENDING SKILL DEVELOPMENT

Explain the goal of this skill to others and ask them to:

1. Post the Steps to Success in the classroom and at home.

2. Observe and identify specific situations where flexibility is useful.

3. Review and rehearse with the child in advance of potential opportunities to be flexible.

4. Set up situations and "surprises" where the child must be flexible.

5. Offer a plan for how to be flexible in a situation when the child is unable to think of one.

6. Use natural situations to foster flexibility.

7. Praise the child for being flexible and point out that he is being friendly.

8. Offer incentives to motivate the child to be flexible if needed, perhaps by earning a token. Tokens can be exchanged for special privileges or treats.

SKILL 8-4: COMPROMISING

STEPS TO SUCCESS

To compromise, you:

1. **Think of a way everyone can do part of what they want:**
   a. **Do each idea.**
   b. **Take turns.**
   c. **Give up part of what everyone wants.**
   d. **Do something different.**
2. **Use a friendly face and voice.**
3. **Exchange suggestions.**
4. **Come to an agreement.**
5. **Do it.**

THOUGHTS BEFORE STARTING

For children who fail to recognize that others might have a different opinion, another way of doing things, or any other preference than their own, compromising is an unfamiliar idea. For them, the suggestion to consider, and perhaps adopt, another's point of view is strange and unusual. These children are not selfish; they simply do not understand that there might be different ideas and that all opinions have equal merit. Furthermore, they do not appreciate that they should have to consider these other opinions and come to an agreement on a solution that is mutually acceptable. This requires some degree of flexibility and being able to "let go," which is also a challenge for children who are rigid in their thinking. A constant emphasis in Super Skills is to help children become more aware of others and to moderate their behavior accordingly. This is fundamental when compromising.

✓ INTRODUCING THE SKILL

Today we are going to practice compromising. When you compromise, you come to a solution that is acceptable to everyone involved, not just you. That means you might have to give up some of what you want.

Discussion Questions

☐ *What does compromise mean?* (Find a way that allows everyone to get some of what they want.)

☐ *Let's pretend that all of you are in the supermarket to buy a package of cookies. Half of you want to buy chocolate chip cookies and the rest of you want to buy frosted cookies. What should you do? Think of a way that everyone can get some of what he or she wants.* Discuss ideas: buy a package of assorted cookies, buy something different such as cake, buy one kind this time and the other kind the next time, look for smaller packages of both kinds, etc.

There are lots of ways to compromise. What would happen if one of you insisted that you buy chocolate chip cookies only? Would that be a compromise? (No.)

✓ READ AND REVIEW STEPS TO SUCCESS

✓ WARM-UP ACTIVITY

Hold three small, unopened bags of different chips or other treats in front of the children. *One of these treats is for the whole group. You can open and eat one of them. Which one should you open?* Proceed to lead the discussion, prompting and guiding the Steps to Success as needed. The end result should be a decision that is acceptable to everyone. Be sure to take time to eat the treat. Additional compromising may be necessary regarding the amount received, who eats the last one, etc.

Problem

✖ One child tries to convince the others to select his favorite snack by crying, arguing or otherwise acting immaturely.

Solution d

☺ Let the discussion proceed to its natural conclusion. If the child succeeds in convincing the others to choose his favorite snack, discuss whether or not this outcome is a "true" compromise. Likely the answer is no, especially if others in the group cannot eat or do not like the preferred snack.

☺ Stop the discussion and remind the child to "use a friendly face and voice." If he continues, ask him to describe how he thinks the other group members are feeling.

☺ Ask the children to answer "What is happening here?" ([Name] is trying to convince the group to select his favorite snack). Ask the group to come up with ideas for how to deal with this problem (let [name] decide, ask [name] to take a break so he can compose himself, talk to [name] about how the others feel in this situation).

ROLE-PLAYS

Review the role-play format presented in Chapter 5.

🎬 Alternative School Scenarios

1. You are working on a class project with a partner. Both of you want the scissors at the same time.

2. You enter music class with a friend. Both of you want to pass out the music books.

3. You get on the school bus with a friend. Both of you want to sit by the window.

4. You and a classmate get to the water fountain at the same time.

🎬 Alternative Home Scenarios

1. You and your brother are ordering pizza. You like ham and hate pepperoni. He hates ham and likes pepperoni.

2. Your mom has directed you and your sister to do the dinner dishes. Both of you want to watch television instead.

3. Your grandma has given you and your brother a puppy. You both want it to sleep in your own room.

4. Your dad is assigning chores for the week. Both you and your sister want to fold the towels.

Alternative Community Scenarios

1. Your friend has come to play at your house. He wants to ride bikes but you want to watch TV.

2. You and your friend are playing a board game at his house. Both of you want to go first.

3. You and your friend are renting a video. He wants to watch *Harry Potter* and you want to watch *The Lord of the Ring*.

4. You and a friend are going to a park. He wants to go to the park with the paddleboats and you want to go to the park with the swimming pool.

PRACTICE ACTIVITIES

Practice Activity 1: Compromising Teams

Copy the table on page 242 onto a flipchart or board, writing large enough so students can see it easily.

Instructions

◆ Call the names of two children. Direct each of them to ask a peer to be his partner. If both children approach the same peer, instruct them to work out a compromise. Continue to call names until everyone has chosen a partner. If there is an odd number of students, do one of the following: (a) make one group a team of three players, or (b) ask for a volunteer to be the reader and recorder.

◆ Direct the players to come up with a name for their team, reaching a compromise if necessary.

◆ Ask the teams to decide which team should go first. Come to an agreement and record the team names in order on a board or flipchart.

◆ Ask the first team on the list to choose a category and letter from the chart.

◆ Using the cards on pages 245-246, read a Compromise game card to the team. Give them 1 minute to come to an agreement on an appropriate compromise for the situation. Use a timer.

◆ If the compromise is excellent (in your opinion), award the team five points. If it is good, award the team three points, and if it is a poor compromise, award one point for effort.

◆ Award bonus points for working together, sharing ideas and listening to a partner's ideas. Record points next to a team's name on the board.

◆ Once a selection has been chosen, cross it off the chart or erase it. Go on to the next team.

SCHOOL	HOME	COMMUNITY
A	A	A
B	B	B
C	C	C
D	D	D
E	E	E
F	F	F

Practice Activity 2: Fish for a Compromise

Play the traditional game of *Go Fish*, except use the Compromise game cards found on pages 245-246 or make up your own. Make two copies and cut them into individual playing cards.

Instructions

◆ Deal three cards to each player and place the remaining cards face down on the table.

◆ On his turn the player requests a card from a peer by asking for it according to the letters in the upper-left corner. For example, "Do you have Compromise card School A?" If the child has the card, he must give it to the player. If not, he says, "go fish," and the player chooses another card from the table.

◆ When the player collects a match, direct him to read the situation aloud to the group and suggest a compromise. If the compromise is acceptable to the group, the child places the cards aside. If the compromise is not acceptable, the child can try again on his next turn. Assist those who need help reading.

◆ The winner is the first child who is out of cards.

Practice Activity 3: Compromise Memory

Use the Compromise game cards on pages 245-246 or make your own. Make two copies and cut them into individual playing cards.

Instructions

◆ Shuffle the cards and place all of them face down on the table.

◆ Direct the group to take turns locating matches. Once a match is found, the child must read the situation aloud to the group and suggest a compromise. If the compromise is acceptable, he can keep the match.

◆ The winner is the child with the most matches once all have been found and collected.

SUPPORTIVE SKILLS TO PROMPT AND REINFORCE

1. Listening (page 143)

2. Giving a Suggestion (page 263)

4. Cooperating (page 255)

5. Staying on Task (page 156)

SUPPLIES

◆ Compromise cards (pages 245-246)

◆ Flipchart or blackboard

◆ Small unopened bags of treats

◆ Timer

☑ EXTENDING SKILL DEVELOPMENT

Explain the goal of this skill to others and ask them to:

1. Post the Steps to Success in the classroom and at home.

2. Observe and identify specific situations where compromising is required.

3. Review and rehearse with the child in advance of potential opportunities to compromise.

4. Set up situations where the child must compromise with others.

5. Offer a suggestion of how to compromise in the situation when the child is unable to think of one.

6. Use natural situations to foster compromising.

7. Praise the child for compromising and point out that he is being friendly.

8. Offer incentives to motivate the child to compromise if needed, perhaps by earning a token. Tokens can be exchanged for special privileges or treats.

Practice Activity 1, 2, 3: Compromise Game Cards

A **SCHOOL** You are working on a class project with a partner. Both of you want the computer at the same time.	**A** **HOME** You are ordering pizza with your sister. She wants plain cheese and you want pepperoni.	**A** **COMMUNITY** Your friend has come to visit. You want to play *Nintendo* and he wants to watch a movie.
B **SCHOOL** You and a friend go to the office. Both of you want to pass out the mail.	**B** **HOME** Your mom is assigning chores for the week. Both you and your sister want to feed the dog.	**B** **COMMUNITY** You and a friend are at the mall. He wants to go to the music store while you want to go to the bookstore.
C **SCHOOL** You want to write a report and your friend wants to make a poster for your joint history project.	**C** **HOME** Your family is driving to your grandma's house. You and your brother want to play the same hand-held video game.	**C** **COMMUNITY** Your friend wants to go trick-or-treating on his street and you want to go trick-or-treating on yours. You only have time for one street.

Practice Activity 1, 2, 3: Compromise Game Cards

D **SCHOOL** It's indoor recess. You want to play *Sorry* and your friend wants to draw cartoons.	**D** **HOME** You and your brother have to clean your room. Both of you want to vacuum.	**D** **COMMUNITY** You are spending the night with a friend. She wants to make popcorn with butter and you want it plain.
E **SCHOOL** Your class is putting on a Thanksgiving program. You and a friend both want to be Pocahontas.	**E** **HOME** You and your sister are making cookies. She wants to make chocolate chip cookies and you want to make sugar cookies.	**E** **COMMUNITY** Your Scout troop is choosing a cake for a party. Some of you want the cake to be white and others want chocolate cake.
F **SCHOOL** You are making a flag for a project with a friend. You want it to be blue and white and she wants it to be red and green.	**F** **HOME** Your dad is fixing breakfast. You want him to make pancakes and your brother wants waffles.	**F** **COMMUNITY** You are at a birthday party. Both you and another guest want to go first at a game.

SKILL 8-5: BEING A GOOD SPORT

STEPS TO SUCCESS

To be a good sport, you:
1. **Keep a friendly face and voice.**
2. **Take a deep breath to stay calm.**
3. **Think: "I'm disappointed, but I can handle this."**
4. **Make a plan:**
   a. **Congratulate the other players.**
   b. **Say, "Good game."**
   c. **Think "Maybe next time."**

THOUGHTS BEFORE STARTING

Learning to cope with disappointment is important to all children, including those with ASD. When a competitive situation is especially difficult, distressing or frustrating, it is hard for most children to be good sports. For children with ASD, some of the difficulty lies in the unpredictable nature of competition. Sometimes you win – sometimes you lose. That's the way life is. However, for a child who is rigid in his thinking and who relies on routines to be able to cope, unpredictability is distressing. In addition, losing is a personal disaster for those who are prone to perfectionism. It is perceived as failure and being "wrong." It is the child's self-focus that interferes. If she cannot predict the actions of others, how can she predict that someone else might win the game? Some children would rather leave a game than finish it if they see they might lose. Others react to disappointment by crying, screaming or becoming aggressive.

Such extreme responses indicate that structured teaching in self-control and good sportsmanship is necessary. One cannot simply remove the child from all competitive activities or protect her by always "letting her win." Although losing may be disappointing, it is not the end of the world. We must work with the child to develop self-control, good sportsmanship and flexibility.

☑

INTRODUCING THE SKILL

Today we are going to practice being a good sport.

Discussion Questions

☐ *What is a sport?* (Game, contest, competition, like soccer, baseball, etc.)

☐ *When I say, "Be a good sport," what does that mean?* (Be kind, considerate, friendly, etc.)

☐ *What are some ways to show you are a good sport?* (Congratulate the other players, let others go first, shake hands, say, "good game," stay calm, smile, etc.)

☐ *When you lose at a game, or lose a contest, how do you feel?* (Disappointed, sad, hurt, angry, etc.)

☐ *Let's list situations where you might feel disappointed.* Write the list on a flipchart or board. Thoughts to include: not receiving a birthday gift you really wanted, an activity or plan is canceled, not being chosen for something, missing an activity because you got sick.

☐ *Disappointment happens when things don't work out like you planned or wanted them to, like losing a game, not getting the birthday present you really wanted or not doing well on a spelling test. Everyone feels disappointed at times. It's normal. Being a good sport applies to all of the situations where you feel disappointed, not just sports.*

☐ *If I play a game of Uno with one of you and I lose, should I cry?* (No.) *Should I throw the cards?* (No.) *What should I do?* (Say, "Good game," and ask to play again if I want to.)

READ AND REVIEW
STEPS TO SUCCESS

WARM-UP ACTIVITY

The traditional game of "musical chairs" is ideal for practicing good sportsmanship. Arrange chairs in a line or circle, using one fewer chairs than the number of players.

Instructions

◆ Begin to play music on a tape or CD player while the children walk around the chairs. Players may not touch the chairs or each other while the music is playing.

◆ When the music stops, the children sit down. One child will be left standing. This child is "out" and must leave the game.

◆ Praise good sportsmanship and reward with bonus points if desired.

◆ Remove one of the chairs and proceed to play until there is one child remaining.

◆ Praise all those who are "out" for being good sports.

Problem

✖ A child is a poor sport (in your judgment).

Solution

☺ Insist that she "rehearse" the Steps to Success, playing the game again.

ROLE-PLAYS

Review the role-play format presented in Chapter 5.

🎬 Alternative School Scenarios

1. You know the answer to the question the teacher has asked and raise your hand. She calls on someone else.

2. You are really good at spelling and enter the spelling contest. You come in third.

3. Your team loses a game of kickball in gym class.

4. You have to miss the class Halloween party because you get sick.

Alternative Home Scenarios

1. Your brother ate the last of your favorite cookies.

2. Your mom promises she will take you to the movies on Saturday. On Saturday morning she tells you she has to work and you cannot go to the movies.

3. Your grandma gives you a sweater for your birthday. You really wanted a baseball glove.

4. You and your dad play a game of cards. He wins.

Alternative Community Scenarios

1. Your bowling game is canceled because of bad weather. It's the last one of the season.

2. You and your friend are playing a board game at his house. He wins the game.

3. You and your friend rent a video. When you get to his house, you find out that his VCR is broken.

4. You miss two days of camp because your cousins are visiting from out of state.

PRACTICE ACTIVITIES

Practice Activity 1: Marble Relay

Determine a relay course through which team members must travel (such as to a wall and back). The course may be easy or made more difficult through the use of obstacles such as furniture, cardboard boxes, etc. Ask for volunteers to be team captains and choose two captains. Praise those who are not chosen for being good sports (or guide them through the Steps to Success if necessary). Direct the captains to take turns choosing team members. Line up each team behind a line taped to the floor. Give the first player on each team a spoon with a marble in it. Give the other players empty spoons.

Instructions

◆ At the start signal, the first player on each team carries the marble as quickly as possible to the destination and back to the second team member. The player may not touch the marble or cover the spoon with his hand.

◆ Should the player drop the marble, she must return to the front of the line and start again.

◆ When the player returns to the team, she transfers the marble to the next person's spoon without touching it. The next player travels the course, transferring the marble to the third person.

◆ The winner is the first team that can move one marble through all the team members and the course without dropping it.

◆ Frequently praise evidence of good sportsmanship and prompt and guide students' efforts when encouragement is needed.

◆ Make sure the losing team congratulates the winning team at the end of the game and that the winning team responds with "good game."

Adapted from Foster, E. S. (1989). Spoon marbles. In *Energizers and icebreakers for all ages and stages.* Minneapolis, MN: Educational Media Corporation.

Practice Activity 2: Egg Hunt

Copy and cut the Egg Notes on page 254. Place one note inside a plastic egg. In addition, place candy inside the egg as directed by the numbers. For example, the first Egg Note, "return this egg to the wall," has 0 pieces of candy with it. If you are working with a large group of children, simply duplicate the notes and fill more eggs accordingly.

Assign children to:

◆ Move furniture out of the way.

◆ Place a piece of tape across the floor about 8-10 feet away from and parallel to a wall (or draw a chalk line).

◆ Pass out one shooting marble to each child.

◆ Wait for the children to ask questions if they do not understand where to put the chairs, etc. Scatter the eggs next to the wall and direct everyone to kneel behind the line.

Instructions

◆ Children take turns shooting marbles at the eggs that have been scattered on the floor.

◆ They may not shoot until the person before them has retrieved his marble, collected his egg and is behind the line again. If anyone shoots out of turn or before everyone is behind the line, she loses the next turn.

◆ Act as referee and call out which egg a marble has hit first.

◆ Children open the egg and follow the instructions inside.

Modified from Jackson, N. F., Jackson, D. A., & Monroe, C. (1983). *Getting along with others: Teaching social effectiveness to children.* Champaign, IL: Research Press.

Practice Activity 3: Assorted Games

Playing games helps to practice good sportsmanship. Some of my favorites are games that also encourage self-control and can be played with partners or small groups. They include:

- *Bingo*
- *Cat Nip*
- *Connect Four*
- *Don't Break the Ice*
- *Hungry, Hungry Hippos*

- *Mr. Mouth*
- *Sorry*
- *Trouble*
- *Twister*
- *Uno*

SUPPORTIVE SKILLS TO PROMPT AND REINFORCE

1. Cooperating (page 255)
2. Being Flexible (page 232)
3. Using Kind Talk (page 217)
4. Compromising (page 238)

SUPPLIES

- Egg Notes (page 254)
- Flipchart or blackboard
- Games
- Marbles
- Music tape/CD

- Plastic eggs
- Small pieces of candy
- Spoons
- Tape/CD player

EXTENDING SKILL DEVELOPMENT

Explain the goal of the skill to others and ask them to:

1. Post the Skills to Success in the classroom and at home.

2. Observe and identify situations where being a good sport is necessary.

3. Review and rehearse with the child in advance of potential opportunities to be a good sport.

4. Set up situations where the child must demonstrate being a good sport.

5. Suggest how to be a good sport in situations when the child is unable to think of one.

6. Use natural situations to foster being a good sport.

7. Praise the child for being a good sport and point out that she is being friendly, for example.

8. Offer incentives to motivate the child to be a good sport, if necessary, perhaps by earning a token. Tokens may be exchanged for special privileges or treats.

Practice Activity 2: Egg Hunt

Egg Notes

0 **Return this egg to the wall.**	**1** **Give me to a friend.**
1 **I'm yours to keep.**	**0** **Sorry, I'm empty.**
1 **Take me home.**	**1** **Eat me.**
1 **Take a green egg.**	**2** **Smile.**
2 **Share me with a friend.**	**0** **All gone!!**
0 **Fooled you.**	**1** **I'm all yours.**
1 **Give me to your teacher.**	**2** **Give me away.**
0 **Take any egg.**	**1** **I'm yours.**
1 **Take a blue egg.**	**3** **Share me.**

Modified from Jackson, N. F., Jackson, D. A., & Monroe, C. (1983). *Getting along with others: Teaching social effectiveness to children.* Champaign, IL: Research Press.

SKILL 8-6: COOPERATING

STEPS TO SUCCESS

To cooperate, you:
1. **Listen to the directions.**
2. **Use a friendly face and voice.**
3. **Listen to other's ideas.**
4. **Tell your ideas.**
5. **Make a plan.**
6. **Do it.**

THOUGHTS BEFORE STARTING

Cooperating is an intricate blend of several social skills, including listening, exchanging conversation, staying on task, offering a suggestion and compromising. It is especially challenging for children with ASD because this is an area where their numerous and wide-ranging social deficits can be most evident.

The inability to read and interpret the subtle cues and nuances of conversation, body language and facial expression, while failing to engage in reciprocal interaction, leads to a breakdown in the communication necessary for successful cooperation. Children with AS have a compounding problem. Their inability to understand another's point of view while insisting upon imposing their own "expert" views, coupled with their inability to think about how their actions affect others, frequently leads to rejection and ostracism (Stewart, 2002).

For all children with ASD, learning how to interact cooperatively with others is essential for social competence. It is not a simple skill to learn because of its very nature as well as the breadth of circumstances where cooperation occurs. Therefore, it requires practice, practice and more practice.

INTRODUCING THE SKILL

Present the group with an envelope that contains the individual letters of the word COOPERATION. (Write the individual letters on small cards in advance or use letter tiles.) Direct the group to work together to unscramble the letters to find out the skill for today. Praise working together, kind talk, taking turns, etc. When they have unscrambled the letters, say something like: *Great job of working together. You have been cooperating. It's a big word. Let's say it together. Cooperating.*

Adapted from Foster, E. S. (1989). Cooperation squares. In *Energizers and icebreakers for all ages and stages*. Minneapolis, MN: Educational Media Corporation.

Note: An alternative introductory activity is to present the group with an envelope of individual words and punctuation marks. Direct them to form a sentence that includes all the words. Suggested sentence: When we exchange ideas and cooperate, we are being friendly.

Discussion Questions

☐ *What does cooperate mean?* (Work together, share, take turns, and listen to others' ideas.)

☐ *When should we cooperate?* (When more than one person is trying to do the same thing, such as playing games, group projects, chores, etc.)

☐ *Why is it important to cooperate?* (So jobs get finished, everyone has a turn, no one feels left out, etc.)

☐ *What does uncooperative mean?* (Being bossy, not giving someone else a turn, not doing your share, etc.)

REVIEW AND PRACTICE
STEPS TO SUCCESS

WARM-UP ACTIVITY

Copy, cut out and place the sentences on page 262 in an envelope. Place one sheet of green paper with the word "cooperating" written on it and one sheet of red paper with the words "not cooperating" written on it on the table.

Instructions

1. One at a time, direct children to pick a sentence from the envelope and read it aloud. (If the child does not read, read it for the child or ask for a volunteer reader. If the non-reader is learning how to ask for help, point out that this would be a good time to do so.)

2. Direct the group to decide whether the sentence belongs with the green (cooperating) pile or the red (not cooperating) pile. Some of the statements are purposefully ambiguous to generate discussion. Direct the child to put the strip on the appropriate pile and proceed until all students have had a turn.

ROLE-PLAYS

Review the role-play format presented in Chapter 5.

🎬 Alternative School Scenarios

1. You are working on a science project with a group; you don't like the others' ideas. Your group has to get started today or the project will not get done in time.

2. The art teacher has asked a group from your class to decorate the hall for St. Patrick's Day. You must come up with a plan.

3. The music teacher directs you and a friend to collect all the music books and take them to the lunchroom. Make a plan for how to accomplish this task.

4. A friend asks to borrow your library book. You need it for your history project.

🎬 Alternative Home Scenarios

1. You and your brother must clean up the kitchen before your parents come home.

2. You and your sister both need to look up information on the computer for different homework assignments before bedtime.

3. Your mom asks you and your dad to set the table for Thanksgiving dinner.

4. Your cousins are visiting and want to play with your trains.

Alternative Community Scenarios

1. You and a friend are collecting cans in the neighborhood for recycling.

2. Your grandma has given you and your older brother a list of things to buy in the grocery store. She is waiting in the car.

3. Your neighbor offers to pay you and a friend to rake the leaves and put them in bags. She has a big yard.

4. Your Scout troop is planning a haunted house for Halloween. Both you and a friend want to make the advertisement posters.

PRACTICE ACTIVITIES

Practice Activity 1: Draw a Shopping Center

Divide the children into small groups and direct them to plan a shopping center. Give each group a large piece of newsprint or drawing paper.

Instructions

◆ Instruct the group to plan a shopping center, deciding where to place each feature.

◆ Each person has one color marker and one job to do. For example, one child makes all the roads; another makes all the stores, etc. Each color marker represents certain features of the shopping center.

>   Green = Grass and trees
>
>   Black = Roads and parking lot
>
>   Red = Cars
>
>   Blue = Buildings
>
>   Yellow = Shoppers

◆ Prompt and guide exchanging ideas. Once a plan has been decided upon and the markers are distributed, the group can begin.

◆ Remind the children to ask the group before making any changes or additions to the shopping center.

Note: If group members have trouble with fine-motor activities such as drawing, some children can be creative and draw roads and shoppers, while others make the stores out of building blocks.

This activity is a variation of the "Draw a Town" activity by Jackson, N., Jackson, D., & Monroe, C. (1983). *Getting along with others. Teaching social effectiveness to children.* Champaign, IL: Research Press.

Problem

✖ Two or more children want the same job (e.g., making the roads).

Solutions

☹ Use two markers of the same color. This is not a good solution in this case because it does not foster problem solving and cooperation. It simply encourages the children to work alone.

☺ Engage the children in problem solving by saying: *(Name) and (Name) have a problem. Both of them want the same job. How can they solve this problem?* Lead a brief discussion of options. These might include taking turns using the marker, job sharing, picking a number, etc. Do not let the group continue until the problem has been solved.

Practice Activity 2: Preparing a Snack

Determine in advance what snack the group will prepare and have the ingredients and preparation items available. Suggested snack items include brownies or cookies made from a mix, cut-up fruit, cut-up cheese and crackers, pizza from a kit, tacos, pudding, drink mix.

Instructions

1. Direct the children to divide the jobs involved so that everyone participates in making the snack.

2. Make a plan and proceed.

Problem

✖ One child becomes overly controlling and tries to dictate who will do what.

Solutions

☹ Let the child continue without intervention during the entire activity. This is not a good solution because it encourages the child to act without consulting others.

😐 Let the child continue, but encourage the other children to express their displeasure to the "boss." Encouraging the other children to express their feelings is important; however, you may have to take a more active role.

☺ Actively intervene to help the child understand how to be a leader without telling others what to do. Remind the child to "ask, not tell" and to use a friendly voice. Encourage problem solving and compromising when necessary.

Practice Activity 3: Collages

Assign the name of a wild animal to each member of the group, such as zebra, giraffe, hippopotamus, cougar, elephant, lion, tiger, bear, etc.

Instructions

◆ Call out three animal names. These will form a small group. Proceed to call out names until everyone is in a group. (Partners may be used instead of small groups when there are too few children to form groups.)

◆ Give groups/pairs a stack of magazines, one pair of scissors, one glue stick, one marker and one piece of paper. Direct each group to create a poster.

◆ Each poster has a different theme. Suggested themes include Healthy Foods, Leisure Activities, Pets, People's Faces, Creatures That Live Outdoors, Sports.

◆ Prompt and guide cooperation as needed.

◆ Share posters with the large group when they are finished.

SUPPORTIVE SKILLS TO PROMPT AND REINFORCE

1. Listening (page 143)

2. Following Directions (page 148)

3. Giving a Suggestion (page 263)

4. Compromising (page 238)

5. Staying on Task (page 156)

SUPPLIES

- ◆ Cooperating/Not Cooperating Statements (page 262)
- ◆ Envelopes
- ◆ Letters to spell COOPERATION
- ◆ Magazines

- ◆ Markers, glue, scissors
- ◆ Newsprint
- ◆ Poster paper
- ◆ Red and green paper (one sheet each)
- ◆ Snack preparation ingredients and items

EXTENDING SKILL DEVELOPMENT

Explain the goal of this skill to others and ask them to:

1. Post the Steps to Success in the classroom and at home.

2. Observe and identify specific cooperative play activities in which the child can participate.

3. Review and rehearse with the child in advance of potential opportunities to cooperate.

4. Set up situations where the child must cooperate and work with others in a group, (e.g., making snacks, cleaning up, completing a project).

5. Make sure the child has a specific job in large group cooperative tasks.

6. Use natural situations to foster cooperation, such as clean-up or chores.

7. Offer incentives to motivate the child to cooperate, perhaps by earning a token for each cooperative activity. Tokens can be exchanged for special privileges or treats.

Warm-Up Activity: Cooperating/Not Cooperating

Let's trade.

You watch me, and then I'll watch you.

Do you want to share markers?

May I have that, please?

I'm not going to give you any.

Do you want some?

Let's ride bikes.

That's a good idea.

Don't do that!

That's mine! Give it back!

That's a terrible idea.

I'm not going to help.

Who says you're the boss?

Shut up!

You're stupid!

SKILL 8-7: GIVING A SUGGESTION

STEPS TO SUCCESS

To give a suggestion, you:

1. **Decide if you have something to suggest.**
2. **Use a friendly face and voice.**
3. **Make the suggestion.**
   a. **I think . . .**
   b. **I wonder . . .**
   c. **What about . . .?**
4. **Remember:**
   a. *There is more than one right way.*

THOUGHTS BEFORE STARTING

Being unable to give relevant suggestions appropriately to others may be the reason for social failure for children with ASD, and therefore is an important skill to master. As with so many other social skills, the problems for these children begin with failure to recognize when a suggestion might be offered, followed by failure to use the right words in a friendly tone of voice. In addition, recognizing that a suggestion is not a demand and may not be followed is often difficult. Many children, those with AS especially, get into trouble when they believe their suggestion is the only way.

INTRODUCING THE SKILL

Today we are going to practice giving suggestions.

Discussion Questions

☐ *What is a suggestion?* (An offer, idea, plan.)

☐ *When might you make a suggestion?* List ideas.

☐ *There are usually two types of suggestions, positive and negative. Positive suggestions are helpful and encourage people to change a behavior or do something different. For example: "Matt, I really like playing with you. It would be nice if I could get to choose what we play some time." This is a positive suggestion. Why is it positive?* (Tone of voice and words used, starting with a positive comment.)

☐ *Negative suggestions are hurtful and insulting. They are demeaning and cause embarrassment. For example, "Matt, what a jerk you are; you always choose what to play. I don't want to play with you any more." This is negative. Why is it negative?* (Tone of voice and words used, attitude.)

☐ *When you make a suggestion, does the other person have to follow it?* (No; it is a suggestion, not a demand or command.) *There is more than one right way to do things.*

☐ *Which suggestion is more likely to be followed, a friendly positive suggestion or a negative suggestion?* (A friendly one.)

REVIEW AND PRACTICE STEPS TO SUCCESS

WARM-UP ACTIVITY

Using a flipchart or blackboard, play the traditional game of "hang man." Think of a word, like "suggestion," "conversation" or "idea" and mark enough spaces for each letter in the word. Draw the gallows. One at a time children suggest a letter of the word using the Steps to Success. If they correctly suggest a letter, write it in the appropriate spot. If they are incorrect, proceed to draw the head, body, legs, arms, etc., of the man. Praise use of friendly voices, turn-taking and cooperation.

ROLE-PLAYS

Review the role-play format presented in Chapter 5.

Alternative School Scenarios

1. Someone behind you keeps talking during class so you can't hear the teacher.

2. The student behind you is kicking his foot against your chair so you can't write your answers to the spelling test.

3. You are playing ball on the playground and someone comes by and takes the ball away from you.

4. You are part of a group making a poster for a science project. You would like to suggest the poster include drawings from an Internet web page.

Alternative Home Scenarios

1. Your mom cleaned out your room and threw away some magazines you wanted to keep.

2. Your brother was in your room playing with your toys. He didn't put them away.

3. Your mom is telling you what to wear to school. You have another idea.

4. Your dad came in and changed the TV channel while you were watching a show.

Alternative Community Scenarios

1. Your friends are deciding what movie to see. You have a suggestion to make.

2. You and your mom are shopping for a birthday present for your friend. You know what you'd like to get.

3. Your friend borrowed your bike but didn't bring it back to your house.

4. Your friend is playing a new computer game. You have a suggestion for how he might win.

PRACTICE ACTIVITIES

Practice Activity 1: Architect and Builder

Provide a supply of building blocks such as Legos and ask group members to find a partner. One partner is the architect; the other is the builder.

Instructions

◆ Give each architect and builder a pile or container of building blocks.

◆ The architect comes up with an idea and suggests to the builder how to build it.

◆ The architect makes the suggestion(s) using the Steps to Success and without touching the blocks.

◆ The builder listens to what the architect says and follows the suggestions.

◆ Give bonus points to teams that give suggestions using the Steps to Success and follow the suggestion.

◆ After 5 minutes of building, have children switch roles.

Problem

✖ The builder may ignore the architect's suggestions.

Solutions

☹ Let the builder continue building. This is not a good solution in this case because it encourages the builder to ignore her partner

😐 Encourage the architect to speak up and assertively say something to the builder like: "You are ignoring me and my suggestions. You are not following the Steps to Success." This is O.K. as long as the architect can say it without anger and has the necessary language skills.

☺ Stop the builder. Point out that he is not following the Steps to Success and ask him to make a plan for receiving suggestions. Practice if necessary.

Note: This activity may also be completed using clay, drawing supplies or other types of building materials.

Practice Activity 2: Statues

Ask for three volunteers – a director, sculptor and statue.

Instructions

◆ Instruct the director to think of a pose for the statue.

◆ The sculptor and the statue are silent throughout the activity.

◆ The director makes suggestions to the sculptor for how to pose the statue's head, arms and legs.

◆ Children take turns being the director, sculptor and statue.

SUPPORTIVE SKILLS TO PROMPT AND REINFORCE

1. Using Kind Talk (page 217)

2. Compromising (page 238)

3. Receiving a Suggestion (page 268)

4. Cooperating (page 255)

SUPPLIES

◆ Building blocks

◆ Flipchart or blackboard

EXTENDING SKILL DEVELOPMENT

Explain the goal of this skill to others and ask them to:

1. Post the Steps to Success in the classroom and at home.

2. Observe and identify specific situations where giving a suggestion is appropriate.

3. Review and rehearse with the child in advance of potential opportunities to give a suggestion.

4. Set up situations where the child must give a suggestion.

5. Offer a plan for how to give a suggestion in a given situation when the child is unable to think of one.

6. Use naturally occurring situations to give suggestions.

7. Praise the child for giving suggestions using the Steps to Success.

8. Offer incentives to motivate the child to give suggestions if needed, perhaps by earning a token. Tokens can be exchanged for special privileges or treats.

SKILL 8-8: RECEIVING A SUGGESTION

STEPS TO SUCCESS

To receive a suggestion, you:

1. **Stay calm.**
2. **Listen carefully to the suggestion.**
3. **Make no excuses.**
4. **Respond to the suggestion:**
   a. **Thanks for the suggestion.**
   b. **Let me think about that for a minute.**
5. **Do.**
   a. **Follow the suggestion.**
   b. **Explain your behavior.**
   c. **Suggest what to do now.**
   d. **Correct a mistake.**
   e. **Apologize.**
6. **Remember:**
   a. *There is more than one right way.*

THOUGHTS BEFORE STARTING

Receiving a suggestion from someone may imply that one is wrong or incorrect. As a result, the first impulse is often to become defensive and reject what is said, assuming one has heard the suggestion in the first place. This is also true for children with ASD, who are prone to perfectionism and have difficulty handling mistakes.

It is easy to take suggestions personally, even when they are not meant to be so. The best response in most circumstances is simply to thank the person for the suggestion and then decide what to do. In order to think clearly, however, it is important to stay calm. This is often difficult for children with impulse control problems.

INTRODUCING THE SKILL

Today we are going to practice receiving suggestions.

Discussion Questions

☐ *Who can tell me the Steps for Success to giving a suggestion?* Review.

☐ *Sometimes when someone gives you a suggestion, it is common to think you have done something wrong. For example, I am working on my math problems and the teacher suggests that I read the problem again. My first impulse is to reject what she said. I might feel guilty that I made a mistake and didn't do the problem right. What other suggestions can you think of that might make you think you have done something wrong?* List.

☐ *Remember when we gave suggestions? The purpose was not to tell someone they were wrong, but to encourage them to do something different or to look at things from a different point of view. So when someone gives you a suggestion, the correct response is to say, "Thanks for the suggestion" or "I need to think about that." Then figure out what to do.*

☐ *Let's look at your choices.* Review choices (Step 5), such as follow the suggestion, explain your behavior, suggest what to do now, etc. Make sure everyone knows what the Step 5 choices mean and give examples if necessary. If more discussion is needed, use the Role-Plays on page 210 to talk about what one might say and do in each situation.

REVIEW AND PRACTICE STEPS TO SUCCESS

WARM-UP ACTIVITY

Show the children a maze taken from any book of mazes. *I have a maze that I'd like to complete. I might need some suggestions.* Begin to complete the maze and wait for suggestions. Respond with *"Thanks for the suggestion, I'll think about that for a minute,* etc. If necessary, correct any mistakes and make an alternate suggestion.

ROLE-PLAYS

Review the role-play format presented in Chapter 5.

Alternative School Scenarios

1. You really like outer space and talk about it whenever you can. Your friend is getting tired of the topic and suggests that you talk about his interests for once.

2. You like to be first in line and always try your hardest to be first. A classmate tells you he likes to be first, too.

3. Your teacher suggests a book to look at to make your report more complete.

4. You have been daydreaming in class. The teacher suggests you pay attention and listen.

Alternative Home Scenarios

1. You like to play on the computer and always choose what to play with your friend when he visits. He would like to choose sometimes.

2. You really like to wear your blue sweat pants. Your mom suggests you wear something different today.

3. Your sister has two friends over. You keep checking on what they are doing. Your sister suggests that you find something else to do.

4. Your dad is helping you with your book report. He thinks you should type it on the computer.

Alternative Community Scenarios

1. You are at a friend's house. He suggests you help clean up before you leave.

2. You are at a birthday party and are alone in the bedroom. The hostess suggests you join the group.

3. Your dad and you are shopping for groceries. The store is really busy and you are tired. Your dad suggests you find the Cheerios in the next aisle.

4. You are at your aunt's house and want to tell her about your new computer game. She is talking to your uncle and you interrupt. She suggests you wait until they are finished talking.

PRACTICE ACTIVITIES

Practice Activity 1: Game of Knowledge

Set up a knowledge game, such as *Go to the Head of the Class* or *Trivial Pursuit for Juniors.*

Instructions

◆ Play by the rules of the game.

◆ After each player receives the question, other players may suggest the answer (following the Steps to Success for giving a suggestion).

◆ The player must receive all suggestions following the Steps to Success before he answers the question and finishes his turn.

◆ Reinforce listening, joining in, using kind talk and cooperating with praise.

◆ If a child has trouble receiving suggestions, guide the child through the Steps to Success.

Practice Activity 2: Architect and Builder B

Provide a supply of building blocks such as Legos and ask the children to find a partner. One partner is the architect and the other is the builder.

Instructions

◆ Give each architect and builder a pile or container of building blocks.

◆ The architect comes up with an idea of what to make and tells the builder.

◆ The builder begins to build, and the architect offers suggestions on how to build according to his original plan, using the Steps to Success and without touching the blocks.

◆ The builder follows the Steps to Success to receive the suggestion.

◆ Praise cooperation.

◆ After 5 minutes of building, have children switch roles.

Note: This activity may also be completed using clay, drawing supplies or other types of building materials.

Problem

✖ The builder may ignore the architect's suggestions.

Solutions

☹ Let the builder continue building. This is not a good solution in this case because it encourages the builder to ignore her partner.

😐 Encourage the architect to speak up and assertively say something to the builder like: "You are ignoring me and my suggestions. You are not following the Steps to Success." This is O.K. as long as the architect can say it without anger and has the necessary language skills.

☺ Stop the builder. Point out that he is not following the Steps to Success and ask him to make a plan for receiving suggestions. Practice if necessary.

Additional Practice Activities

Crossword puzzles, mazes and word searches may also be used to practice receiving suggestions. Divide the children into pairs and have them take turns giving and receiving suggestions.

SUPPORTIVE SKILLS TO PROMPT AND REINFORCE

1. Compromising (page 238)

2. Giving a Suggestion (page 263)

3. Listening (page 143)

4. Cooperating (page 255)

SUPPLIES

◆ Building blocks

◆ Flipchart or blackboard

◆ *Go to the Head of the Class* or *Trivial Pursuit for Juniors*

◆ List of Role-Plays (page 210)

◆ Maze

EXTENDING SKILL DEVELOPMENT

Explain the goal of this skill to others and ask them to:

1. Post the Steps to Success in the classroom and at home.

2. Observe and identify specific situations to practice receiving a suggestion.

3. Review and rehearse with the child in advance of potential opportunities to receive a suggestion, reviewing choices of what to say and do.

4. Set up situations where the child must receive a suggestion.

5. Offer a plan for how to receive a suggestion in a given situation when the child is unable to think of one.

6. Use natural situations to receive suggestions.

7. Praise the child for receiving suggestions using the Steps to Success.

8. Offer incentives to motivate the child to receive suggestions if needed, perhaps by earning a token. Tokens can be exchanged for special privileges or treats.

SKILL 8-9: DEALING WITH A PROBLEM

STEPS TO SUCCESS

To deal with a problem, you:

1. **Stay calm.**
2. **Think: "This is a problem. What is happening here?"**
3. **Sort out the problem.**
4. **Think of different ways to manage the problem.**
5. **Try the best way.**
6. **Choose another way if the first way doesn't work.**

THOUGHTS BEFORE STARTING

Problems are a challenge for everyone in everyday life, including children with ASD. For children with ASD, it may be more useful to think in terms of lessening, reducing, coping with or managing problems, rather than solving them. Since it is not always a realistic option to solve a problem, it is better not to present this expectation to children who are concrete thinkers as it may reinforce their feelings of failure when they are unable to do so. Sometimes one can only tackle part of a problem because many others are involved. At other times problems can seem so overwhelming that one does not know where to begin, much less how to solve them. Therefore, for the benefit of children with ASD, it may be better to think in different terms than "problem solving."

INTRODUCING THE SKILL

Today we are going to practice dealing with problems.

☐ *What is a problem?* (When something does not go as you expect, when you hit a snag, have difficulty, have questions, run into trouble, reach an obstacle.)

☐ *Sometimes you can predict when you might have a problem, like when you are going to a friend's house and you forget the directions for how to get there. At other times you can't predict problems. They happen "out of the blue," which means they are a surprise, like when you are going to your friend's house and there is a traffic accident blocking the highway you usually take to get there.*

☐ *Problems come in all sizes, and some are easier to deal with than others. Who can tell me a problem? Let's see what different kinds of problems you can think of.* List problems, such as breaking a shoe lace, getting a paper cut, losing or forgetting homework, breaking something that belongs to someone else, getting lost, etc. *The first thing you do when faced with a problem is to sort it out. Think, "What is happening here anyway? Exactly what is the problem?"*

☐ Show a picture of a problem situation. (Drawings of problem situations involving children may be found in DeGaetano, J. G. (1996). *Problem solving activities.* Wrightsville Beach, NC: Great Ideas for Teachers Inc.). *"What is happening here? What is the problem?"* Discuss responses.

☐ *Dealing with a problem is like solving a puzzle. There are lots of pieces and many ideas for how to put them together. First you try one idea, and if that idea doesn't work, you try another. How can you deal with the problem in this picture?* Show the picture again and discuss ideas. Be sure to talk about ideas that show respect for others and do not harm anyone.

☐ *Other people have ideas too. So if you run out of ideas, you can ask someone for help. Who can you ask for help when you have a problem?* (Parent, teacher, sibling, friend.)

REVIEW AND PRACTICE
STEPS TO SUCCESS

WARM-UP ACTIVITY

Wrap up a small prize in many layers of gift wrap. Present the children with a problem, such as one from the Role-Plays, or one you know they have had to deal with in the past. Ask the children to think of ways to manage the problem. The first person who offers a suggestion removes the top layer of gift wrap. Each child who offers a different suggestion removes one more layer until the gift is unwrapped. The child to unwrap the last layer shares the gift with those who continued to offer solutions.

Prompt with, *What else can you do?* when necessary. Don't censor solutions unless they are harmful. If a child presents a negative solution, reply with *What might happen next?* For example, if a child believes he could solve a problem by hitting, he might get into a fight, get into more trouble, etc. Let the child unwrap a layer if he responds to this question.

ROLE-PLAYS

Review the role-play format presented in Chapter 5.

🎬 Alternative School Scenarios

1. You can't figure out how to do a math problem. The teacher is busy helping someone else.

2. You are in the library and someone checked out the book you need.

3. The teacher announces that book reports are due tomorrow. You haven't started yet.

4. The teacher calls on you to read but you don't know where to begin.

🎬 Alternative Home Scenarios

1. Your family is ordering pizza for dinner. You don't like pizza.

2. It's time to get ready for bed. You haven't started your homework.

3. Your brother is playing his music really loud. It bothers your ears.

4. You want to make a birthday present for your mom but don't know what to make.

🎬 Alternative Community Scenarios

1. While at the playground, someone starts to tease you and call you "stupid."

2. While running, you trip and fall at the park. You tear a hole in your new pants.

3. You made plans to go skating with a friend. He calls and says he can't go.

4. You are at the mall and get separated from your dad. You don't know where he is.

PRACTICE ACTIVITIES

Practice Activity 1: *Tic-Tac-Toe*

Draw a tic-tac-toe grid on the board or flipchart and ask for two volunteer players. One is X and the other O.

Instructions

◆ Present the players with a problem.

◆ The players take turns brainstorming reasonable solutions to the problem.

◆ If the solution is acceptable, the players make an X or an O, respectively, on the grid.

◆ As long as a player can continue to think of a new solution, the player keeps on playing and making an X or an O, as appropriate.

◆ When a player cannot think of any more solutions, the player sits down and a new player takes over.

◆ Continue replacing players until the game is over.

◆ The winner begins a new game with a different partner. Play again with another problem.

Modified from Shore, M. B. (1992). *I can problem solve.* Champaign, IL: Research Press.

Practice Activity 2: What Is the Problem?

Use photo pictures of problems from magazines, and set up a game such as *Jenga, Wheel of Fortune,* or *Don't Break the Ice.*

Instructions

◆ On each player's turn, present the player with a photograph or picture of a problem.

◆ When the player correctly identifies the problem, he takes his turn at the game.

◆ Continue playing using different photographs until the game is over.

Note: An alternate activity is to present the pictures and ask the player to identify what might happen next.

Practice Activity 3: Board Game Sabotage

Sabotage several board games by removing the spinner, playing pieces, directions, etc.

Instructions

◆ Present the children with the choice of games and encourage them to solve the problem of how to play without the missing pieces.

◆ Encourage them to solve any other problems that arise, such as too many players want to play the same game, etc.

◆ Do not predict problems for them; let them occur naturally. If a prompt is needed, say something like, *It looks like you have a problem.*

SUPPORTIVE SKILLS TO PROMPT AND REINFORCE

1. Compromising (page 238)

2. Giving a Suggestion (page 263)

3. Receiving a Suggestion (page 268)

4. Cooperating (page 255)

5. Joining In (page 82)

6. Being a Good Sport (page 247)

SUPPLIES

◆ Assorted games

◆ Flipchart or blackboard

◆ Gift wrap

◆ Pictures of problem situations

◆ Small prize

☑ EXTENDING SKILL DEVELOPMENT

Explain the goal of this skill to others and ask them to:

1. Post the Steps to Success in the classroom and at home.

2. Observe and identify specific problems.

3. Review and rehearse with the child in advance of potential problems how to manage them.

4. Set up problems that the child must deal with.

5. Offer a plan for how to manage a problem when the child is unable to think of one.

6. Use natural problem situations to practice dealing with them.

7. Praise the child for managing problems.

8. Offer incentives to motivate the child to deal with problems if needed, perhaps by earning a token. Tokens can be exchanged for special privileges or treats.

SKILL 8-10: DEALING WITH TEASING

STEPS TO SUCCESS

To deal with teasing, you:

1. **Take a deep breath.**
2. **Keep calm.**
3. **Think: "I can handle this."**
4. **Choose:**
   a. **Ignore.**
   b. **Walk away.**
   c. **In a friendly way ask the person to stop.**
   d. **Accept it gracefully.**
   e. **Make a joke of it.**
   f. **Seek help.**
5. **Do it.**

THOUGHTS BEFORE STARTING

Teasing is difficult for children with ASD to handle. It is often abstract and subtle, but can be blatant and hurtful. Children with ASD are very susceptible to teasing and are frequently targets of bullies (Moore, 2002). Their difficulty recognizing and understanding humor, as well as determining others' intentions, increases this vulnerability. Teasing can be friendly, such as joking and kidding around, or unfriendly, such as mocking and making fun of someone. Children with ASD have trouble determining the difference and may perceive all teasing as bad. They are not usually "teasers" themselves. For these reasons, this skill is difficult to teach and difficult to learn. Distinguishing between good and bad teasing, as well as learning how to respond appropriately, are ongoing struggles for many children with ASD.

INTRODUCING THE SKILL

Today we are going to practice dealing with teasing.

Discussion Questions

☐ *What is teasing?* (Name calling, put-downs, threats, sarcasm, bullying, harassment, whispering, laughing, making faces.)

☐ *Can teasing be fun?* (Good teasing: joking, kidding and trying to make someone laugh.) Read a few simple jokes from a joke book to illustrate how telling jokes might make someone laugh.

☐ *Can teasing be hurtful?* (Bad teasing: mocking, making fun of, annoying, cruel, starting a fight.) *Teasing can be good or bad. It depends upon the purpose of the teasing and how the person being teased feels about it.*

☐ *Why might someone tease?* (To hurt someone, be mean, get attention, make someone laugh, start a fight, feel important, to see people get upset.)

☐ *How do you feel when you are teased?* (Angry, frustrated, embarrassed or sad.)

☐ *Is it O.K. to tease back? Why? Why not?* (You may end up in trouble, problems escalate, and it does not stop the teasing.)

☐ *Your reaction may determine whether someone will continue teasing or stop. If what you do amuses the teaser, then the teasing will likely continue. Teasers (and bullies) often know how you will act (cry, scream, run away), and they are delighted by your response. If you respond in this way, the teaser succeeds. If you want teasing to stop, you must choose a different way to respond. How do you usually respond to teasing?* Discuss.

☐ *What is ignoring?* (Pay no attention, turn away, look away, not speaking, or walk away.)

REVIEW AND PRACTICE STEPS TO SUCCESS

WARM-UP ACTIVITY

Pass out three to four animal puppets to students who volunteer to act as "puppet masters." Choose one of the scenarios below and assign roles to the puppet masters. Direct them to act out the scenario using the puppets.

Scenario 1: Animal 1 is reading aloud in reading group. He reads very slowly because he does not want to make any mistakes. The other animals start sighing because he is taking so long. He comes to a word he isn't sure of and stops for a long time. Animal 2 laughs and calls him a "slow poke." He adds that Animal 1 should be in the "baby reading group." Animal 1 takes a deep breath and says, "Yeah, I do read carefully. Can you help me with this word?"

Scenario 2: Animal 1 does not know how to tie his shoes. It's the first week of school and time for gym class. The class changes into gym shoes. Animal 1 starts walking down the hall with his shoes untied. Some of the other animals point at his shoes and start laughing. "Hey look, he can't tie his shoes. He didn't learn to tie his shoes in kindergarten. He's a baby." Animal 1 looks at his shoes, takes a deep breath, smiles, and says to one of the animals, "Can you help me?"

ROLE-PLAYS

Review the role-play format presented in Chapter 5.

 Alternative School Scenarios

1. You are in computer class and the kids across from you are whispering and making faces at you.

2. You bring a book about trains to school and can't find it. You think someone might have hidden it from you.

3. You are on a special diet and bring your lunch to school every day. At lunch someone across from you starts teasing you about the food you eat.

4. You are playing outside at recess when someone grabs your favorite hat off your head and runs away.

Alternative Home Scenarios

1. You have just finished building a big tower of blocks. Your brother walks by and knocks it over.

2. Your sister teases you about your pants, saying they are "girl pants." You don't like to wear blue jeans.

3. Your brother turns on the vacuum when your mom is shopping. You hate the sound of the vacuum cleaner.

4. Your cousin, whom you haven't seen in a while, is visiting. It takes you some time to think of what to say. He says you talk like a baby.

Alternative Community Scenarios

1. While at the park someone starts to throw sand at you.

2. A friend comes to visit and starts to tease you because you are separating different kinds of food on your plate.

3. You are walking on the sidewalk and a bully starts calling you names.

4. You like to wear a knit hat, even in the summer. While at the mall, you see some kids pointing at your hat and laughing.

PRACTICE ACTIVITIES

Practice Activity 1: Card Rehearsal

Instructions

◆ Duplicate two sets of the game cards on page 286 onto card stock. Cut them apart and place them face down in front of the group.

◆ Choose a Role-Play scenario from pages 282-283 and read it to the first player.

◆ The player picks a card from the table, turns it over and responds to the Role-Play scenario according to the directions on the card. For example, if the Role-Play scenario is the first one under community scenarios, and the card directs the youngster to "make a joke," he must think of a way to humorously respond to someone who is throwing sand.

◆ If the player successfully follows the Steps to Success and demonstrates the strategy depicted on the card, award two points, and proceed to the next player.

Practice Activity 2: *Hungry, Hungry Hippos* and Teasing Eggs

Instructions

◆ Copy the Teasing cards on page 287, cut them apart and place them, one at a time, into plastic eggs.

◆ Set up the *Hungry, Hungry Hippos* game with three to four volunteer players.

◆ Place the remaining group members in between the players. They are the "teasers." Remind everyone to follow the Steps to Success when they are teased.

◆ Begin to play *Hungry, Hungry Hippos* as directed in the instructions to the game.

◆ While the children are playing, give an egg to one of the "teasers." The teaser opens the egg and follows the instructions, teasing as directed without the other players knowing what the directions said.

◆ The person who is teased must respond according to the Steps to Success. If he is successful, he continues to play the game. If he is unsuccessful, he loses his playing chair to the "teaser" and becomes a "teaser."

◆ Begin again, continuing to pass out plastic eggs one at a time to the teasers, who tease the players.

SUPPORTIVE SKILLS TO PROMPT AND REINFORCE

1. Dealing with a Problem (page 274)

2. Reading Body Language (page 168)

3. Being a Good Sport (page 247)

4. Dealing with Anger (page 208)

5. Giving a Suggestion (page 263)

6. Asking for Help (page 101)

SUPPLIES

- ◆ Animal puppets
- ◆ Flipchart or blackboard
- ◆ Game cards (page 286)
- ◆ *Hungry, Hungry Hippos*

- ◆ Joke book
- ◆ List of Role-Play scenarios (page 282-283)
- ◆ Plastic eggs
- ◆ Teasing cards (page 287)

EXTENDING SKILL DEVELOPMENT

Explain the goal of this skill to others and ask them to:

1. Post the Steps to Success in the classroom and at home.

2. Observe and identify situations where teasing occurs.

3. Review and rehearse with the child in advance of potential teasing situations how to manage them.

4. Set up friendly teasing so that the child can practice dealing with it.

5. Offer a plan for how to deal with teasing when the child is unable to think of one.

6. Use natural situations to practice using humor.

7. Praise the child for dealing with teasing.

8. Offer incentives to motivate the child to deal with teasing appropriately if needed, perhaps by earning a token. Tokens can be exchanged for special privileges or treats.

Practice Activity 1: Card Rehearsal

Game Cards

Ignore	**Walk away**
Ask to stop	**Accept it gracefully**
Make a joke	**Seek help**

Practice Activity 2: *Hungry, Hungry Hippos* **and Teasing Eggs**

Teasing Game Cards

Bump the chair of a person playing next to you.	*Look at the person across from you and make faces at him/her.*	*Whisper to the person next to you while looking at a player.*
Take a game piece of the person on your left.	*Bump the elbow of the person on your right.*	*Take a game piece from any person who is not looking.*
Put your face close to the person sitting next to you and make a face.	*Rest your hand on the arm of the person sitting next to you.*	*Point at someone's game pieces and start laughing.*

REFERENCES, SOCIAL SKILLS MATERIALS & RESOURCES

Anderson, J. (1982). *Thinking, changing, rearranging: Improving self-esteem in young people*. Eugene, OR: Timberline Press.

Attwood, T. (1998). *Asperger's syndrome: A guide for parents and professionals*. Philadelphia, PA: Jessica Kingsley Publishers.

Baker, J. E. (2003). *Social skills training for children and adolescents with Asperger Syndrome and social-communication problems*. Shawnee Mission, KS: Autism Asperger Publishing Company.

Ballare, A., & Lampros, A. (1994). *Behavior smart: Ready-to-use activities for building personal and social skills for grades K-4*. West Nyack, NY: Center for Applied Research in Education.

Begun, R. W. (1995). *Social skills lessons and activities for grades pre K-K*. West Nyack, NY: Center for Applied Research in Education.

Boardmaker. Solana Beach, CA: Mayer-Johnson, Inc. www.mayer-johnson.com

Borba, M. (1989). *Esteem builders: A K-8 self-esteem curriculum for improving student achievement, behavior and school climate*. Rolling Hills Estates, CA: Jalmar Press.

Cardon, T. A. (2004). *Let's talk emotions: Helping children with social cognitive deficits, including AS, HFA, and NVLD, learn to understand and express empathy and emotions*. Shawnee Mission, KS: Autism Asperger Publishing Company.

Carter, M. A., & Santomauro, J. (2004). *Space travelers: An interactive program for developing social understanding, social competence and social skills for students with Asperger Syndrome, autism and other social cognitive challenges*. Shawnee Mission, KS: Autism Asperger Publishing Company.

Dalrymple, N. J . (1995). Environmental supports to develop flexibility and independence. In K. A. Quill (Ed.), *Teaching children with autism: Strategies to enhance communication and socialization* (pp. 243-264). New York: Delmar Publishers, Inc.

Devencenzi, J., & Pendergast, S. (1988). *Belonging: Self and social discovery for children and all ages*. San Luis Obispo, CA: BELONGING.

Emotions. (chartlet) Carson-Dellosa Publ. www.carsondellosa.com

Foster, E. S. (1989). *Energizers and icebreakers for all ages and stages*. Minneapolis, MN: Educational Media Corporation.

Frost, L. A., & Bondy, A. S. (1994). *The picture exchange communication system.* Cherry Hill, NJ: Pyramid Educational Consultants, Inc.

Fouse, B., & Wheeler, M. (1997). *A treasure chest of behavioral strategies for individuals with autism.* Arlington, TX: Future Horizons.

DeGaetano, J. G. (1996) *Problem solving activities.* Wrightsville Beach, NC: Great Ideas for Teaching, Inc.

Freeman, S., & Dake, L. (1997). *Teach me language.* Langley, BC: SKF Books.

Gajewski, N., Hirn, P., & Mayo, P. (1993). *Social star: General interaction skills (Book 1).* Eau Claire, WI: Thinking Publications.

Gajewski, N., Hirn, P., & Mayo, P. (1994). *Social star: General interaction skills (Book 2).* Eau Claire, WI: Thinking Publications.

Gajewski, N., Hirn, P., & Mayo, P. (1996). *Social star: Conflict resolution and community interaction skills (Book 3).* Eau Claire, WI: Thinking Publications.

Ghaziuddin, M. (2002). Asperger syndrome: Associated psychiatric and medical conditions. *Focus on Autism and Other Developmental Disabilities,17*(3),138-144.

Goldstein, A. P., Sprafkin, R. P., Gershaw, N. J., & Klein, P. (1980). *Skillstreaming the adolescent: A structured learning approach to teaching prosocial skills.* Champaign, IL: Research Press.

Gregson, B. (1982). *The incredible indoor games book.* Carthage, IL: Fearon Teacher Aids.

Gregson, B. (1984). *The outrageous outdoor games book.* Torrance, CA: Fearon Teacher Aids.

Gutstein, S. E., & Whitney, T. (2002). Asperger syndrome and the development of social competence. *Focus on Autism and Other Developmental Disabilities, 17*(3), 161-171.

Hausman, B., & Fellman, S. (1999). *A to S – Do you ever feel like me?* New York: Dutton Children's Books.

Hodgdon, L. A. (1995). *Visual strategies for improving communication, Volume 1: Practical supports for school and home.* Troy, MI: QuirkRoberts Publishing.

Hodgdon, L. A. (1999). *Solving behavior problems in autism: Improving communication with visual strategies.* Troy, MI: QuirkRoberts Publishing.

Jackson, D., & Jackson, N. et al. (1991). *Learning to get along: Social effectiveness training for people with developmental disabilities.* Champaign, IL: Research Press.

Jackson, N. F., Jackson, D. A., & Monroe, C. (1983). *Getting along with others: Teaching social effectiveness to children.* Champaign, IL: Research Press.

Klin, A., Volkmar, F. R., & Sparrow, S. S. (Eds.). (2000). *Asperger Syndrome.* New York: The Guilford Press.

Mannix, D. (1993). *Social skills activities for special children.* West Nyack, NY: The Center for Applied Research in Education.

Mattes, L., & Schuchardt, P. (1996). *Verbal problem solving in social situations.* Oceanside, CA: Academic Communication Associates.

McGinnis, E., & Goldstein, A. P. (1990). *Skillstreaming in early childhood: Teaching prosocial skills to the preschool and kindergarten child.* Champaign, IL: Research Press.

McGinnis, E., & Goldstein, A. P. (1984). *Skillstreaming the elementary school child: A guide for teaching prosocial skills.* Champaign, IL: Research Press.

McGinnis, E., & Goldstein, A. P. (1997). *Skillstreaming the elementary school child: New strategies and perspectives for teaching prosocial skills* (rev. ed.). Champaign, IL: Research Press.

Meyer, J., & Minshew, N. (2002). An update on neurocognitive profiles in Asperger syndrome and high-functioning autism. *Focus on Autism and Other Developmental Disabilities,17*(3),152-160.

Moore, S. T. (2002). *Asperger Syndrome and the elementary school experience: Practical solutions for academic and social difficulties.* Shawnee Mission, KS: Autism Asperger Publishing Company.

Myles, B. S., & Simpson, R. L. (2002). Asperger Syndrome: An overview of characteristics. *Focus on Autism and Other Developmental Disabilities,17*(3),132-137.

Myles, B. S., & Southwick, J. (2005). *Asperger Syndrome and difficult moments: Practical solutions for tantrums, rage and meltdowns (new expanded edition).* Shawnee Mission, KS: Autism Asperger Publishing Company.

Nichols, P. (1996). *Clear thinking – Clearing dark thought with new words and images.* Iowa City, IA: River Lights Publishers.

Nowicki, S., & Marshall, P. D. (1992). *Helping the child who doesn't fit in.* Atlanta, GA: Peachtree Publishers, Ltd.

Patterson, G. (1975). *Families: Applications of social learning to family life* (rev. ed.). Champaign, IL: Research Press.

Photo Emotions. Salem, OR: Living and Learning Company; (800)521-3218.

Quill, K. (Ed.). (1995). *Teaching children with autism: Strategies to enhance communication and socialization.* Albany, NY: Delmar Publishers, Inc.

Quill, K. (2000). *Do-watch-listen-say: Social and communication intervention for children with autism.* Baltimore: Brookes Publishing.

Redl, F., & Wineman, D. (1957). *The aggressive child.* New York: Free Press.

Reese, P., & Nena, C. (1999). *Autism and PDD: Social skills lessons.* East Moline, IL: Lingui Systems.

Richardson, R. (1996). *Connecting with others: Lessons for teaching social and emotional competence grades 3-5.* Champaign, IL: Research Press.

Rules for Good Listening (chartlet). Carson-Dellosa Publishing Company; www.carson-dellosa.com

Schwartz, L. (1988). *Feelings about friends grades 3-6.* Santa Barbara, CA: The Learning Works.

Show, S., & Beisler, J. (1997*). Blending approaches to support communication, play and social skills in young children with autism and related disorders.* Cedar Rapids, IA: Grant Wood AEA.

Shure, M. B. (1992). *I can problem solve. An interpersonal cognitive problem-solving program for kindergarten and primary grades.* Champaign, IL: Research Press.

Stewart, K. (2002). *Helping a child with nonverbal learning disorder or Asperger's Syndrome.* Oakland, CA: New Harbinger Publications, Inc.

We All Have Feelings (poster). Frank Schaffer Publications, Inc.; www.teacherspecialty.com

Weiss, M., & Harris, S. L. (2001). *Reaching out, joining in: Teaching social skills to young children with autism.* Bethesda, MD: Woodbine House.

Wilde, J. (1997). *Hot stuff to help kids chill out. The anger management book.* East Troy, WI: LGR Publishing.

Wing, L. (1972). *Autistic children. A guide for parents and professionals.* Secaucus, NJ: The Citadel Press.

Zimmerman, T. (1997). *The cooperation workbook.* King of Prussia, PA: Center for Applied Psychology.

APPENDIX

CREATING SUCCESS: KNOW THE STUDENT CHECKLIST

Child's Name: _____   **Date:** _____

Current Interests: What are the child's current interests and favorite activities? Check all that apply and list or highlight as needed.

☐ Art: clay, crafts, drawing, painting, sand, wood Other:	☐ Sports activities: Baseball, basketball, bike riding, hockey, horseback riding, outdoor play, skating, soccer, swimming, tennis, gymnastics Other:
☐ Pet(s):	☐ Movies: (list)
☐ Collections: beads, books, dolls, cards, coins, comics, insects, rocks, stamps, t-shirts Other:	☐ Television show(s): (list)
☐ Play activities/games: (list)	☐ Music: (list)
☐ Computer activities: (list)	☐ Transportation: airplanes, boats, cars, trains, trucks, ships
☐ Special topics: animals, dinosaurs, event(s), famous person(s), geography, historical era, insects, plants, solar system Other:	☐ Other comments:
☐ Electronic games: (list)	

Stress Response: How does the child usually indicate he/she is becoming anxious or stressed? Check all that apply and add details as needed.

☐ Asks inappropriate questions/ makes inappropriate comments	☐ Distractibility increases
☐ Leaves seat/room	☐ Shuts down
☐ Becomes off task	☐ Facial expression/posture changes
☐ Meltdown	☐ Stares off
☐ Becomes silly	☐ Fidgeting/restlessness Increase
☐ Noises/humming Increase	☐ Voice tone/volume changes
☐ Blurts out, calls names	☐ Hurts self/others
☐ Reduces eye contact	☐ Yells out
☐ Cries/tearful	☐ Other comments:
☐ Refuses requests	
☐ Damages property	
☐ Repeats self	

Academic Skills: Indicate the child's broad reading and writing skills. Check those that apply and add details as needed.

- ❑ Reads at age/grade level
- ❑ Reads below age/grade level
- ❑ Reading skills minimal
- ❑ Does not like to read aloud
- ❑ Likes to read aloud
- ❑ Writes at age/grade level

- ❑ Writes below age/grade level
- ❑ Writing skills minimal
- ❑ Does not like to write
- ❑ Likes to write
- ❑ Other comments: math above grade. Slow to complete school work

Language Ability: In general, how do the child's language expression and comprehension abilities relate to typical peers? Are there specific problems with language use? Check all that apply and add details as needed.

- ❑ Language expression at age/grade level
- ❑ Language expression slightly below age/grade level
- ❑ Language expression below age/grade level
- ❑ Comprehension of spoken language at age/grade level
- ❑ Comprehension of spoken language slightly below age/grade level
- ❑ Comprehension of spoken language below age/grade level
- ❑ Argues
- ❑ Blurts out

- ❑ Monopolizes conversation
- ❑ Repeats self (perseverates)
- ❑ Slow to respond (needs more time)
- ❑ Script required for discussion/role plays
- ❑ Difficult to understand when speaks
- ❑ Voice volume: soft, loud
- ❑ Visual supports helpful but not required
- ❑ Visual supports required: pictures/ written words
- ❑ Other comments:

Sensory Issues: Does the child have any significant sensory issues? Check those that apply and add details as needed.

- ❑ Sensitive to bright lights
- ❑ Sensitive to touch
- ❑ Sensitive to loud sounds/voices
- ❑ Sensitive to infringement into personal space
- ❑ Sensitive to textures

- ❑ Sensitive to smells/tastes
- ❑ Other comments:

Health Concerns:

- ❑ Activity restrictions:
- ❑ Medications:
- ❑ Allergies:
- ❑ Seizures:

- ❑ Diet restrictions:
- ❑ Sleep problems:
- ❑ Other comments:

Social Profile: Complete the POSD.

Misc:

FUNCTIONAL ANALYSIS

Name: _____

Challenging/Disruptive Behavior: + _____

Date	Place/Circumstances *(Describe what the child is doing)*	Time Began	Time Ended	Antecedent: *What happened immediately prior to the behavior?*	Intensity (0-5) low – high	Consequence: *What happened immediately after the behavior? (adult action)*

HOMEWORK COUPONS

Work with a family member to make something together. Ideas: Bake cookies, Make an art project, draw a picture or build a Lego house. Remember to share, take turns and cooperate.	Write out a question you can ask each of these family members that shows an interest in them. Grandparent, Parent, Brother, Sister, Aunt, Uncle, Cousin.
Offer to help three different people. Write down their names and what you offered to help them do.	Play charades with a family member. Take turns acting out a feeling (no words) and guessing the feeling. (At least 5 different feelings).
Think of a compliment to give each of the following people and give them the compliment: your mother, your father, your teacher and a friend.	Pick a feeling and write about a situation during the past week when someone you know felt that feeling. Describe what happened.
Start a conversation with your teacher. Find out where she went to school.	Draw pictures of how you might look when you are feeling the following emotions (one picture per feeling): Worried, Sad, Angry, Proud, Excited, Afraid, Confused.

Pick a feeling and write about a situation during the past week when you felt that feeling. Describe what happened.

Bring a photograph of your last vacation to show the group.

Find or draw pictures of people that exhibit the following emotions. Glue the pictures onto a large piece of paper. Label each picture: Happy, Depressed, Enraged, Bored, Frustrated, Elated, Overwhelmed, Calm, Upset.

Cut out pictures of people from magazines and label each picture with how you think the person in the picture is feeling based upon their body language. Glue the pictures onto a large piece of paper. Try to find pictures that display at least 7 different feelings.

Interview a relative to find out: where the relative grew up, went to school, favorite food, best friend's name, and favorite place to travel.

Make a collage or drawing of your personal interests, hobbies, and favorites.

Start a conversation with 3 different friends. Write down their names and what you talked about.

Invite a friend to play at your house. Take turns deciding what to play.

LIST OF GAMES AND MANUFACTURERS

Allowance: Lakeshore/Toys to Grow On
Bingo: Toys 'R' Us
Cat Nip: Milton Bradley Company
Chutes and Ladders: Milton Bradley Company
Clue Junior: Parker Brothers
Colors and Shapes Bingo: Trend Enterprises, Inc.
Connect Four: Milton Bradley Company
Don't Break the Ice: Milton Bradley Company
Go Fish: Toys 'R' Us
Go to the Head of the Class: Milton Bradley Company
Hot Potato: Parker Brothers
Hungry, Hungry Hippos: Milton Bradley Company
Jenga: Milton Bradley Company
Lego Creator: Rose Art Industries
Light Bright: Rose Art Industries
Lucky Ducks: Milton Bradley Company
Monopoly: Parker Brothers
Monopoly Junior: Parker Brothers
Mr. Mouth: Milton Bradley Company
Mr. Potato Head Pals: Hasbro, Inc.
Oreo Matchin' Middles: Fisher-Price
Sorry: Parker Brothers
The Talking, Feeling, Doing Game: Creative Therapeutics
Trivial Pursuit Juniors Game: Horn Abbot
Trouble: Milton Bradley Company
Twister: Milton Bradley Company
Uno: Mattel
Wheel of Fortune: Mattel

SUPER SKILLS
PARENT FINAL EVALUATION AND COMMENTS

What did you like most about Super Skills?

What did you like least about Super Skills?

How much progress has your child made with his/her target behaviors since the group began?

Target Behavior 1: _____ : none, some, moderate, a lot

Target Behavior 2: _____ : none, some, moderate, a lot

Target Behavior 3: _____ : none, some, moderate, a lot

What would you like to see changed about the group, or done differently?

What suggestions do you have for future groups?

Any other comments or suggestions.

SUPER SKILLS FINAL EVALUATION

Date: _____

Please rate the degree to which you agree or disagree with the following statements:

	Strongly Agree	Agree	Neither Agree nor Disagree	Disagree	Strongly Disagree
1. The leader demonstrated a working knowledge of the subject matter.					
2. The leader gave information that was at a level my child could understand.					
3. The leader was well organized.					
4. Written materials were helpful to my child and to me.					
5. Practice activities were helpful to my child.					
6. Homework activities helped my child with practice at home.					
7. I believe my child has made progress with his/her social skills in the past 3 months.					
8. My child's teacher reports an improvement in my child's social skills.					
9. My child enjoyed coming to Super Skills.					
10. I will use information from Super Skills with my child at home.					
11. Overall, Super Skills was well conducted.					
12. I would re-enroll my child in Super Skills if offered.					
13. I would recommend Super Skills to other parents.					

Additional comments: _____

STEPS TO SUCCESS

Asking for Help

It is OK to ask for help. Sometimes other people have <u>different</u> ideas and information that might help to make your task easier.

To ask for help, you:

1. **Recognize you need help.**
2. **Think who can help.**
3. **Move close to the person.**
4. **Say the person's name.**
5. **Ask in a friendly voice.**
6. **Say: "Thank you."**

Asking for Help

It is OK to ask for help. Sometimes other people have <u>different</u> ideas and information that might help to make your task easier.

To ask for help, you:

1. **Recognize you need help.**
2. **Think who can help.**
3. **Move close to the person.**
4. **Say the person's name.**
5. **Ask in a friendly voice.**
6. **Say: "Thank you."**

Being a Good Sport

Everyone likes to win. Sometimes you win and feel happy. Sometimes you lose and feel disappointed. It's O.K. Everyone tries to be a good sport when they lose.

To be a good sport, you:

1. **Keep a friendly face and voice.**
2. **Take a deep breath to stay calm.**
3. **Think: "I'm disappointed but I can handle this."**
4. **Make a plan:**
   a. **Congratulate the other players.**
   b. **Say, "Good game."**
   c. **Think: "Maybe next time."**

Being a Good Sport

Everyone likes to win. Sometimes you win and feel happy. Sometimes you lose and feel disappointed. It's O.K. Everyone tries to be a good sport when they lose.

To be a good sport, you:

1. **Keep a friendly face and voice.**
2. **Take a deep breath to stay calm.**
3. **Think: "I'm disappointed but I can handle this."**
4. **Make a plan:**
   a. **Congratulate the other players.**
   b. **Say, "Good game."**
   c. **Think: "Maybe next time."**

Being Flexible

There are many ways to do something. Being flexible is very important when working with others and when solving problems.

To be flexible, you:

1. **Stop.**
2. **Take a deep breath.**
3. **Let it go.**
4. **Think: "What is happening here?"**
5. **Make a plan.**
6. **Remember:**
   a. **There is more than one right way.**
   b. **There is always another way.**

Being Flexible

There are many ways to do something. Being flexible is very important when working with others and when solving problems.

To be flexible, you:

1. **Stop.**
2. **Take a deep breath.**
3. **Let it go.**
4. **Think: "What is happening here?"**
5. **Make a plan.**
6. **Remember:**
   a. **There is more than one right way.**
   b. **There is always another way.**

Compromising

Compromising is coming to an agreement with others that is acceptable to everyone.

To compromise, you:

1. **Think of a way everyone can do part of what they want:**
   a. **Do each idea.**
   b. **Take turns.**
   c. **Give up part of what everyone wants.**
   d. **Do something different.**
2. **Use a friendly face and voice.**
3. **Exchange suggestions.**
4. **Come to an agreement.**
5. **Do it.**

Compromising

Compromising is coming to an agreement with others that is acceptable to everyone.

To compromise, you:

1. **Think of a way everyone can do part of what they want:**
   a. **Do each idea.**
   b. **Take turns.**
   c. **Give up part of what everyone wants.**
   d. **Do something different.**
2. **Use a friendly face and voice.**
3. **Exchange suggestions.**
4. **Come to an agreement.**
5. **Do it.**

Cooperating

Cooperating is working together on the same activity. When people cooperate, everyone has a job and no one is left out. It means making a plan that everyone can accept. The plan may not be the one you like most.

To cooperate, you:

1. **Listen to the directions.**
2. **Use a friendly face and voice.**
3. **Listen to others' ideas.**
4. **Tell your ideas.**
5. **Make a plan.**
6. **Do it.**

Cooperating

Cooperating is working together on the same activity. When people cooperate, everyone has a job and no one is left out. It means making a plan that everyone can accept. The plan may not be the one you like most.

To cooperate, you:

1. **Listen to the directions.**
2. **Use a friendly face and voice.**
3. **Listen to others' ideas.**
4. **Tell your ideas.**
5. **Make a plan.**
6. **Do it.**

Dealing with a Problem

Problems are like surprises that can happen to anyone at anytime. There are many ways to deal with problems. When one way doesn't work, try another way.

To deal with a problem, you:

1. Stay calm.
2. Think: "This is a problem. What is happening here?"
3. Sort out the problem.
4. Think of different ways to manage the problem.
5. Try the best way.
6. Choose another way if the first way doesn't work.

Dealing with a Problem

Problems are like surprises that can happen to anyone at anytime. There are many ways to deal with problems. When one way doesn't work, try another way.

To deal with a problem, you:

1. Stay calm.
2. Think: "This is a problem. What is happening here?"
3. Sort out the problem.
4. Think of different ways to manage the problem.
5. Try the best way.
6. Choose another way if the first way doesn't work.

Dealing with Anger

Being angry is O.K. Everyone gets angry sometimes. Dealing with anger appropriately is important to maintaining friendships.

To deal with anger, you:

1. **Stop.**
2. **Take a deep breath.**
3. **Let it go.**
4. **Think: "What is happening here?"**
5. **Make a plan:**
   - **Wait it out.**
   - **Talk it out.**
   - **Walk it out.**
   - **Apologize if you need to.**
6. **Do it.**

Dealing with Anger

Being angry is O.K. Everyone gets angry sometimes. Dealing with anger appropriately is important to maintaining friendships.

To deal with anger, you:

1. **Stop.**
2. **Take a deep breath.**
3. **Let it go.**
4. **Think: "What is happening here?"**
5. **Make a plan:**
   - **Wait it out.**
   - **Talk it out.**
   - **Walk it out.**
   - **Apologize if you need to.**
6. **Do it.**

Dealing with Mistakes

Making mistakes is O.K. Everyone makes mistakes sometimes.

To deal with a mistake, you:

1. **Take a deep breath.**
2. **Keep calm.**
3. **Think, "It's a mistake; I can handle it."**
4. **Choose:**
   a. **Ask for help.**
   b. **Try again.**
   c. **Admit your mistake, apologize and try to correct it.**
   d. **Accept another's apology.**

Dealing with Mistakes

Making mistakes is O.K. Everyone makes mistakes sometimes.

To deal with a mistake, you:

1. **Take a deep breath.**
2. **Keep calm.**
3. **Think, "It's a mistake; I can handle it."**
4. **Choose:**
   a. **Ask for help.**
   b. **Try again.**
   c. **Admit your mistake, apologize and try to correct it.**
   d. **Accept another's apology.**

Dealing with Teasing

Teasing can be friendly, such as joking around or unfriendly, such as name-calling and making fun of someone.

To deal with teasing, you:

1. Take a deep breath.
2. Keep calm.
3. Think: "I can handle this."
4. Choose:
   a. Ignore.
   b. Walk away.
   c. Ask the person to stop in a friendly way.
   d. Accept it gracefully.
   e. Make a joke of it.
   f. Seek help.
5. Do it.

Dealing with Teasing

Teasing can be friendly, such as joking around or unfriendly, such as name-calling and making fun of someone.

To deal with teasing, you:

1. Take a deep breath.
2. Keep calm.
3. Think: "I can handle this."
4. Choose:
   a. Ignore.
   b. Walk away.
   c. Ask the person to stop in a friendly way.
   d. Accept it gracefully.
   e. Make a joke of it.
   f. Seek help.
5. Do it.

Ending a Conversation

To end a conversation, it is courteous to give a simple explanation and use a farewell.

To end a conversation, you:

1. **Wait for a pause.**
2. **Look.**
3. **Give a short, simple explanation.**
4. **End with a friendly farewell.**

Ending a Conversation

To end a conversation, it is courteous to give a simple explanation and use a farewell.

To end a conversation, you:

1. **Wait for a pause.**
2. **Look.**
3. **Give a short, simple explanation.**
4. **End with a friendly farewell.**

Entering a Conversation

When you enter a conversation, it is polite to briefly talk on the same topic that the others are talking about, not a different topic.

To enter a conversation, you:

1. **Listen.**
2. **Watch.**
3. **Wait for a pause.**
4. **Smile.**
5. **Speak for a short time on the topic.**

Entering a Conversation

When you enter a conversation, it is polite to briefly talk on the same topic that the others are talking about, not a different topic.

To enter a conversation, you:

1. **Listen.**
2. **Watch.**
3. **Wait for a pause.**
4. **Smile.**
5. **Speak for a short time on the topic.**

Exchanging Conversation

When you exchange conversation, it is courteous to take turns talking and listening.

To exchange conversation, you:

1. **Look.**
2. **Listen.**
3. **Talk about yourself.**
4. **Ask about others.**
5. **Take turns talking and listening.**

Exchanging Conversation

When you exchange conversation, it is courteous to take turns talking and listening.

To exchange conversation, you:

1. **Look.**
2. **Listen.**
3. **Talk about yourself.**
4. **Ask about others.**
5. **Take turns talking and listening.**

Following Directions

When someone tells you what to do, they are giving you directions.

To follow directions, you:

1. **Look.**
2. **Listen.**
3. **Ask questions if you need to.**
4. **Do it now.**

Following Directions

When someone tells you what to do, they are giving you directions.

To follow directions, you:

1. **Look.**
2. **Listen.**
3. **Ask questions if you need to.**
4. **Do it now.**

Giving a Suggestion

A suggestion is an idea spoken to another person in a respectful way.

To give a suggestion, you:

1. **Decide if you have something to suggest.**
2. **Use a friendly face and voice.**
3. **Make the suggestion.**
   a. **I think . . .**
   b. **I wonder . . .**
   c. **What about . . . ?**
4. **Remember:**
   There is more than one right way.

Giving a Suggestion

A suggestion is an idea spoken to another person in a respectful way.

To give a suggestion, you:

1. **Decide if you have something to suggest.**
2. **Use a friendly face and voice.**
3. **Make the suggestion.**
   a. **I think . . .**
   b. **I wonder . . .**
   c. **What about . . . ?**
4. **Remember:**
   There is more than one right way.

Giving and Receiving Compliments

Compliments make people feel good.

To give a compliment, you:

1. **Look.**
2. **Use a friendly face.**
3. **Use a sincere voice.**
4. **Say what you like about what the person did.**

To receive a compliment, you:

1. **Smile.**
2. **Look.**
3. **Say "thank you."**

Giving and Receiving Compliments

Compliments make people feel good.

To give a compliment, you:

1. **Look.**
2. **Use a friendly face.**
3. **Use a sincere voice.**
4. **Say what you like about what the person did.**

To receive a compliment, you:

1. **Smile.**
2. **Look.**
3. **Say "thank you."**

Giving Encouragement

Sometimes people feel sad or discouraged, especially when things are not going as they expect them to. It is friendly to show concern and give encouragement to others.

To give encouragement, you:

1. **Read the person's feelings.**
2. **Look.**
3. **Use a friendly face and voice.**
4. **Make a hopeful comment such as,**
   a. **"Nice try."**
   b. **"You can do it."**
   c. **"It will be O.K."**
   d. **"You'll get it."**

Giving Encouragement

Sometimes people feel sad or discouraged, especially when things are not going as they expect them to. It is friendly to show concern and give encouragement to others.

To give encouragement, you:

1. **Read the person's feelings.**
2. **Look.**
3. **Use a friendly face and voice.**
4. **Make a hopeful comment such as,**
   a. **"Nice try."**
   b. **"You can do it."**
   c. **"It will be O.K."**
   d. **"You'll get it."**

Greetings

When you enter a room, see someone you know or meet someone new, it is polite to greet him or her.

To greet someone, you:

1. **Smile.**
2. **Use a friendly voice.**
3. **Look at the person.**
4. **Say "Hi" and the person's name.**

Greetings

When you enter a room, see someone you know or meet someone new, it is polite to greet him or her.

To greet someone, you:

1. **Smile.**
2. **Use a friendly voice.**
3. **Look at the person.**
4. **Say "Hi" and the person's name.**

Introducing

When you meet someone new, it is polite to introduce yourself to him or her.

To introduce yourself, you:

1. **Smile.**
2. **Look at the person.**
3. **Say: "Hi, my name is ___. What's your name?"**
4. **Listen to the answer and say: "Hi, ___, it's nice to meet you."**

Introducing

When you meet someone new, it is polite to introduce yourself to him or her.

To introduce yourself, you:

1. **Smile.**
2. **Look at the person.**
3. **Say: "Hi, my name is ___. What's your name?"**
4. **Listen to the answer and say: "Hi, ___, it's nice to meet you."**

Inviting Someone to Play

It is fun to play with others rather than alone. To play with others, you ask someone to join you.

To invite someone to play, you:

1. **Choose someone.**
2. **Walk close.**
3. **Smile.**
4. **Ask.**
5. **If "yes," go play**
6. **If "no," ask someone else.**

To answer someone who wants to play, you:

1. **Smile.**
2. **Look.**
3. **Answer.**

Inviting Someone to Play

It is fun to play with others rather than alone. To play with others, you ask someone to join you.

To invite someone to play, you:

1. **Choose someone.**
2. **Walk close.**
3. **Smile.**
4. **Ask.**
5. **If "yes," go play**
6. **If "no," ask someone else.**

To answer someone who wants to play, you:

1. **Smile.**
2. **Look.**
3. **Answer.**

Joining In

Sometimes it is fun to join a group and do what the others are doing.

To join others, you:

1. **Move close.**
2. **Watch.**
3. **Wait.**
4. **Ask.**
5. **If "yes," join in.**
6. **If "no," do something else.**

Joining In

Sometimes it is fun to join a group and do what the others are doing.

To join others, you:

1. **Move close.**
2. **Watch.**
3. **Wait.**
4. **Ask.**
5. **If "yes," join in.**
6. **If "no," do something else.**

Listening

Showing you are listening helps the speaker know that you are paying attention to what he or she is saying.

To show someone you are listening, you:

1. **Look at the speaker.**
2. **Use a friendly face.**
3. **Stay still, quiet and calm.**
4. **Think about what is being said.**

Listening

Showing you are listening helps the speaker know that you are paying attention to what he or she is saying.

To show someone you are listening, you:

1. **Look at the speaker.**
2. **Use a friendly face.**
3. **Stay still, quiet and calm.**
4. **Think about what is being said.**

Offering Help

It is kind to notice when others might need your help and then offer to help them.

To offer help, you:

1. Notice if someone needs help.
   a. Look at what they are doing.
   b. Look at their body language.
   c. Listen to their words and voice tone.
2. Use a friendly voice.
3. Ask if you can help.
4. If the person says "yes," then help.
5. If the person says "no," do not help.

Offering Help

It is kind to notice when others might need your help and then offer to help them.

To offer help, you:

1. Notice if someone needs help.
   a. Look at what they are doing.
   b. Look at their body language.
   c. Listen to their words and voice tone.
2. Use a friendly voice.
3. Ask if you can help.
4. If the person says "yes," then help.
5. If the person says "no," do not help.

Reading Body Language

A person's face and body give clues to what he or she is feeling and thinking. These clues – body language – help you decide what to do and say.

To read body language, you:

1. **Look for clues in:**
   a. **the face**
   b. **gestures**
   c. **what the body does**
2. **Recognize the clue.**
3. **Understand the clue.**
4. **Respond to the clue.**

Reading Body Language

A person's face and body give clues to what he or she is feeling and thinking. These clues – body language – help you decide what to do and say.

To read body language, you:

1. **Look for clues in:**
   a. **the face**
   b. **gestures**
   c. **what the body does**
2. **Recognize the clue.**
3. **Understand the clue.**
4. **Respond to the clue.**

Reading the Feelings of Others

A person's body language and voice give clues to what he or she is feeling. Reading these feelings helps you to respond correctly.

To read feelings of others, you

1. **Look for clues:**
   a. **Read body language.**
   b. **Listen to the tone of voice.**
   c. **Listen to the words.**
2. **Recognize the clue.**
3. **Understand the clue.**
4. **Respond to the clue.**

Reading the Feelings of Others

A person's body language and voice give clues to what he or she is feeling. Reading these feelings helps you to respond correctly.

To read feelings of others, you

1. **Look for clues:**
   a. **Read body language.**
   b. **Listen to the tone of voice.**
   c. **Listen to the words.**
2. **Recognize the clue.**
3. **Understand the clue.**
4. **Respond to the clue.**

Receiving a Suggestion

A suggestion is an idea spoken in a respectful way. Sometimes a suggestion is given to encourage someone to do something different.

To receive a suggestion, you:

1. **Stay calm.**
2. **Listen carefully to the suggestion.**
3. **Make no excuses.**
4. **Respond to the suggestion.**
   a. **Thanks for the suggestion.**
   b. **Let me think about that for a minute.**
5. **Do.**
   a. **Follow the suggestion.**
   b. **Explain your behavior.**
   c. **Suggest what to do now.**
   d. **Correct a mistake.**
   e. **Apologize.**
6. **Remember:**
   a. **There is more than one right way.**

Receiving a Suggestion

A suggestion is an idea spoken in a respectful way. Sometimes a suggestion is given to encourage someone to do something different.

To receive a suggestion, you:

1. **Stay calm.**
2. **Listen carefully to the suggestion.**
3. **Make no excuses.**
4. **Respond to the suggestion.**
   a. **Thanks for the suggestion.**
   b. **Let me think about that for a minute.**
5. **Do.**
   a. **Follow the suggestion.**
   b. **Explain your behavior.**
   c. **Suggest what to do now.**
   d. **Correct a mistake.**
   e. **Apologize.**
6. **Remember:**
   a. **There is more than one right way.**

Showing Interest in Others

It is friendly to show interest in others, especially when you want to be a friend to someone.

To show interest in others, you:

1. **Use a friendly face and voice.**
2. **Look.**
3. **Ask a question, or comment about:**
   a. **What the person is doing.**
   b. **What the person is thinking.**
   c. **How the person is feeling.**

Showing Interest in Others

It is friendly to show interest in others, especially when you want to be a friend to someone.

To show interest in others, you:

1. **Use a friendly face and voice.**
2. **Look.**
3. **Ask a question, or comment about:**
   a. **What the person is doing.**
   b. **What the person is thinking.**
   c. **How the person is feeling.**

Starting a Conversation

When you see someone you know, or meet someone new, it is polite to converse on a topic that both of you can talk about.

To start a conversation, you:

1. **Look friendly (relax) and smile.**
2. **Choose a common, shared topic.**
3. **Begin with a greeting.**
4. **Ask a polite question or make a polite comment.**

Starting a Conversation

When you see someone you know, or meet someone new, it is polite to converse on a topic that both of you can talk about.

To start a conversation, you:

1. **Look friendly (relax) and smile.**
2. **Choose a common, shared topic.**
3. **Begin with a greeting.**
4. **Ask a polite question or make a polite comment.**

Staying on Task

Staying on task means paying attention and continuing to work until the task is finished, or until it is time to do something else.

To stay on task, you:

1. **Listen carefully to the directions.**
2. **Ask questions when you do not understand.**
3. **Look at the task.**
4. **Show you are working.**

Staying on Task

Staying on task means paying attention and continuing to work until the task is finished, or until it is time to do something else.

To stay on task, you:

1. **Listen carefully to the directions.**
2. **Ask questions when you do not understand.**
3. **Look at the task.**
4. **Show you are working.**

Using Kind Talk

It is friendly to use kind talk when speaking to others, especially when you want others to think you are friendly.

To use kind talk you:

1. **Look at the person.**
2. **Use a friendly face.**
3. **Use a calm voice.**
4. **Use nice words.**

Using Kind Talk

It is friendly to use kind talk when speaking to others, especially when you want others to think you are friendly.

To use kind talk you:

1. **Look at the person.**
2. **Use a friendly face.**
3. **Use a calm voice.**
4. **Use nice words.**

Waiting

Sometimes you have to wait. When this happens, you can make a waiting plan and do something else for a little while.

To wait, you:

1. **Stay still, quiet and calm.**
2. **Think: "It's hard to wait, but I can do it."**
3. **Make a waiting plan.**
4. **Do it.**

Waiting

Sometimes you have to wait. When this happens, you can make a waiting plan and do something else for a little while.

To wait, you:

1. **Stay still, quiet and calm.**
2. **Think: "It's hard to wait, but I can do it."**
3. **Make a waiting plan.**
4. **Do it.**

SAMPLE STEPS TO SUCCESS USING PICTURE SUPPORTS

Compromising

Think of a way everyone can do part of what want.

Do each idea.

Take turns.

Give up something

Do something different
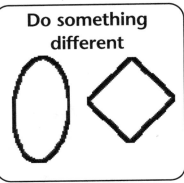

Use a friendly face and voice.

Exchange suggestions.
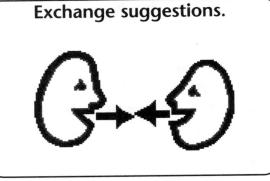

Come to an agreement.

Do it.

Dealing with Teasing

Take a deep breath.	Keep calm.	Think: I can handle this.

Choose:

Ignore.	Walk away.	Ask the person to stop.

Accept it gracefully: "Thank you."	Make a joke of it.	Seek help.

Do it.

Ending a Conversation

Wait for a pause.

Look.

Give a short, simple explanation.

Say, "Goodbye."

Exchanging Conversation

Look.

Listen.

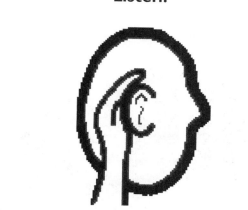

Talk about yourself.

Ask about others.

Take turns talking and listening.

my turn   *your turn*

You've got it!

Greetings

Smile.

Use a friendly voice.

Look at the person.

Say "Hi (name)."

Listening

Look at the speaker.

Use a friendly face.

Stay still, quiet and calm.

Think about what is being said.

We have a spelling test Friday.

Using Kind Talk

Look at the person.

Use a friendly face.

Use a calm voice.

Do not yell.

Do not whine.

Use nice words.

Do not curse.

Do not be mean.

STEPS TO SUCCESS RATING FORM

Date: _____

_____ is learning the skill of: _____

The steps involved in this skill are:

1.

2.

3.

4.

5.

1. Did he or she demonstrate this skill in your presence?
   ☐ Yes
   ☐ No

2. How well did he or she do in performing the skill? (Check one)
   ☐ Poor
   ☐ Below average
   ☐ Average
   ☐ Above average
   ☐ Excellent

3. How difficult was it for him or her to perform the skill? (Check one)
   ☐ Very difficult
   ☐ Difficult
   ☐ Somewhat difficult
   ☐ Neither difficult or easy
   ☐ Somewhat easy
   ☐ Easy
   ☐ Very easy

4. Does he or she need continued practice with this skill?
   ☐ Yes
   ☐ No

Comments:

Please sign and return this form to Super Skills at the next session.

Signature: _____ Date: _____

Adapted from McGinnis, E., & Goldstein, A. P. (1997). *Skillstreaming the elementary school child.* Champaign, IL: Research Press.

SUPER SKILLS GROUPING PROFILE OF SOCIAL DIFFICULTY

To identify shared social skill difficulty among a group of children, summarize their POSD scores below. Assign a numerical value to each level of difficulty on the POSD, starting with 0 for very difficult and ending with 6 for very easy. The higher the total score the easier it is for a child to perform.

Children's Names							
Fundamental Skillsf							
Eye Contact							
Correct Facial Expression							
Correct Voice Volume							
Correct Voice Tone							
Correct Timing							
Social Initiation Skills							
Using Person's Name							
Using Farewells							
Greeting							
Introducing Self							
Asking for Help							
Giving a Compliment							
Starting a Conversation							
Entering a Conversation							
Ending a Conversation							
Exchanging Conversation							
Inviting Someone to Play							
Introducing Others							
Joining In							
Talking About Self							
Making a Complaint							
Asking Appropriate Questions							
Offering an Opinion							
Expressing Basic Feelings							
Expressing Complex Feelings							
Social Response Skills							
Responding to Greeting							
Responding to Compliments							
Listening							

Children's Names		
Social Response Skills (cont.)		
Following Directions		
Making Short Comments		
Staying on the Topic		
Waiting		
Staying on Task		
Offering Help		
Giving Encouragement		
Reading Body Language		
Reading Feelings of Others		
Dealing with Mistakes		
Dealing with Anger		
Refusing Appropriately		
Getting Along with Others		
Taking Turns		
Sharing		
Playing by the Rules		
Apologizing		
Being Fair		
Being a Good Sport		
Using Kind Talk		
Being Flexible		
Asking Permission		
Cooperating		
Dealing with "No"		
Compromising		
Dealing with a Problem		
Receiving a Suggestion		
Giving a Suggestion		
Letting Others Talk		
Showing Interest in Others		
Using Humor		
Disagreeing Politely		
Dealing with Teasing		

SUPER SKILLS PROFILE OF SOCIAL DIFFICULTY (1 of 2)

Name: _____ **Age:** _____ **Date:** _____

Recorder: _____ **Relationship to child:** _____

Here are some social skills that people sometimes have difficulty with. Please mark the column you think applies to this child at present.

	Very Difficult	Difficult	Somewhat Difficult	Neither Difficult nor Easy	Somewhat Easy	Easy	Very Easy
Fundamental Skills	0	1	2	3	4	5	6
Eye Contact							
Correct Facial Expression							
Correct Voice Volume							
Correct Voice Tone							
Correct Timing							
Social Initiation Skills	0	1	2	3	4	5	6
Using Person's Name							
Using Farewells							
Greeting							
Introducing Self							
Asking for Help							
Giving a Compliment							
Starting a Conversation							
Joining a Conversation							
Ending a Conversation							
Exchanging Conversation							
Inviting Someone to Play							
Introducing Others							
Joining In							
Talking About Self							
Making a Complaint							
Asking Appropriate Questions							
Offering an Opinion							
Expressing Basic Feelings							
Expressing Complex Feelings							
Social Response Skills	0	1	2	3	4	5	6
Responding to Greeting							

SUPER SKILLS PROFILE OF SOCIAL DIFFICULTY (2 of 2)

	Very Difficult	Difficult	Somewhat Difficult	Neither Difficult nor Easy	Somewhat Easy	Easy	Very Easy
	0	1	2	3	4	5	6
Social Response Skills (cont.)							
Responding to Compliments							
Listening							
Following Directions							
Making Short Comments							
Staying on the Topic							
Waiting							
Staying on Task							
Offering Help							
Giving Encouragement							
Reading Body Language							
Reading the Feelings of Others							
Dealing with Mistakes							
Dealing with Anger							
Refusing When Appropriate							
Getting Along with Others	0	1	2	3	4	5	6
Taking Turns							
Sharing							
Playing by the Rules							
Apologizing							
Being Fair							
Being a Good Sport							
Using Kind Talk							
Being Flexible							
Asking Permission							
Cooperating							
Dealing with "No"							
Compromising							
Dealing with a Problem							
Receiving a Suggestion							
Giving a Suggestion							
Letting Others Talk							
Showing Interest in Others							
Using Humor							
Disagreeing Politely							
Dealing with Teasing							

SUPER SKILLS PROFILE OF SOCIAL DIFFICULTY SELF-REPORT (1 of 2)

Name: _____ **Age:** _____ **Date:** _____

Here are some social skills that people sometimes have difficulty with. Please mark the column you think applies to you at present.

	Very Difficult	Difficult	Somewhat Difficult	Neither Difficult nor Easy	Somewhat Easy	Easy	Very Easy
Fundamental Skills							
Eye Contact							
Correct Facial Expression							
Correct Voice Volume							
Correct Voice Tone							
Correct Timing							
Social Initiation Skills							
Using Person's Name							
Using Farewells							
Greeting							
Introducing Self							
Asking for Help							
Giving a Compliment							
Starting a Conversation							
Joining a Conversation							
Ending a Conversation							
Exchanging Conversation							
Inviting Someone to Play							
Introducing Others							
Joining In							
Talking About Self							
Making a Complaint							
Asking Appropriate Questions							
Offering an Opinion							
Expressing Basic Feelings							
Expressing Complex Feelings							
Social Response Skills							
Responding to Greeting							

SUPER SKILLS PROFILE OF SOCIAL DIFFICULTY SELF-REPORT (2 of 2)

	Very Difficult	Difficult	Somewhat Difficult	Neither Difficult nor Easy	Somewhat Easy	Easy	Very Easy
Social Response Skills (cont.)							
Responding to Compliments							
Listening							
Following Directions							
Making Short Comments							
Staying on the Topic							
Waiting							
Staying on Task							
Offering Help							
Giving Encouragement							
Reading Body Language							
Reading the Feelings of Others							
Dealing with Mistakes							
Dealing with Anger							
Refusing When Appropriate							
Getting Along with Others							
Taking Turns							
Sharing							
Playing by the Rules							
Apologizing							
Being Fair							
Being a Good Sport							
Using Kind Talk							
Being Flexible							
Asking Permission							
Cooperating							
Dealing with "No"							
Compromising							
Dealing with a Problem							
Receiving a Suggestion							
Giving a Suggestion							
Letting Others Talk							
Showing Interest in Others							
Using Humor							
Disagreeing Politely							
Dealing with Teasing							

SUPER SKILLS TARGET BEHAVIOR PRACTICE CHART

Name:_____

Each time you practice one of your target behaviors you receive credit towards a bonus prize. Write in the target behavior that you practiced below. Tell me where you practiced it and how well you think you did. Have your parent, teacher, or friends initial it. Return the completed chart to me for credit. The more you practice the more you earn!!

Date	Target behavior	Situation	How did I do?	Initials

Awesome!! You did it!!

YESTERDAY'S STORY

Yesterday I went _____

_____

_____

_____

I saw _____

_____

_____

_____

I felt _____

_____

_____

_____

I thought _____

_____

_____

_____

Tomorrow I will _____

_____

_____

_____

Signed _____

OTHER SOCIAL SKILLS RESOURCES PUBLISHED BY AAPC

Asperger Syndrome and Difficult Moments: Practical Solutions for Tantrums, Rage, and Meltdowns; NEW EXPANDED EDITION
Brenda Smith Myles and Jack Southwick

When My Autism Gets Too Big!
A Relaxation Book for Children with Autism Spectrum Disorders
Kari Dunn Buron; foreword by Brenda Smith Myles

Perfect Targets: Asperger Syndrome and Bullying;
Practical Solutions for Surviving the Social World
Rebekah Heinrichs

The Incredible 5-Point Scale – Assisting Students with Autism Spectrum Disorders
in Understanding Social Interactions and Controlling Their Emotional Responses
Kari Dunn Buron and Mitzi Curtis

Let's Talk Emotions: Helping Children with Social Cognitive Deficits, Including
AS, HFA, and NVLD, Learn to Understand and Express Empathy and Emotions
Teresa A. Cardon

Social Skills Training for Children and Adolescents
with Asperger Syndrome and Social-Communication Problems
Jed E. Baker

Joining In! A Program for Teaching Social Skills
Created by: Linda Murdock and Guru Shabad Khalsa

Space Travelers: An Interactive Program for Developing Social Understanding,
Social Competence and Social Skills for Students with Asperger Syndrome, Autism
and Other Social Cognitive Challenges; teacher and student guides
M. A. Carter and J. Santomauro

Peer Play and the Autism Spectrum – The Art of Guiding Children's
Socialization and Imagination
Pamela J. Wolfberg

Difficult Moments for Children and Youth with Autism Spectrum Disorders – DVD
Brenda Smith Myles

AAPC Autism Asperger Publishing Company

In the US: To order, call **913-897-1004**, fax to **913-681-9473**
visit our website at **www.asperger.net** or mail to AAPC • P.O. Box 23173 Shawnee Mission, KS 66283-0173

CODE	TITLE	PRICE	QTY.	TOTAL
9901a	Asperger Syndrome and Difficult Moments	$21.95		
9935	When My Autism Gets Too Big!	$15.95		
9918	Perfect Targets: Asperger Syndrome and Bullying	$21.95		
9936	The Incredible 5-Point Scale	$18.95		
9934	Let's Talk Emotions	$24.95		
9924	Social Skills Training	$34.95		
9701	Joining In! A Program for Teaching Social Skills (Video)	$79.95		
9931	Space Travelers Teacher's Guide	$29.95		
9931S	Space Travelers Student's Manual	$12.00		
9921	Peer Play and the Autism Spectrum	$39.95		
9720	Difficult Moments for Children and Youth with ASD (DVD)	$44.95		

NAME

ADDRESS

CITY

STATE **ZIP**

PHONE

EMAIL

SHIPPING AND HANDLING/USA

Order Total	Ground
$1 – $50	$5
$51 – $100	$8
$101 – $200	$10
$201 – $300	$20
$301 – $400	$30
Over $400	10% of subtotal

For rush, international or Canadian deliveries, please call toll-free 1-877-277-8254.

METHOD OF PAYMENT
☐ AMEX ☐ VISA ☐ DISCOVER ☐ MASTERCARD ☐ P.O. ATTACHED
☐ CHECK/MONEY ORDER ENCLOSED (PAYABLE TO AAPC)

ACCOUNT #

EXP. DATE ☐☐–☐☐ SIGNATURE _____ *(Required to process your order)*

SUBTOTAL $ _____

7.525% KS SALES TAX + _____
(Kansas Residents Only)

SHIPPING & HANDLING + _____

TOTAL _____